UNITED STATES MIGRANT INTERDICTION AND THE DETENTION OF REFUGEES IN GUANTÁNAMO BAY

This book provides a thorough legal analysis of the United States Migrant Interdiction Program, examining the United States' compliance with its obligations under municipal and international law as it interdicts individuals at sea, conducts status determinations and returns those interdicted to their home countries. This book also examines the rights of the small number of refugees and individuals at risk of torture detained in Guantánamo Bay, Cuba, awaiting resettlement in third countries.

Policy makers, students and scholars will benefit from this book's clarification of the legal obligations of nations engaged in extraterritorial status determination and detention, as well as its blueprint for compliance with international human rights and refugee law. As the first book of its kind devoted to the U.S. interdiction program, this work represents an important contribution to scholarship in refugee law and policy, U.S. constitutional law, international maritime law and international human rights law.

Dr. Azadeh Dastyari is Lecturer in the Faculty of Law at Monash University, Australia, specialising in refugee and immigration law. Research for this book was supported by the WG Walker Scholarship, granted to the highest-ranked postgraduate Fulbright Scholar in Australia.

United States Migrant Interdiction and the Detention of Refugees in Guantánamo Bay

Azadeh Dastyari

Monash University

CAMBRIDGE
UNIVERSITY PRESS

CAMBRIDGE
UNIVERSITY PRESS

32 Avenue of the Americas, New York, NY 10013-2473, USA

Cambridge University Press is part of the University of Cambridge.

It furthers the University's mission by disseminating knowledge in the pursuit of education, learning and research at the highest international levels of excellence.

www.cambridge.org
Information on this title: www.cambridge.org/9781107101005

First published 2015

A catalog record for this publication is available from the British Library.

Library of Congress Cataloging in Publication Data
Dastyari, Azadeh, author.
United States migrant interdiction and the detention of refugees in Guantánamo Bay / Azadeh Dastyari, Monash University.
pages cm
Includes bibliographical references and index.
Based on author's thesis (doctoral – Monash University).
ISBN 978-1-107-10100-5 (hardback)
1. Refugees – Legal status, laws, etc. – United States. 2. Haitians – Cuba – Guantánamo Bay Naval Base. I. Title.
KF4836.D37 2015
342.7308'2–dc23 2015003111

ISBN 978-1-107-10100-5 Hardback

Contents

Acknowledgements

This book has benefitted from the support of the Australian American Fulbright Commission, Lionel Murphy Foundation and the Australian Postgraduate Award. I am grateful to Harvard University Law School, the Institute for the Study of International Migration at Georgetown University and Hastings College of the Law for hosting my period of research in the United States. I would like to thank Professors Gerald Neuman, Karen Musallo and Andrew Shoenholtz for their invitations, valuable assistance and helpful guidance during this period. I would also like to thank Bill Frelick of Human Rights Watch and Professor Niels Frenzen for their generosity with information and resources.

I owe a special thank you to Dr. Patrick Emerton, Professor Susan Kneebone and Associate Professor Adam McBeth for the work they put into supervising the Ph.D. on which this book is based. I would also like to thank Professor François Crépeau and Associate Professor Angus Francis for their detailed feedback on my thesis and their encouragement to publish the work in monograph form.

This book would not have been possible without the support of Monash University and my wonderful colleagues in the Faculty of Law. I am grateful for their open doors, vast knowledge and encouragement of the people I am lucky enough to work with. I am indebted to Professor Sarah Joseph and Associate Professor Douglas Guilfoyle for reading chapters of this book and sharing their expertise and time with me. I also owe a big thank you to the numerous other friends I am fortunate to call colleagues who assisted me with this project: Dr. Heli Askola, Dr. Becky Batagol, Dr. Nicole Bieske, Dr. Nina Boughey, Melissa Castan, Adam Fletcher, Dr. Kathryn James, Dr. Alison Kesby, Dr. Joanna Kyriakakis and Dr. Lisa

Spagnolo. It certainly helps to have friends who are not only kind but brilliant! It goes without saying that my academic start in this field was nurtured by Professor Mary Crock at the University of Sydney, and I am thankful for her support and guidance over the years.

I would like to thank my brother-in-law Elia Vecellio who was not intimidated by legal scholarship and has a way with maps. This book has benefitted from his enviable attention to detail. I would also like to thank my sister Alison Davidian, upon whose support and love I have relied for almost everything I have tackled in the last decade. I am grateful for the support of my brother, Sam Dastyari, my parents, Ella and Naser Dastyari, and the kind members of the community of which my family and I have been blessed to be a part. During the course of writing this book I lost my grandparents. The thirst for knowledge which drove this book was inspired by my grandfather who continued to learn to his last days, and it was my grandmother's kindness and concern for others which led me to this field of study.

Most of all, I am grateful to the extraordinary patience, hard work and support of Lorien Vecellio. It would be impossible for me to have written this book without his remarkable backing and assistance. He is a partner, in the very true sense of the word, and for that no words of gratitude are sufficient. Finally, I am grateful for the patience of my son Oli. I must be the only mother who has had a song written for her by her then three-year-old, asking her to stay home and not go back to her work. I am happy to say, Oli, that it is finally done. Mummy can play now.

Abbreviations

CAA	*Cuban Adjustment Act*
CAT	*Convention against Torture and Other Cruel, Inhuman or Degrading Treatment or Punishment*
CAT Committee	Committee against Torture
CERD	*International Convention on the Elimination of All Forms of Racial Discrimination*
CERD Committee	Committee on the Elimination of Racial Discrimination
CIA	Central Intelligence Agency
D Conn	United States District Court for the District of Connecticut
DC Cir	United States Court of Appeals for the District of Columbia Circuit
DHS	Department of Homeland Security
DNJ	United States District Court for the District of New Jersey
DTA	*Detainees Treatment Act of 2005*
ECHR	*European Convention for the Protection of Human Rights and Fundamental Freedoms*
ECtHR	European Court of Human Rights
ED Va	United States District Court for the Eastern District of Virginia
ED Wash	United States District Court for the Eastern District of Washington
EDNY	District Court for the Eastern District of New York

EEZ	Exclusive Economic Zone
EMT	Emergency Medical Technician
ExCom	Executive Committee of the High Commissioner's Programme
F 2d	Federal Reporter, 2nd Series
F 3d	Federal Reporter, 3rd Series
F Supp	Federal Supplement
FARRA	*Foreign Affairs Reform and Restructuring Act* 1998
HR Committee	Human Rights Committee
HRC	Haitian Refugee Center
ICCPR	International Covenant on Civil and Political Rights
ICJ	International Court of Justice
ICJ Rep	International Court of Justice Reports
INA	*Immigration and Nationality Act*
INS	Immigration and Naturalization Service
IOM	International Organization for Migration
MIP	Migrant Interdiction Program
MITS	Migrant Information Tracking System
MOC	Migrant Operations Center
MOU	Memorandum of Understanding
NCG	National Council of Government
ND Cal	United States District Court for the Northern District of California
ND Ill	United States District Court for the Northern District of Illinois
OAS	Organization of American States
PNG	Papua New Guinea
PSO	Protection Screening Officer
Refugee Convention	*Convention Relating to the Status of Refugees*
Refugee Protocol	*Protocol Relating to the Status of Refugees*
SAR	*International Convention on Maritime Search and Rescue*
SD Fla	United States District Court for the Southern District of Florida

SDNY	United States District Court for the Southern District of New York
Smuggling Protocol	*Protocol against the Smuggling of Migrants by Land, Sea and Air*
SOLAS	*International Convention on Safety of Life at Sea*
UK	United Kingdom
UNCLOS	*United Nations Convention on the Law of the Sea*
UNHCR	United Nations High Commissioner for Refugees
UNTS	United Nations Treaty Series
U.S.	United States
US (in the context of court reports)	United States Supreme Court Reports
USCIS	United States Citizenship & Immigration Services
VCLT	*Vienna Convention on the Law of Treaties*

Glossary of Terms

Cutter	Sea vessel 19.8 metres (65 feet) in length or greater, having adequate accommodations for crew to live onboard.
Interdictees	Individuals interdicted by the United States as part of the United States' Migrant Interdiction Program.
International waters	Waters outside the territorial sea of any country, including the contiguous zone and exclusive economic zone of the United States and neighbouring countries, as well as the high seas.
Protected person	Individuals (including refugees) who are owed a *non-refoulement* obligation under international human rights and refugee law.
Protected population	Refugees and individuals at risk of *refoulement* to torture who have undergone a status determination procedure in Guantánamo Bay and have been recognised by the United States as having protection needs.
Protection seekers	Individuals who seek protection from *refoulement* under international human rights and/or refugee law (this broad category includes both protected persons and individuals to whom a state does not in fact owe a *non-refoulement* obligation).

U.S. mainland	U.S. territory as defined under INA § 101(a)38; 8USC § 1101(a)(38) – that is, continental United States, Alaska, Hawaii, Puerto Rico, Guam, the Virgin Islands of the United States and the Commonwealth of the Northern Mariana Islands.

1

Introduction

> I am a Cuban mother who finds herself in the U.S. Naval Base in Guantánamo Bay, Cuba. My name is Arelys Valladares Prado. I am here with my husband and my two daughters, one who is 5 years old, the other who is 15. Today, as sadness and isolation grip my heart, having spent more than a year and a half in this labyrinth, I take the liberty to write to you, to tell you how desperately lost we are.... To those of us who abandoned our homes and risked our lives at sea, it's hard to conceive that all this time that has been lost will never be recovered.... Please, I am desperate. Don't forget me.[1]
>
> This is not a polite, bloodless process which is going on.... Mr Bertrand and Mr Remy ... were interdicted on the high seas. Their boats were destroyed by the Coast Guard. They were taken to Guantánamo, where they were held behind barbed wire in U.S. captivity for months. And then, when they asked for lawyers, before they had an asylum hearing, they were forced back onto the boats and returned to Haiti ... at Port-au-Prince, Mr Bertrand was driven off the boat with fire hoses. He was fingerprinted, identified by the Haitian military. That night he was taken from his bed, beaten, his left arm was fractured, and he fled into hiding. And he would now flee again, but for this [Migrant Interdiction Program].[2]

U.S. President Barack Obama has stated that Guantánamo Bay is 'a symbol around the world for an America that flouts the rule of law'.[3] President

1 'A refugee mother opens her heart', *Miami Herald*, 19 February 2001 <www.latinamericanstudies.org/immigration/arelys.htm>.

2 Harold Koh, Oral testimony before the U.S. Supreme Court, *Chris Sale, Acting Commissioner, Immigration and Naturalization Service, et al., Petitioners v Haitian Centers Council et. al.*, No 92–344, 2 March 1993.

3 President Barack Obama, *Remarks by the President at the National Defense University* (23 May 2013) <www.whitehouse.gov/the-press-office/2013/05/23/remarks-president-national-defense-university>.

Obama was referring to the imprisonment of non-citizens in the 'war on terror' in the U.S. naval base that has garnered unprecedented international attention and has been the subject of much scholarship. Yet the same quotation is also applicable to the detention of refugees and individuals fleeing torture in the U.S. immigration detention facility in Guantánamo Bay. However, the continuing operation of an immigration detention facility, across the bay from the facilities used in the 'war on terror', is virtually unknown both in the United States and internationally. The immigration detention facility in Guantánamo Bay has received almost no media or scholarly attention since the mid-1990s.[4] Indeed, the majority of scholars believe the facility has not been used since 1996, and the few scholars who acknowledge its continuing operation harbour significant misconceptions about its current role.[5] Despite an expressed intention to close down the detention facilities used in the 'war on terror' at Guantánamo Bay,[6] at no point has the U.S. executive indicated any intention to close down the immigration detention facility there. On the contrary, there is some evidence of plans to expand the facility.[7]

The immigration detention facility in Guantánamo Bay has been in operation since 1991 as part of the U.S. 'Migrant Interdiction Program'

4 The lack of reporting is in part because media representatives are prohibited from speaking to individuals transferred to Guantánamo Bay under the Migrant Interdiction Program (MIP) without specific approval: Department of Defense, 'Media Ground Rules for Guantanamo Bay, Cuba' (10 September 2010), H.2. Three pieces of scholarship which constitute a notable exception to the silence on the rights of Haitian and Cuban nationals detained in Guantánamo Bay under the MIP in recent years are Sonia Farber, 'Forgotten at Guantánamo: The *Boumediene* Decision and Its Implications for Refugees at the Base under the Obama Administration' (2010) 98 *California Law Review* 989; Christina Frohock, '"Brisas Del Mar": Judicial and Political Outcomes of the Cuban Rafter Crisis in Guantánamo Bay' (2012) 15 *Harvard Latin Law Review* 302; and Niels Frenzen, 'US Migrant Interdiction Practices in International and Territorial Waters' in Bernard Ryan and Valsamis Mitsilegas (eds), *Extraterritorial Immigration Control: Legal Challenges* (Martinus Nijhoff Publishers, 2010).

5 Some scholars wrongly believe, for example, that all Cubans interdicted by the United States are sent to Guantánamo Bay for status determinations during interdiction operation: see Stephen Legomsky, 'The USA and the Caribbean Interdiction Program' (2006) 18 *International Journal of Refugee Law* 677, 684; Lori Nessel, 'Externalized Borders and the Invisible Refugee' (2009) 40 *Columbia Human Rights Law Review* 625, 695; Maryellen Fullerton, 'Cuban Exceptionalism: Migration and Asylum in Spain and the United States' (2004) 35 *University of Miami Inter-American Law Review* 527, 531. In fact, between 1996 and 2013, less than 1.7 per cent of all Cuban nationals interdicted were identified as having any form of protection needs under the MIP and were transferred to Guantánamo Bay. The vast majority were simply repatriated. See Section 5.6.

6 Executive Order 13492, 74 *Federal Register* 4897 (2009).

7 See Section 2.4.

(MIP), also referred to by the United States as Alien Migration Interdiction Operations,[8] in the Caribbean region.[9] Interdiction has been aptly defined by Ryan as action taken by states to prevent non-citizens 'from reaching their intended destination'.[10] Under the MIP, the United States intercepts sea vessels outside U.S. waters to prevent non-citizens from entering the municipally defined territory of the United States (U.S. mainland) without authorisation.[11] The vast majority of interdictions under the MIP take place in and around the Straits of Florida, the Windward Passage and the Mona Passage, where the United States maintains a persistent presence of U.S. Coast Guard vessels.[12] This area is represented in the map in Figure 1.

The vast majority of people interdicted at sea, referred to in this book as 'interdictees', are returned to their point of origin. However, the U.S. Coast Guard identifies a very small percentage of interdictees as having a credible fear of persecution or torture and transfers them to Guantánamo Bay. Once in Guantánamo Bay, interdictees are detained for further processing to determine whether or not they have a well-founded fear of persecution (are refugees) or are more likely than not to be tortured if returned home. Anyone found not to have protection needs in Guantánamo Bay

8 See, for example, U.S. Coast Guard, *Statistics: Alien Migrant Interdiction* <www.uscg.mil/hq/cg5/cg531/AMIO/amio.asp>.

9 As discussed in Section 4.2, the use of the term 'migrant' by the United States to refer to its interdiction program is misleading because not all individuals interdicted by the United States are, in fact, 'migrants'. Some individuals interdicted by the United States are refugees, which is a legally defined status that carries certain obligations under international refugee law. On this issue, see James Hathaway, 'Forced Migration Studies: Could We Agree Just to "Date"?' (2007) 20 *Journal of Refugee Studies* 349. See also Erica Feller, 'Refugees Are Not Migrants' (2005) 24 *Refugee Survey Quarterly* 27, 28. The use of the term 'Migrant Interdiction Program' and references in this book to 'migrant interdictions' should not be seen as an endorsement of the terminology adopted by the United States. The terms are utilised in this book to avoid confusion by retaining consistency with literature produced by the U.S. executive.

10 Bernard Ryan, 'Extraterritorial Immigration Control: What Role for Legal Guarantees?' in Bernard Ryan and Valsamis Mitsilegas (eds.), *Extraterritorial Immigration Control: Legal Challenges* (Martinus Nijhoff Publishers, 2010), 22.

11 The 'United States' is defined under U.S. municipal law as 'Alaska, Hawaii, Puerto Rico, Guam, the Virgin Islands of the United States, and the Commonwealth of the Northern Mariana Islands': INA § 101(a)38; 8 USC § 1101(a)(38). See Section 1.2. It is U.S. policy to interdict vessels 'as far as possible from the US border': Presidential Decision Directive 9, 'Alien Smuggling', White House, 18 June 1993.

12 See Testimony of Rear Admiral Vincent Atkins, U.S. Coast Guard, before the House Subcommittee on Homeland Security, on Department of Homeland Security Air and Marine Operations and Investments, 19 April 2010 <www.dhs.gov/ynews/testimony/testimony_1271690315007.shtm>.

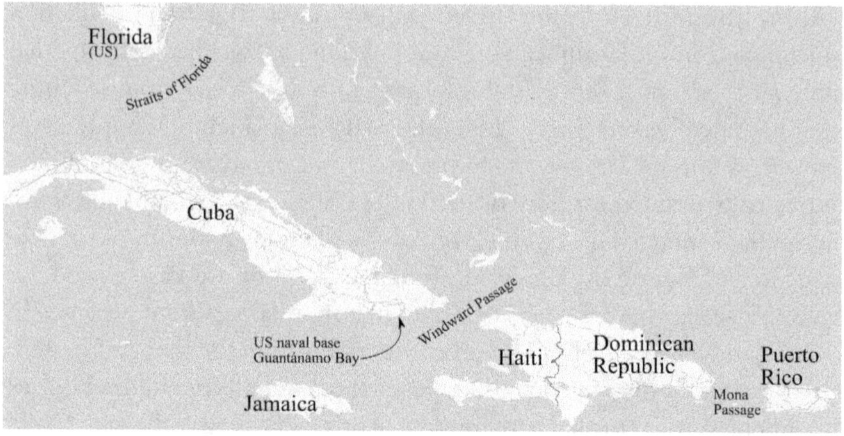

Figure 1. Map showing the Straits of Florida, the Windward Passage and the Mona Passage. Open Street Maps <www.openstreetmap.org/>. Markings made by author.

is repatriated. However, refugees and individuals at risk of torture remain in Guantánamo Bay until they can be resettled. It is U.S. policy that individuals interdicted under the MIP will not be paroled or admitted onto the U.S. mainland.[13] As a result, the majority of refugees and individuals at risk of torture remain in Guantánamo Bay until they can be resettled in a third country.[14]

As Brouwer and Kumin argue, 'in terms of numbers, the U.S. would appear to be the leader in maritime interception'.[15] The numbers are indeed striking. Between the fiscal years 1982 and 2014,[16] the United States interdicted

[13] However, individuals in need of emergency medical attention during interdiction operations, for whom adequate care cannot be provided on board a Coast Guard vessel, are taken to the hospital of nearest convenience, which may be on the U.S. mainland: Friedman et al., *Maritime Interception: History, Practice and Emerging Issues*, Yale Law School, Allard K. Lowenstein International Human Rights Clinic (Unpublished, 2002), 26. Copy on file with the author.

[14] A very small number of individuals have in fact been paroled or admitted to the U.S. mainland despite this general policy. Between the fiscal years 2009 and 2014, five Cuban nationals were the only individuals to be admitted to the U.S. mainland from Guantánamo Bay. They constituted 5 per cent of all individuals found to have protection needs in Guantánamo Bay during the period: U.S. Immigration and Customs Enforcement, ICE FOIA Case Number 2014-ICFO-03555 (30 September 2014), copy on file with the author.

[15] Andrew Brouwer and Judith Kumin, 'Interception and Asylum: When Migration Control and Human Rights Collide' (2003) 21 *Refuge: Canada's Journal on Refugees* 6.

[16] The U.S. fiscal year is from 1 October to 30 September.

244,488 people under the MIP.[17] Yet the number of individuals transferred to Guantánamo Bay for further status determination and potential resettlement is extraordinarily small compared to the total number interdicted. For example, between the fiscal years 1996 and 2014, only 425 individuals were transferred to Guantánamo Bay for further processing.[18] The small number of individuals found to have protection needs during interdiction operations at sea is consistent with the substantial evidence that the screening procedures adopted by the U.S. Coast Guard on board Coast Guard vessels are inadequate and fail to identify many refugees and individuals at risk of torture. As a result, there is a high probability that the United States is not complying with its international obligation to protect refugees and individuals at risk of torture from being returned to harm.[19]

The largest groups of individuals interdicted by the United States under the MIP are nationals of Haiti, Dominican Republic, China, Cuba, Mexico and Ecuador.[20] Only Haitians, Cubans and Chinese nationals are known to have been transferred to Guantánamo Bay following an interdiction. However, only Haitian and Cuban nationals have been, and continue to be, systematically transferred to Guantánamo Bay, in very small numbers, as part of the MIP and are the only groups confirmed to have been resettled in third countries after having been taken to Guantánamo Bay for full status determinations.[21] In contrast, two groups of Chinese nationals were transferred to Guantánamo Bay in 1996 and 1997. These were ad hoc events that ended with the repatriation of the interdictees.[22] No Chinese national is known to have been transferred to Guantánamo Bay after 1997. This book therefore focuses on the implications of the U.S. interdiction program in the Caribbean region for Haitian and Cuban nationals.

The MIP has an important role within U.S. immigration law and policy. For example, the MIP denies thousands of individuals from nations such as Haiti and Cuba access to the U.S. in-country processing regimes.

17 U.S. Coast Guard, *Statistics*, *'Alien Migrant Interdiction'* <http://www.uscg.mil/hq/cg5/cg531/AMIO/FlowStats/currentstats.asp>.

18 Email to author from PRM Press, Bureau of Population, Refugees, and Migration, U.S. Department of State, 15 July 2014 (on file with author).

19 See discussion in Chapter 5.

20 See the source in n 17 to this chapter.

21 In the fiscal years 2009 and 2014, 114 Cubans and 1 Haitian were the only individuals to be transferred to Guantánamo Bay under the MIP. See the source in n 14 to this chapter.

22 See Section 2.3.

The MIP is also the cornerstone of the U.S. 'wet-foot, dry-foot' policy under which Cuban nationals interdicted at sea are prevented from entering the U.S. mainland. In contrast, any Cuban national who reaches the U.S. mainland is, as a matter of policy, paroled into the United States and is permitted to apply for an adjustment of status to a permanent resident after one year of being physically present in the country.[23] Furthermore, as the oldest extraterritorial interdiction, processing and detention regime in the world, the MIP is highly significant. It predates interdiction operations coordinated by the European Union's border agency (FRONTEX), interdiction measures adopted by European States such as Italy and Spain, and Australia's policy of extraterritorial processing and detention.

1.1 The United States' Exercise of Jurisdiction and Control in Guantánamo Bay, Cuba

A unique feature of the U.S. MIP, which is not shared by the interdiction and extraterritorial detention regimes that preceded it, is that individuals found to have a credible fear of persecution or torture during interdiction operations at sea are transferred to Guantánamo Bay, territory under the 'ultimate sovereignty of the Republic of Cuba',[24] where the United States exercises 'complete jurisdiction and control'.[25] To understand the position of Guantánamo Bay in international law and U.S. municipal law, it is important to understand the history of the area.

Cuba was Spanish territory when Spain declared war on the United States on 24 April 1898.[26] After sixteen weeks of fighting, the Spanish surrendered in July 1898 and relinquished control of Cuba by signing the *Treaty of Paris* on 10 December 1898.[27] Following the end of the war, Cuba came under U.S. military occupation.[28] The United States did not attempt

[23] This is pursuant to the *Cuban Adjustment Act* of 1966, Pub L No 89–414, 732, 80 Stat. 1161 (1966).

[24] *Agreement between the United States and Cuba for the Lease of Lands for Coaling and Naval Stations; Lease to the United States of Lands in Cuba for Coaling and Naval Stations*, 16–23 February 1903, U.S.-Cuba, T.S. No 418, Art 3.

[25] Ibid. This issue will be explored further in subsection 6.3.1.

[26] *An Act Declaring that War Exists Between the United States of America and the Kingdom of Spain*, 30 Stat. 364.

[27] *Treaty of Paris*, 30 Stat. 1754.

[28] For commentary, see Marion Murphy, *History of Guantánamo Bay 1494–1964* (District Publications, 1962).

to annex Cuba and its territory of Guantánamo Bay outright. However, in 1901, an amendment to an Army Appropriation Bill was proposed by Orville Platt, Chairman of the Senate Committee on Foreign Relations. The 'Platt amendment' stipulated conditions that had to be met before the United States would grant Cuba its independence, including Article VII which states

> That to enable the United States to maintain the independence of Cuba, and to protect the people thereof, as well as for its own defense, the government of Cuba *will sell or lease to the United States lands necessary for coaling or naval stations* at certain specified points to be agreed upon with the President of the United States.[29]

The Platt amendment, including Article VII, was approved by the U.S. Congress on 2 March 1901 and became an appendix to the Constitution of Cuba on 20 May 1902.[30]

Pursuant to the Platt amendment, the first lease agreement for Guantánamo Bay as a coaling and naval station[31] was signed by Cuban President Estrada Palma on 16 February 1903 and by U.S. President Theodore Roosevelt on 23 February 1903.[32] Article III of the lease agreement states in part that

> While on the one hand the United States recognizes the continuance of the *ultimate sovereignty* of the Republic of Cuba over the above described areas of land and water, on the other hand the Republic of Cuba consents that during the period of the occupation by the United States of said areas under the terms of this agreement the *United States shall exercise complete jurisdiction and control over and within* said areas ...[33]

[29] *Treaty Between the United States of America and Cuba*, 29 May 1934, U.S.-Cuba, T.S. No 866. Emphasis added.

[30] See n 28 in this chapter.

[31] Coaling stations were needed when Navy ships were fuelled by coal. They became obsolete with the First World War as the Navy began to use petroleum to fuel ships. See Gabrielle Hech, *Entangled Geographies: Empire and Technopolitics in the Global Cold War* (MIT Press, 2011), 30.

[32] *Agreement between the United States and Cuba for the Lease of Lands for Coaling and Naval Stations; Lease to the United States of Lands in Cuba for Coaling and Naval Stations*, 16–23 February 1903, U.S.-Cuba, T.S. No 418.

[33] Emphasis added.

A supplementary agreement dated 2 July 1903[34] stipulated under Article I that the United States agreed to pay Cuba two thousand dollars in gold annually for the occupation and use of Guantánamo Bay. The Lease Agreement and the Supplementary Agreement of 1903 formed the basis for the U.S. occupation of Guantanamo Bay until 1934.

In 1934, an additional agreement was signed in the *Treaty Between the United States of America and Cuba*,[35] which made the lease of Guantánamo Bay indefinite so that the lease agreement could only be broken by mutual agreement or by abandonment of the property by the United States.[36]

The United States exercises jurisdiction over Guantánamo Bay to this day. The Cuban Supreme Court has stated that under Cuban law, 'the territory of that naval station is for all legal effects regarded as foreign' in Cuba.[37] As the U.S. Supreme Court declared in *Boumediene v Bush* (*Boumediene*),[38] 'the United States, by virtue of its complete jurisdiction and control over the base, maintains *de facto* sovereignty over this territory'.[39]

1.2 Structure of This Book

While the United States exercises de facto sovereignty over Guantánamo Bay, Guantánamo Bay does not constitute U.S. territory for the purposes of U.S. municipal law. The *Immigration and Nationality Act* (INA)[40] defines the 'United States', when used in a 'geographical sense', as 'the continental United States, Alaska, Hawaii, Puerto Rico, Guam, the Virgin Islands of the United States and the Commonwealth of the Northern Mariana Islands'[41] – what this book refers to as the 'U.S. mainland'. This definition excludes the territory of Guantánamo Bay.[42]

[34] *Lease to the United States by the Government of Cuba of Certain Areas of Land and Water for Naval or Coaling Stations in Guantánamo and Bahia Honda*, U.S.-Cuba, T.S. No 426, Art III. The United States discontinued the lease of Bahia Honda under the 1902 Supplementary Agreement.

[35] 29 May 1934, U.S.-Cuba, T.S. No 866.

[36] Ibid Art III.

[37] *In Re Guzman & Latamble*, Annual Digest, 1933–34, Case No 43 p 112. See subsection 6.3.1.

[38] 553 U.S. 723 (2008).

[39] Ibid 755. See subsection 6.3.1.

[40] Pub L No 82–414, 66 Stat. 163.

[41] INA § 101(a)38; 8 USC § 1101(a)(38).

[42] For simplicity, this book refers to the municipally defined territory of the United States as the 'U.S. mainland', even though it includes islands such as Hawaii and Guam.

The status of Guantánamo Bay, as an area under the jurisdiction of the United States but outside its municipally defined territory, has enabled the United States to deny interdictees protections that would be due to them under U.S. municipal law if they were located on the U.S. mainland. The English Court of Appeal in the case of *R* (*on the application of Abbasi et al.*) *v Secretary of State for Foreign and Commonwealth Affairs* referred to Guantánamo Bay as a space governed solely by the will of the U.S. government, 'immune from review in any court or independent forum'.[43] This statement was a reference to the operation of the detention facilities in the 'war on terror', but it is equally relevant to the immigration detention facility on the U.S. naval base. However, it is misleading to categorise Guantánamo Bay as a 'legal black hole'.[44] The United States is bound by legal obligations both under municipal law and international law when it exercises jurisdiction in Guantánamo Bay. In fact, this book will show that Guantánamo Bay constitutes U.S. territory for the purposes of international human rights and refugee law.[45] The lack of effective enforcement mechanisms under international law should not be confused with a lack of applicable law. The challenge for interdictees and their advocates is not overcoming a legal vacuum, but ensuring that the United States abides by its existing international human rights and refugee law obligations.

The lack of effective avenues for the enforcement of the U.S.' international legal obligations has been an issue for individuals interdicted under the MIP from the program's inception. Chapter 2 discusses the historical and political context of the MIP. The chapter begins by examining the evolution of the MIP from initially targeting the irregular movement of Haitians to its extension to include the interdiction of Cuban nationals. The chapter also briefly discusses the interdiction of individuals from the Dominican Republic, Ecuador and China under the program. Furthermore, the chapter provides a background and context to the largely unsuccessful attempts by interdictees to challenge the operation of the MIP in U.S. courts. The specific legal arguments raised in these litigations

43 [2002] EWCA Civ 1598, [66].

44 Ibid [64]. See also Ralph Wilde, 'Legal Black Hole – Extraterritorial State Action and International Treaty Law on Civil and Political Rights' (2006) 26 *Michigan Journal of International Law* 739; George Fletcher, 'Black Hole in Guantánamo Bay' (2004) 2 *Journal of International Criminal Justice* 121.

45 See, for example, discussion of Articles 12(1) and 13 of the ICCPR in subsection 6.3.1.

are further analysed in subsequent chapters to show the lack of avenues for challenging the MIP under municipal law. Finally, Chapter 2 considers the very few occasions where the MIP has been amended in favour of individuals interdicted under the program, showing that the changes occurred primarily as a result of effective public advocacy campaigns rather than litigation in the courts.

Chapters 3 and 4 examine the municipal and international legal frameworks governing the MIP. Chapter 3 analyses the municipal legal foundations of the MIP as well as the legal foundations of the MIP under the international law of the sea. The exercise of jurisdiction over individuals interdicted by the United States is largely compliant with both U.S. municipal law and the international law of the sea. The only exception is that the United States sometimes turns rescue operations into interdiction operations and destroys unseaworthy vessels flagged to another State with which it does not have an agreement. These practices are not authorised under the international law of the sea.

The international law of the sea is not, however, the only international law that governs the MIP. In Chapter 4, this book argues that U.S. obligations under international human rights and refugee law apply wherever the U.S. exercises jurisdiction, including outside its territorial waters and in Guantánamo Bay. It goes on to explore the extent to which the United States has implemented relevant international human rights and refugee law treaties in its municipal law. The chapter shows that individuals interdicted by the United States have no effective means of compelling the U.S. executive to abide by its obligations under international human rights and refugee law. U.S. courts will not recognise such rights unless they have been implemented in U.S. municipal law, and many of the obligations in question have not been implemented by the United States. Furthermore, when implementing legislation does exist, it has been found (or is likely to be found) by U.S. courts not to apply outside the U.S. mainland. In addition, the international legal arena does not provide any effective mechanisms for the enforcement of the U.S.' international obligations.

The specific rights under international human rights and refugee law that are violated by the United States during migrant interdiction operations are analysed in Chapters 5 and 6. This book is concerned with two particularly significant components of the MIP: status determinations and the plight of individuals whose protection needs are recognised by the United States but who remain detained in Guantánamo Bay. With respect to the former, Chapter 5 analyses the United States' compliance with its international obligations when undertaking status determinations. It shows that the United States is in violation of its non-discrimination obligations, and there is strong evidence that the United States is in violation of its *non-refoulement* obligations, under international human rights and refugee law.

Chapter 6 analyses the United States' compliance with its international obligations to refugees and individuals at risk of *refoulement* to torture, who have undergone status determinations in Guantánamo Bay and await resettlement. The chapter analyses the concept of detention within international law, arguing that individuals awaiting resettlement in Guantánamo Bay are arbitrarily detained and are denied the right to an effective review of their detention by a court empowered to release them. Even if individuals awaiting resettlement in Guantánamo Bay are not detained (as the U.S. executive contends), they are clearly denied freedom of movement, which is also prohibited. The chapter goes on to show that the resettlement of interdictees in third countries from Guantánamo Bay constitutes expulsion, which requires certain procedural safeguards in the case of individuals at risk of torture, and is prohibited for refugees. Finally, the chapter considers the denial of the facilitation of the naturalisation to refugees who are resettled in third countries.

Chapter 7 concludes the book. While the MIP is largely compliant with U.S. municipal law and the international law of the sea, the program places the United States in breach of numerous obligations under international human rights and refugee law. The United States would best meet its international obligations by processing protection seekers in the U.S. mainland and resettling individuals in need of protection from *refoulement* in the United States itself. However, individuals interdicted by the United States and their advocates cannot look to the courts of the U.S. or the international legal regime to compel the U.S. executive to abide by its international obligations. As such, the book concludes that public advocacy aimed at the full implementation of the U.S.' international obligations (including the extraterritorial reach of such obligations) is the most effective tool for ensuring individuals interdicted by the United States under the MIP are afforded their rights.

By analysing the violations of international law under the MIP and highlighting the futility of engaging in litigation in U.S. courts (in the absence of law reform or public advocacy) as a means of ensuring the U.S. executive complies with its international obligations, it is hoped that this book will pave the way for more creative challenges to current U.S. law and policy. It is also hoped that this study will reignite interest in a vulnerable group whose plight has been ignored or misunderstood in recent years.

2

Political and Historical Background

Since 1981, the U.S. Coast Guard has regularly patrolled the coast of the United States, and the transit routes that are used by sea vessels, to 'interdict undocumented migrants at sea, denying them entry via maritime routes to the United States, its territories and possessions'.[1] This chapter outlines the political and historical events in Haiti and Cuba that have come to shape the U.S. MIP, including the operation of a detention facility in Guantánamo Bay, Cuba. The chapter begins with a discussion of Haiti and Haitian migration. Denying entry to undocumented Haitians entering the United States was the impetus for the creation of the interdiction program. This chapter then provides an examination of the historical and political events in Cuba that have influenced Cuban movement to the United States, and the U.S. response through the MIP. As will be shown, Cubans have enjoyed privileged status in the United States since the Cuban revolution of 1959. The extension of the MIP to Cuban nationals in 1994 was a departure from this favoured treatment (although it has not completely removed this privileged status).[2] This chapter then briefly outlines the interdiction of other nationals under the MIP and concludes with a discussion of the future of the MIP.

The chapter also provides a background to the important legal challenges to the MIP in the U.S. courts. The chapter shows that in only two cases,[3]

1 U.S. Coast Guard, *Statistics: Alien Migrant Interdiction* <www.uscg.mil/hq/cg5/cg531/AMIO/amio.asp>.

2 Cubans who enter the United States enjoy rights that are not available to nationals of other states under the *Cuban Adjustment Act* of 1966 (discussed in Section 2.2). As will be shown in subsection 5.3.1, Cubans are also provided greater procedural safeguards during interdiction operations than are their Haitian counterparts.

3 *Haitian Centers Council, Inc. v Sale*, 823 F Supp 1028 (EDNY, 1993). Abrogation recognised by *Cuban American Bar Association v Christopher*, 43 F 3d 1412 (11th Cir, 1995); *Haitian*

which now hold no precedential value, have interdictees and their advocates been successful in challenging the MIP through litigation. Furthermore, of the two successful challenges to the MIP, only one led to any improvements in the plight of the interdictees in question, and the success of that ligation was largely attributable to public pressure that stopped the executive from appealing a decision to a higher court (which would likely have reversed the decision).[4] Advocates have had greater success in achieving results for the betterment of those affected by the U.S. MIP through public advocacy than through litigation.

2.1 Haiti

Haiti is the poorest country in the Western Hemisphere.[5] It also has had a long history of political persecution and violence. Movement of people from Haiti to the United States is closely tied to the history of the small nation. In 1791, Haiti (then called St. Domingue) was a slaveholding colony of France that derived its sizeable wealth from trade in sugar, molasses, rum, coffee, tobacco, indigo and cotton.[6] From 1791 until 1804, a revolutionary war drove the French colonialists out of Haiti, bringing freedom to the slaves. In 1804, the new country of Haiti gained its independence in a region of slave-owning colonies. France, the defeated party in the revolution, forced Haiti to pay substantial indemnities before it recognised the new country. Haiti was poor after the revolution and marked by class differences. The plantation system was nearly in ruins, and there was no longer a coerced labour force. The majority of Haiti's population was illiterate, and the country had limited natural resources. The country was also plagued by political instability most evident in the frequent changes of leadership. Between 1843 and 1915, Haiti had twenty-two presidents. Only one president served his full term.[7] Six Haitian presidents died or

Centers Council, Inc. v McNary, 969 F 2d 1326 (2nd Cir, 1992) vacated as moot sub nom. *Sale v Haitian Centers Council, Inc.*, 509 US 155 (1993).

4 *Haitian Centers Council, Inc. v Sale* 823 F Supp 1028, 1038 (EDNY, 1993).

5 World Bank, 'Haiti Country Brief' <www.worldbank.org/en/country/haiti>.

6 Columbus came to Haiti in 1492. It was originally inhabited by the Arawak Indians, who were virtually exterminated during the first twenty-five years of Spanish occupation. St. Domingue, modern Haiti, was ceded to France by Spain in 1697. See Sidney Mintz, 'Can Haiti Change' (1995) 74 *Foreign Affairs* 73.

7 Joyce Hughes and Linda Crane, 'Haitians: Seeking Refuge in the United States' (1993) 7 *Georgetown Immigration Law Journal* 747, 751.

were killed in office, one resigned and the other fourteen were deposed by revolution.[8]

Haiti's fate has also been much influenced by its close, powerful neighbour, the United States.[9] The United States occupied Haiti in July 1915 and continued its military occupation of the country for nineteen years.[10] Under the occupation, which aimed to bring stability to Haiti, U.S. officials seized customs houses and took over the country's finances. The Haitian legislature was dissolved and martial law was imposed. The United States had the power to veto all government decisions, and figureheads were installed in important offices.[11] One of the most lasting features of the U.S. occupation of Haiti was the creation of a new centralised Haitian army.[12] The Haitian military was to turn on its own citizens in the years that followed.[13]

After the end of the U.S. occupation, Haiti suffered a series of authoritarian rulers. In 1957, François 'Papa Doc' Duvalier took power in Haiti and ruled with an iron fist. In 1964, he declared himself President for Life and formed a brutal paramilitary force, the *Tontons Macoutes*, to solidify his power. It is believed that more than 40,000 Haitians lost their lives as victims of official brutality during 'Papa Doc' Duvalier's reign.[14] In 1971, 'Papa Doc' Duvalier arranged a referendum in which his son, Jean-Claude 'Baby Doc' Duvalier, was made his successor. 'Baby Doc' Duvalier was almost as brutal as his father was, instituting further violent repression of political opponents.

2.1.1 The Creation of the Migrant Interdiction Program

As a result of the political repression in Haiti, many Haitians fled the brutality of the Baby Doc regime to seek asylum in the United States. Between 1972 and 1979, 7,837 undocumented Haitians reached the United States.

8 Ibid.

9 Hans Schmidt, *The United States Occupation of Haiti, 1915–1934* (Rutgers University Press, 1995), 28.

10 For an in-depth discussion of this period, see Mary Renda, *Taking Haiti: Military Occupation and the Culture of US Imperialism, 1915–1940* (The University of North Carolina Press, 2001).

11 Hughes and Crane, n 7 in this chapter, 751.

12 Irwin Stotzzky argues that the Haitian army was designed specifically to keep the Haitians in line: Irwin Stotzzky, *Silencing the Guns in Haiti* (University of Chicago Press, 1986), 24.

13 Ibid.

14 Ibid.

In January 1981, Ronald Reagan was inaugurated as the President of the United States, coming to power with a hard-line policy towards preventing the irregular entrance of undocumented Haitians into the United States. On 29 September 1981, President Reagan issued two Presidential Decrees – a Presidential Proclamation, and an Executive Order – that fundamentally changed the United States' approach to irregular arrivals by sea in the Caribbean region.[15] Under Proclamation 4865,[16] President Reagan declared that

> The ongoing migration of persons to the United States in violation of [U.S.] laws is a serious national problem detrimental to the interests of the United States. A particularly difficult aspect of the problem is the continuing illegal migration by sea of large numbers of undocumented aliens into the southeastern United States ... [I]nternational cooperation to intercept vessels trafficking in illegal migrants is a necessary and proper means of insuring the effective enforcement of [US] laws.

The Proclamation was accompanied by Executive Order 12324,[17] which required the Secretary of Transportation to instruct the Coast Guard to enforce '[t]he suspension of the entry of undocumented aliens and the interdiction of any defined vessels carrying such aliens'.[18] Section 3 of the Executive Order also stated that

> The Attorney General shall, in consultation with the Secretary of State and the Secretary of the Department in which the Coast Guard is operating, take whatever steps are necessary to ensure the fair enforcement of our laws relating to immigration (including effective implementation of this Executive Order) and *the strict observance of our international obligations* concerning those who genuinely flee persecution in their homeland.[19]

In 1981, the relevant international obligations to which the Executive Order referred were the United States' obligations under the *Protocol*

[15] The Executive Order and Presidential Proclamation will be discussed and analysed in more detail in Section 3.2.

[16] 46 *Federal Register* 48, 107 (1981).

[17] 46 *Federal Register* 48, 109 (1981).

[18] Ibid § 2(a).

[19] Emphasis added.

Relating to the Status of Refugees, (Refugee Protocol)[20] which mandates that the United States abide by the *non-refoulement* obligation under Article 33(1) of the *Convention Relating to the Status of Refugees* (Refugee Convention).[21] However, the broad reference to 'international obligations' under the Executive Order suggests an intention to comply with any new obligations under international law that arose.[22]

The defined vessels that were to be stopped were U.S. vessels, vessels without nationality or vessels assimilated to vessels without nationality and flagged vessels of foreign nations with whom the United States had arrangements authorising stopping and boarding.[23] As discussed further in Section 3.3, the limitations placed on the interdiction of vessels by the Coast Guard are significant because under the international law of the sea, the United States is only permitted to interfere with foreign flagged vessels under certain conditions.

Pursuant to the Presidential Decrees of 29 September 1981, the Reagan administration negotiated an agreement with Haiti and the regime of Jean-Claude 'Baby Doc' Duvalier to establish a cooperative interdiction program.[24] Under this first incarnation of the MIP, the U.S. Coast Guard was to stop and board Haitian or stateless vessels outside the territorial sea of the United States. Haitians were to be interviewed or 'screened' for their protection needs. If any Haitians were found to have a 'credible fear' of persecution, they were to be taken to the United States where they could lodge an asylum claim. Refugees whose status was recognised by the United States were permitted to remain

[20] Opened for signature 31 January 1967, 606 UNTS 267 (entered into force 4 October 1967).

[21] Opened for signature 28 July 1951, 189 UNTS 150 (entered into force 22 April 1954). The United States' *non-refoulement* obligation will be discussed and analysed in Section 5.3.

[22] The United States' *non-refoulement* obligations under Article 3 of the *Convention Against Torture and Other Cruel, Inhuman or Degrading Treatment or Punishment* (CAT), opened for signature 10 December 1984, 1465 UNTS 85 (entered into force 26 June 1987), and Articles 6 and 7 of the *International Covenant on Civil and Political Rights* (ICCPR) opened for signature, 19 December 1966, 999 UNTS 171 (entered into force 23 March 1976), discussed and analysed in Section 5.3 and subsection 5.3.1, respectively, did not arise until after Executive Order 12324 was revoked and replaced by Executive Order 12807 (Kennebunkport Order), 57 *Federal Register* 23133 (1992) in May 1992. As discussed further in subsection 2.1.3, the Kennebunkport Order did not mandate observance of the United States' international *non-refoulement* obligations during interdictions.

[23] Executive Order 12324, 46 *Federal Register* 48, 109 (1981), § 2(b).

[24] *Agreement Effected by Exchange of Notes Regarding Migrants and Interdiction*, 23 September 1981, US-Haiti, 33 U.S.T. 3559, TIAS. No 10, 241.

in the country.[25] All other undocumented Haitians on the boats, and any Haitians transferred to the United States who were found not to be refugees, were to be returned to Haiti.[26] The United States received an assurance from the Republic of Haiti that Haitians returned to their country who were not traffickers were not to be subject to persecution for their departure.[27]

Legal challenges to the interdiction program soon followed. The first of these legal challenges was *Haitian Refugee Center v Gracey* (*Gracey*),[28] in which the Haitian Refugee Center (HRC), a community-based, non-profit organisation in the United States, brought an action challenging interdiction by U.S. officials. The plaintiffs sought two forms of relief: (1) an injunction permanently stopping the Coast Guard and the Immigration and Naturalization Service (INS) from continuing the interdiction program; and (2) a judgment declaring the interdiction program illegal.

The District Court for the District of Columbia found that although the HRC had standing to bring a suit, it did not have a cause of action to rely upon that could grant it relief. The Court in *Gracey* rejected the notion that the United States' statutory *non-refoulement* obligation to refugees extended to refugees outside the United States,[29] that refugees had a right to refugee status determination and that they had any rights under the Fifth Amendment of the U.S. Constitution.[30] The Court also found that the Refugee Protocol was not self-executing – that is, the Refugee Protocol requires further action from the legislature and is not directly enforceable by the municipal courts without legislative implementation.[31] The Court thus found that the interdicted Haitians had no right to enter the United

[25] Ibid.

[26] Ibid.

[27] Ibid. Once returned to Haiti, the interdicted Haitians were met by the U.S. Coast Guard and Department of State officials, Haitian officials and a representative of the Red Cross. The name of each interdicted individual was recorded, and the Red Cross provided people with some money (50 Haitian gourds, approximately US $10.00) to use for travel home. Embassy personnel performed occasional and informal follow-up interviews, but returnees were generally difficult to locate. Lawyers Committee for Human Rights, *Refugee Refoulement: The Forced Return of Haitians Under the US-Haitian Interdiction Agreement* (1990) 24.

[28] *Haitian Refugee Center v Gracey* 600 F Supp 1396 (DDC, 1985).

[29] The United States' denial of its *non-refoulement* obligations under the MIP is analysed in subsection 4.2.1.

[30] The denial of the Fifth Amendment of the U.S. Constitution to non-citizens outside the United States is analysed in Section 5.2.

[31] The non-self-executing nature of the Refugee Protocol is explored in detail in Section 4.6.

States, and the complaint was dismissed. The HRC appealed the decision to the U.S. Court of Appeals for the Eleventh Circuit. The Court of Appeals affirmed the District Court's dismissal of the case but ruled that the HRC had no standing.[32]

2.1.1.1 End of the Duvalier Era in Haiti

Following the failed legal challenge in *Gracey*, the interdiction program continued unchanged. However, 'Baby Doc' Duvalier was removed from power in Haiti on 7 February 1986,[33] and a provisional National Council of Government (NCG) was formed to organise elections and rule the country in the interim. The NCG was controlled by the army. A new Constitution was adopted in Haiti that guaranteed fundamental human rights and established a separation of powers between branches of the government. A provisional Electoral Council (CEP) was also established.

As a response to the political change, the U.S. embassy in Haiti completely discontinued any monitoring of returned interdicted Haitians in 1986 on the grounds that

> Any legitimate expectation that persecution might occur based on the general character of the Haitian government was removed when the National Governing Council succeeded President Jean-Claude Duvalier on February 7 [1986] and immediately made several key changes in the government of Haiti's human rights policy.[34]

America Watch and the National Coalition for Haitian Refugees reported, however, that harassment of returned interdicted Haitians had been observed in Haiti.[35] This was unsurprising because, as the Lawyers Committee for Human Rights reported,[36] there was much violence in Haiti following the adoption of the Constitution. The army-controlled NCG did not wish the CEP to organise elections. Former supporters of the Duvaliers were also reluctant to give up the power they had acquired

32 *Haitian Refugee Center v Gracey* 809 F 2d 794 (DC Cir,1987).

33 Jean-Claude 'Baby Doc' Duvalier fled to the south of France with his family on 7 February 1986. See Lawyers Committee for Human Rights, n 27 in this chapter, 26.

34 Ibid., 24–25.

35 Americas Watch & National Coalition for Haitian Refugees, *Half the Story: The Skewed US Monitoring of Repatriated Haitian Refugees* (1992) National Coalition of Haitian Rights <www.nchr.org/mnd/reptlist.htm>.

36 Now Human Rights First.

under both 'Papa Doc' and 'Baby Doc' Duvalier.[37] Between 1986 and 1990, Haiti was plagued by bloodshed and a series of coups.[38]

The clause prohibiting the persecution of returned Haitians in the agreement between the United States and Haiti was thus ineffective because it did not call for reporting and contained no remedial mechanisms. Despite documented political persecution in Haiti, 23,551 interdicted Haitians were returned to Haiti between September 1981 and September 1991.[39] In the same period, only twenty-eight Haitians were 'screened in' and taken to the United States to apply for asylum.[40] Given the documented political persecution in Haiti, it is implausible that only 0.1 per cent of the individuals fleeing Haiti were refugees in need of protection from *refoulement*. As such, it appears that the guarantee that refugees would not be returned to Haiti under the interdiction program was not upheld.

2.1.1.2 Aristide and Changes to the MIP under the George H.W. Bush Administration

The situation changed in Haiti once more when in 1990, Jean-Bertrand Aristide, a popular Catholic priest, became Haiti's first democratically elected president.[41] Following Aristide's rise to power, the number of Haitians fleeing Haiti fell dramatically.[42]

The U.S. asylum policy towards Haiti was forced to change yet again, however, when Aristide was overthrown by the military in September 1991. According to Amnesty International, the Haitian military attacked and killed 1,500 of Aristide's supporters immediately after the coup.[43] Following the overthrow of President Aristide, the United States adopted mandatory

[37] Lawyers Committee for Human Rights, n 27 in this chapter, 26.

[38] Ibid.

[39] Arthur Helton, 'The United States Government Program of Intercepting and Forcibly Returning Haitian Boat People to Haiti: Policy Implications and Prospects' (1993) 10 *New York Law School Journal of Human Rights* 325.

[40] Howard French, 'US is holding 200 Haitians on 2 Ships', *New York Times*, 8 November 1991 <www.nytimes.com/1991/11/08/world/us-is-holding-200-haitians-on-2-ships.html>.

[41] For an in-depth study of Aristide's rise to power in Haiti and his demise, see Alex Dupuy, *The Prophet and Power: Jean-Bertrand Aristide, the International Community, and Haiti* (Rowman & Littlefield Publishers, 2007).

[42] Cheryl Little, 'InterGroup Coalitions and Immigration Politics: The Haitian Experience in Florida' (1998) 53 *University of Miami Law Review* 717, 722–23.

[43] Amnesty International, 'Haiti: The Human Rights Tragedy: Human Rights Violations Since the Coup' (1992).

sanctions, while the Organization of American States (OAS) instituted voluntary sanctions aimed at restoring constitutional government in Haiti. The OAS and the United Nations declared the rule of the junta leader, Raoul Cédras, to be illegal under international law.[44]

In the eight-month period following the coup, 38,000 Haitians fleeing their country were intercepted at sea by the United States.[45] The United States found itself in a political bind. It had publicly denounced the coup that had removed Aristide and had placed sanctions on Haiti, but it did not wish to give asylum to Haitians who were fleeing the very same coup. The administration of George H.W. Bush feared that bringing Haitians interdicted at sea to the United States might lead to a mass exodus of people from Haiti.[46]

The United States initially responded by ceasing repatriations and holding all Haitians intercepted by the United States en route to the United States in Coast Guard cutters,[47] outside U.S. territorial waters.[48] That is, rather than returning Haitians to their home country, the United States sought to hold them indefinitely at sea. As more Haitians fled Haiti, more Coast Guard cutters were deployed in the area.[49] By mid-November 1991, the Coast Guard cutters were full to capacity. Holding Haitians intercepted at sea became increasingly impractical. In response to the inability of the Coast Guard cutters to hold all the Haitians intercepted at sea, the United States sought regional arrangements with its neighbours to share the perceived burden of the interdicted Haitians. U.S. diplomats began negotiating with Caribbean and South American countries, but few of the countries approached were willing to take Haitian nationals that had been interdicted by the United States. Many Caribbean and South American

44 Organization of American States, *Resolution MRE/RES*. 1/91 OEA/SER. F/V.1 (3 October, 1991); Organization of American States Resolution MRE/RES. 2/91 OEA/SER. F/V.1 (8 October 1991); The Situation of Democracy and Human Rights in Haiti, GA Res 46/7, 51st Plen mtg, UN Doc A/RES/46/7 (11 October 1991).

45 Helton, n 39 in this chapter.

46 Vernon Briggs, 'US asylum policy and the new world order' (1993)1 *People and Place* 1.

47 The Coast Guard defines a 'cutter' as 'any [Coast Guard] vessel 19.8 metres (65 feet) in length or greater, having adequate accommodations for crew to live onboard': US Coast Guard, *The Maritime Counter Drug and Alien Migrant Interdiction Operations Manual*, COMDTINST M16247.4/NWP 3-07-4. 46 USC, 13.

48 Victoria Clawson, Elizabeth Detweiler and Laura Ho 'Litigating as Law Students: An Inside Look at Haitian Center Council' (1994) 103 *The Yale Law Journal* 2337.

49 Briggs, n 46 in this chapter.

countries were sceptical about the United States' claim that the influx of Haitians attempting to enter the United States constituted an 'emergency'. They argued that the wealth disparity between their countries and the United States made it illogical for them to be responsible for persons interdicted by the United States.[50] After much negotiation, Honduras, Trinidad and Tobago, Venezuela and Belize agreed to host the intercepted Haitians. However, the numbers were small: only 550 Haitians were transferred to these countries.[51]

Faced with growing numbers of Haitians fleeing Haiti and the refusal of Caribbean countries to take more than a token number of Haitians, as well as a firm resolution to refuse Haitians fleeing by sea entry into the United States, the George H.W. Bush administration made the highly contentious decision to resume the repatriation of Haitians from 18 November 1991. The resumption of repatriations was accompanied by screening-in interviews to determine if the Haitians had a 'credible fear' of persecution. The interviews were often shorter than five minutes and, according to Cheryl Little, then an attorney at the HRC,

> [t]he INS officers interviewing the Haitians had virtually no knowledge of Haitian politics or culture and could not name or recognize the following: The President and Prime Minister of the de facto regime, the General (Cédras) at the head of the military coup, the popular name for President Aristide (Titid), Ti-Legliz (church movement of President Aristide), Lafanmi Selavi (orphanage established by President Aristide), and many others. A high-ranking government official at one point even said the interviews were so defective they needed to be halted.[52]

Those 'screened out' during the interviews were to be returned to Haiti. Those 'screened in' were permitted to enter the United States and lodge an application for asylum.[53]

The HRC responded to what they believed to be inadequate screening procedures with a new lawsuit filed in the U.S. District Court for the Southern District of Florida. The HRC requested declaratory and

50 Arthur Helton, Haitian Refugees in Political Limbo, *Miami Herald*, 24 November 1991, L1.

51 Briggs, n 46 in this chapter.

52 Little, n 42 in this chapter, 723.

53 Michael Ratner, 'How We Closed the *Guantánamo* HIV Camp: The Intersection of Politics and Litigation' (1998) 11 *Harvard Human Rights Journal* 187.

injunctive relief against the U.S. government and agencies engaged in the interdiction of Haitians, seeking to end repatriations subject to only cursory status determinations.

On 3 December 1991, in *Haitian Refugee Center v Baker* (*Baker I*),[54] the U.S. District Court for the Southern District of Florida issued a preliminary injunction that prevented the United States from forcibly repatriating the Haitians until the merits of the HRC's claims had been adjudicated.[55] The U.S. government sought expedited review of the injunction in the U.S. Court of Appeals for the Eleventh Circuit. In *Haitian Refugee Center v Baker* (*Baker II*),[56] the Court of Appeals reversed the District Court's order.[57] The District Court issued two more injunctions against the government's conduct, which the Eleventh Circuit reversed.[58] On 4 February 1992, the Court of Appeals for the Eleventh Circuit considered an appeal by the U.S. government against an injunction and a cross-appeal from the HRC. In *Haitian Refugee Center v Baker* (*Baker III*),[59] the Court of

54 789 F Supp 1552 (SD Fla, 1991).

55 The injunction was granted on the grounds that the refugees showed they would be subjected to a substantial threat if injunctive relief was not issued, and that the threatened injury to the refugees outweighed the threat to the U.S. government. The Court also found that the injunction was in the public interest. *Haitian Refugee Center, Inc v Baker*, 789 F Supp 1552, 1576–1577 (SD Fla, 1991).

56 949 F 2d 1109 (11th Cir, 1991).

57 The preliminary injunction was dissolved, and the case was remanded to the trial court because the U.S. Court of Appeals for the Eleventh Circuit found that Haitian refugees had no enforceable rights under Article 33 of the Refugee Convention: *Haitian Refugee Center, Inc. v Baker*, 949 F 2d 1109, 1110 (11th Cir, 1991). The Court did not make any determination as to whether there was in fact any *refoulement*. On this issue, see Bill Frelick, 'Haitian Boat Interdiction and Return: First Asylum and First Principles of Refugee Protection' (1993) 26 *Cornell International Law Journal* 675, 679.

58 On the night the Eleventh Circuit dissolved the District Court's injunction, the District Court issued a temporary restraining order, which, like the previous order, prevented the United States from repatriating interdicted Haitians. The U.S. government once again appealed the decision of the District Court to the Court of Appeals for the Eleventh Circuit. On 19 December 1991, the Court of Appeals for the Eleventh Circuit rejected the District Court's second attempt at halting repatriations. On 20 December 1991, the District Court issued a Limited Preliminary Injunctive Relief. This time the District Court based its decision on the finding that the HRC – the lawyers attempting to see their clients – showed a substantial likelihood of success on the claim that they had, under the First Amendment of the U.S. Constitution, the right to meet with the interdicted Haitians. *Haitian Refugee Center, Inc. v Baker*, 789 F Supp 1579 (SD Fla, 1991). The attempt to address the First Amendment rights of the lawyers in the 3 December 1991 injunction had been dismissed previously by the Eleventh Circuit as being too broad.

59 953 F 2d 1498 (11th Cir, 1992).

Appeals for the Eleventh Circuit found for the U.S. government on every point and declared that the repatriations were lawful. Most importantly, the Court found that the statutory right to *non-refoulement* did not extend to refugees processed extraterritorially and rejected the application of the First and Fifth Amendments of the U.S. Constitution to non-citizens outside of the United States. The Supreme Court denied a petition for the writ of *certiorari*.[60]

The findings of the Court in *Baker II* and *Baker III* are discussed and analysed later in the book.[61] For present purposes, it suffices to note that the *Baker* litigation is significant because it reaffirmed the decision in *Gracey* that interdictees do not enjoy statutory or constitutional protections that are available to their counterparts in the United States. As such, the case once again reaffirms the difficulty of using litigation as a strategy for challenging the MIP.

2.1.2 The Opening of Guantánamo Bay

The injunction imposed at the end of 1991 by the District Court temporarily stopped the United States from returning Haitians to Haiti. Reluctant to allow Haitians into the country but unable to keep them on Coast Guard cutters, the United States responded to overcrowding on its ships by building a series of tent cities as shelters on its base in Guantánamo Bay. Thus the *Baker* litigation not only shaped the legal rights of interdictees but created a political impasse that led to the creation of the first permanent status determination and detention facility in Guantánamo Bay.

The detention centre in Guantánamo Bay was guarded by U.S. troops and surrounded by barbed wire.[62] The United States conducted status determinations in Guantánamo Bay through INS Asylum Officers. The first major screening program in Guantánamo Bay, referred to by the United States as a 'migrant screening program',[63] was fully functional

60 112 S Ct 1245 (1992).

61 The finding that the Refugee Protocol is not self-executing in the U.S. courts is discussed and analysed in subsection 4.6.1. The rejection of the constitutional rights of interdictees is discussed and analysed in Section 5.2.

62 Jane Franklin, *How Did Guantánamo Become a Prison* (2005) History News Network <http://hnn.us/articles/11000.html>.

63 For a discussion of the use of the word 'migrant' by the United States, see Section 4.2.

by the end of November 1991.[64] Under the 'migrant screening program', the Coast Guard would transfer all interdicted Haitians to Guantánamo Bay where INS Asylum Officers would then make a determination as to whether the individual had a 'credible fear' of persecution. Haitians who were found to have a 'credible fear' of persecution were further transferred to the U.S. mainland to determine if they had a 'well-founded fear' of persecution and were thus refugees in need of protection from *refoulement*. Individuals who were not found to have a 'credible fear' of persecution during status determinations in Guantánamo Bay were repatriated. Between November 1991 and May 1993, the United States interviewed 34,000 interdicted Haitians in Guantánamo Bay. More than 10,500 Haitians established a 'credible fear' of persecution and were transferred to the U.S. mainland.[65]

2.1.2.1 HIV-Positive Haitians in Guantánamo Bay

In addition to its role as a status determination facility, Guantánamo Bay also became the site of a detention centre for Haitians who tested positive for the Human Immunodeficiency Virus (HIV). The United States adopted a policy in June 1987 that mandated the exclusion of HIV-positive immigrants from entry into the U.S. mainland.[66] More than 7,300 Haitians ages fifteen years and older held in Guantánamo Bay were tested for HIV. The HIV-positive Haitians who were found to have a 'credible fear' of persecution were not permitted to enter the U.S. mainland and lodge a protection claim. This was in contrast with Haitians who tested HIV-negative, who were permitted to enter the U.S. mainland if they satisfied the 'credible fear' requirement. The HIV-positive Haitians were instead detained in a separate section of Guantánamo Bay called Camp Bulkeley. Judge Johnson of the District Court described the living conditions of the HIV-positive detainees in the following way:

> They live in camps surrounded by razor barbed wire. They tie plastic garbage bags to the sides of the building to keep the rain out. They

64 Karen Musalo, *Chronology of US Policy on Haitian Refugees – 1980 to the Present* UC Hastings (1993) <www.uchastings.edu/site_files/musalo/chronology.pdf>.

65 United Nations High Commissioner for Refugees (UNHCR), *The State of the World's Refugees: A Humanitarian Agenda* (Oxford University Press, 1997).

66 Peter Barta 'Lambskin Borders: An Argument for the Abolition of the United States' 'Exclusion of HIV Positive Immigrants' (1998) 12 *Georgetown Immigration Law Journal* 323.

> sleep on cots and hang sheets to create some semblance of privacy. They are guarded by the military and are not permitted to leave the camp, except under military escort. The Haitian detainees have been subjected to predawn military sweeps as they sleep by as many as 400 soldiers dressed in full riot gear. They are confined like prisoners and are subject to detention in the brig without a hearing for camp rule infractions.[67]

A new policy was introduced in February 1992, which led to the second round of interviews of HIV-positive Haitians. In this round, in order to avoid repatriation and remain in Guantánamo Bay, HIV-positive Haitians had to prove that they had a 'well-founded fear' of persecution (and thus were recognised as refugees) rather than the less demanding 'credible fear' of persecution. HIV-positive Haitians who refused the second interviews or who were found to have a 'credible fear' but not a 'well-founded fear' were returned to Haiti. This was in direct contrast with Haitians who tested negative for the HIV virus; they were not required to undergo a 'well-founded fear' assessment before they were brought to the U.S. mainland for refugee determinations.[68] Furthermore, the HIV-positive refugees who satisfied the 'well-founded fear' test remained detained in Guantánamo Bay. That is, even when the United States recognised their refugee status, the HIV-positive Haitians were not resettled in the U.S. mainland, but instead were kept in limbo in Guantánamo Bay.

A number of Haitians in Guantánamo Bay responded to the situation by contacting Yale University's Lowenstein Clinic and requesting counsel.[69] The Lowenstein Clinic initiated litigation seeking access to the Haitians in Guantánamo Bay. The District Court for the Eastern District of New York awarded the Lowenstein Clinic a temporary restraining order, denying the U.S. executive the right to refuse lawyers access to Guantánamo Bay and temporarily stopping the repatriation of screened in Haitians.[70] The U.S. executive made a number of unsuccessful attempts before the Court of Appeals to obtain a stay of the District Court's order before appealing to the Supreme Court.[71]

67 *Haitian Centers Council, Inc. v Sale*, 823 F Supp 1028 (EDNY, 1993).

68 Barta, n 66 in this chapter.

69 Clawson, Detweiler and Ho, n 48 in this chapter, 2342.

70 *Haitian Centers Council, Inc. v McNary* 789 F Supp 541, 548 (EDNY, 1992).

71 On 3 April 1992, the U.S. executive filed a notice of interlocutory appeal requesting that the District Court stay the preliminary injunction pending the appeal. The District Court

In their call for a stay on the injunction, the U.S. executive argued that the injunction could have a 'magnet' effect on Haitians fleeing Haiti.[72] The Supreme Court awarded the U.S. government a stay.[73] On 23 April 1992, only twelve hours after the Supreme Court granted the government the stay on the injunction, the INS began returning to Haiti HIV-positive Haitians who had demonstrated a 'credible fear' but who had not been successful in establishing a 'well-founded fear' of persecution. Only 120 HIV-positive refugees and their relatives who had demonstrated that they had a 'well-founded' fear of persecution remained in Guantánamo Bay.[74]

On 10 June 1992, the Court of Appeals for the Second Circuit handed down its decision in *Haitian Centers Council Inc v McNary* (*McNary*).[75] The Court of Appeals for the Second Circuit affirmed the District Court's preliminary injunction and ordered the government to refrain from repatriating Haitians without first providing 'screened-in' individuals with counsel.[76] *McNary* was a landmark decision for it found that lawyers based in the U.S. mainland had rights under the First Amendment of the U.S. Constitution to speak to their clients in Guantánamo Bay. However, the decision in *McNary* has no precedential weight since the U.S. Justice Department negotiated with the litigators for the plaintiffs to have the Second Circuit opinion vacated, in return for the executive refraining from appealing the decision.[77] The applicants, fearing that an appeal to the Supreme Court would result in a defeat, agreed.[78]

However, legal counsel were not in fact given access to their clients in Guantánamo Bay. The Second Circuit's decision in *McNary* permitted 'screened-in' HIV-positive Haitians legal counsel in their 'well-founded fear' hearings.[79] The U.S. government responded by ending 'well-founded

denied the executive the stay. The executive responded by asking the Second Circuit Court of Appeals for a stay. This was also denied on 14 April 1992.

72 Brandt Goldstein, *Storming the Court: How a Band of Yale Law Students Sued the President – And Won* (Simon and Schuster, 2005), 115.

73 *McNary v Haitian Centers Council, Inc.*, 503 US 1000 (1992).

74 Goldstein, n 72 in this chapter, 119.

75 969 F 2d 1326 (2nd Cir, 1992) *vacated as moot sub nom. Sale v Haitian Centers Council, Inc.* 509 US 155 (1993).

76 Ibid., 1347.

77 Goldstein, n 72 in this chapter, 158–59. The deal did not guarantee that refugees would be resettled in the United States.

78 Ibid.

79 *Haitian Centers Council, Inc, v McNary* 969 F 2d 1326 (2nd Cir, 1992) vacated as moot sub nom. *Sale v Haitian Centers Council, Inc.*, 509 US 155 (1993).

fear' hearings and transporting all HIV-positive Haitians who had satisfied the 'credible fear' screening interview to the HIV camp. That is, the United States no longer conducted both 'credible fear' determinations and 'well-founded fear' determinations before holding HIV-positive Haitians in Guantánamo Bay, but moved all who had a 'credible fear' of persecution to the HIV camp whilst repatriating all HIV-positive Haitians who did not have a 'credible fear' of persecution. Because there were no further 'well-founded fear' hearings, the U.S. government reasoned that it did not have to provide 'screened-in' Haitians with legal counsel after all.

In essence, therefore, there was no real victory for Haitians or their advocates in *McNary*, despite a Second Circuit decision that ruled in favour of the Haitian litigants. The U.S. government was successful in vacating the decision and thus removing the precedential weight of the decision without providing lawyers access to their clients in Guantánamo Bay. The case highlights the difficulty of challenging the MIP in U.S. courts and shows that even in rare cases where there has been a legal victory for Haitians or Cubans under the program, such a victory has not necessarily result in an improvement for interdictees under the MIP.

2.1.3 'Kennebunkport Order' and *Sale v Haitian Centers Council*

As the litigation played out in the courts, the United States continued to be faced with high numbers of persons fleeing Haiti, overcrowding on Coast Guard cutters, and increasing overcrowding in Guantánamo Bay. In response, on 24 May 1992, George H.W. Bush made one of his most controversial migration decisions. Under Executive Order 12807, the President ordered the repatriation of all individuals interdicted by the United States.[80] The Executive Order came to be popularly known as the Kennebunkport Order because it was made from the President's holiday house in Maine. Under the order, the Coast Guard is permitted to repatriate individuals interdicted outside U.S. territorial waters without determining if the interdicted person is in fact a refugee or in need of protection from *refoulement* under international human rights law.[81] The order states that

[80] Executive Order 12807, 57 *Federal Register* 23133 (1992).

[81] See discussion of the United States' *non-refoulement* obligation in Section 5.3.

> [t]he international legal obligations of the United States under the United Nations Protocol Relating to the Status of Refugees … to apply Article 33 of the United Nations Convention Relating to the Status of Refugees do not extend to persons located outside the territory of the United States.[82]

The Attorney General retains the discretion to protect refugees from *refoulement*, but that discretion is not reviewable.[83] Prior to the Kennebunkport Order, the United States had not denied the applicability of its obligations to refugees. The Kennebunkport Order, however, fundamentally changed the landscape. For the first time the United States explicitly denied the rights of refugees it interdicts in international waters. The Kennebunkport Order continues to be in operation today and is relied on by the U.S. executive as legal authority for the continuing operation of the MIP.[84]

The legality of the Kennebunkport Order was tested domestically in 1993 in the U.S. Supreme Court in the case of *Sale v Haitian Centers Council* (*Sale I*).[85] In that case, Haitian Centers Council and a number of other organisations representing interdicted Haitians[86] sought a temporary restraining order against *refoulement* of refugees to Haiti. The District Court denied relief.[87] The Court of Appeals for the Second Circuit reversed the District Court's decision on appeal.[88] On further appeal, the Supreme Court found for the U.S. government and upheld the Kennebunkport Order. The Court concluded that neither Article 33(1) of the Refugee Convention nor the United States implementing legislation prohibited the *refoulement* of refugees extraterritorially.[89]

This seminal decision, which has been widely criticised by the United Nations High Commissioner for Refugees (UNHCR), scholars and the international community more generally, is analysed in subsection 4.2.1.1. For present purposes, it suffices to note that it is widely believed, including

[82] See n 80 in this chapter, [2].
[83] Ibid § 3. See discussion in subsection 4.6.1.
[84] See discussion in Section 5.2.
[85] 509 US 155 (1993).
[86] The organisations included the National Coalition for Haitian Refugees, Inc. and the Immigration Law Clinic of the Jerome N. Frank Legal Services Organization of New Haven, Connecticut.
[87] *Haitian Centers Council, Inc. v McNary*, No 92 -CV-1258 (EDNY, June 5, 1992).
[88] *Haitian Centers Council, Inc. v McNary*, 969 F 2d 1350 (2nd Cir, 1992).
[89] *Sale v Haitian Centers Council, Inc.*, 509 US 155 (1993).

by the author, that *Sale I* was wrongly decided both in the construction of the Refugee Convention and the *Immigration and Nationality Act* (INA).[90] Nevertheless, the case remains authority for the proposition that protections under municipal law and international law against *refoulement*, available to refugees within U.S. territory, do not extend to refugees under the MIP.

2.1.3.1 Migrant Interdiction Program under Clinton

In the two years following the decision of the Supreme Court in *Sale I*, 53,735 Haitians were interdicted and returned to Haiti without status determinations.[91] This included individuals held in Guantánamo Bay who had not been granted a status determination interview. HIV-positive Haitians whose refugee status had been recognised through status determinations prior to the Kennebunkport Order remained detained at Camp Bulkeley and were not repatriated to Haiti. There is evidence that many repatriated Haitians, forcibly returned to Haiti without status determinations, were persecuted upon their return.[92]

There was strong opposition in the United States to the forced repatriation without status determination under the Kennebunkport Order. As a presidential candidate, Bill Clinton denounced President George H.W. Bush's policy, calling the Kennebunkport Order 'cruel'.[93] However, a week after his inauguration, President Clinton broadcast a radio message to Haiti announcing that interdiction and forced return of Haitians to Haiti without status determinations would continue under his administration. As such, President Clinton confirmed that the Kennebunkport Order would remain unchanged.[94] HIV-positive

[90] Pub L No 82–414, 66 Stat. 163 (1952).

[91] Americas Watch/National Coalition For Haitian Refugees/Jesuit Refugee Service USA, No Port in a Storm, 7 cited in UNHCR, *Haiti: Prospects for Democracy* (1995) <www.unhcr.org/refworld/country,,WRITENET,,HTI,4562d94e2,3ae6a6c30,0.html>.

[92] Anne Fuller, 'Persecution of Haitian Refugees Forcibly Returned to Haiti', Memorandum, National Coalition for Haitian Refugees, 21 April 1994, cited in UNHCR, *Haiti: Prospects for Democracy* (1995) <www.unhcr.org/refworld/country,,WRITENET,,HTI,4562d94e2,3ae6a6c30,0.html>.

[93] Michael McBride, 'Migrants and Asylum Seekers: Policy Responses in the United States to Immigrants and Refugees from Central America and the Caribbean' (1999) 37 *International Migration* 289.

[94] Philip Schrag, *A Well-Founded Fear: The Congressional Battle to Save Political Asylum in America* (Routledge, 2000), 37–38.

refugees who were found to have satisfied the 'well-founded fear' test under the previous administration, prior to the Kennebunkport Order, would also remain in Guantánamo Bay and would not be transferred to the U.S. mainland.

Advocates responded to President Clinton's about-face with public campaigns challenging the continued detention of HIV-positive refugees in Guantánamo Bay. On 29 March 1993, Actress Susan Sarandon and actor Tim Robbins gave a speech against the continuing detention of the HIV-positive refugees at the 65th annual Academy Awards in Los Angeles. The speech seen by millions around the world was not, however, the only advocacy around the issue.[95] Refugee and immigrant advocates, along with many public health officials, sought the resettlement of HIV-positive Haitians in the United States.[96] A number of physicians, most notably those associated with Doctors of the World, a New York–based international medical relief organisation, also repeatedly travelled to Guantánamo Bay to provide medical care to Haitians on the naval base and vocally spoke out against the treatment of the refugees in U.S. care, demanding their resettlement in the United States.[97]

2.1.3.2 A Successful Challenge on Behalf of HIV-Positive Refugees – Sale II

Lawyers also responded to the continuing detention of HIV-positive refugees through litigation. The parties to the *Sale I* hearing on the issue of *non-refoulement* made an oral application in September 1992 for a bifurcated trial so that issues pertaining to the detention of HIV-positive Haitians in Guantánamo Bay could be heard separately from the evidence on *non-refoulement*. The District Court for the Eastern District of New York heard evidence regarding camp conditions in Guantánamo, medical issues raised by the detention of HIV-positive non-citizens and an attack on the HIV ground for exclusion of aliens.[98] During the hearings

95 Lisa Ocker, 'Haitians at Guantánamo Bay Exempt from HIV Legislation', *South Florida Sun Sentinel*, 20 February 1993 <http://articles.sun-sentinel.com/1993-02-20/news/9301100780_1_guantanamo-haitians-haitian-refugees-guantanamo-bay>.

96 Sid Mohn, 'Haitians in Cuba Need Compassion', *Chicago Tribune*, 18 March 1993 <http://articles.chicagotribune.com/1993-03-18/news/9303180009_1_haitian-refugees-hiv-positive-detainees>.

97 Andrew Skolnick, 'Doctors Help HIV-Positive Haitian Refugees Gain Freedom from US Government Detention Camp' (1993) 270 *Journal of American Medical Association* 563.

98 *Haitian Centers Council, Inc. v Sale*, 823 F Supp 1028 (EDNY, 1993). Abrogation recognised by *Cuban American Bar Association v Christopher*, 43 F 3d 1412 (11th Cir, 1995).

the defendant counsel admitted that 'the medical facilities at Guantánamo [were] not … sufficient to provide treatment for … AIDS patients under the medical care standard applicable to the United States itself'.[99] The Court ordered that the Attorney General exercise her statutory parole power to release HIV-positive plaintiffs from detention.[100] The Court also ordered immediate access for service organisations to Guantánamo Bay to communicate with their clients.

As with the earlier victory by refugees and their advocates in *McNary*, the U.S. government successfully negotiated to have the precedential value of the decision removed by offering to refrain from appealing the decision if the Haitians and their advocates would agree to vacate the case. The refugees and their advocates believed that a successful appeal to a higher court could not be risked. As shown in Chapters 4, 5 and 6 of this book, they were correct to assume a high likelihood of defeat in the Supreme Court had the U.S. executive appealed the decision of the Second Circuit. The plaintiffs thus agreed and the case was vacated.[101] Therefore, as with *McNary*, *Sale II* cannot be relied on as precedent. However, unlike *McNary*, *Sale II* resulted in a tangible victory for the Haitians affected by the decision. Their resettlement in the United States ensured that they received better medical attention and were protected from harm in Haiti.

The significant difference between *McNary* and *Sale II* is the public advocacy that surrounded the detention of HIV-positive Haitians by the United States. Had the Clinton administration appealed the decision of the Second Circuit in the Supreme Court, this already highly public issue would have received even more adverse attention. Thus, the very visible advocacy was effective in ensuring that HIV-positive Haitians were in fact provided with greater rights. Without this public advocacy, it is arguable that the U.S. executive could have simply challenged the Second Circuit decision in the Supreme Court and refused to resettle the Haitians.

[99] Ibid., 1038.

[100] The decision was handed down on 8 June 1993.

[101] The case was vacated by Stipulated Order Approving Class Action Settlement Agreement on 22 February 1994. Abrogation was recognised by *Cuban American Bar Association v Christopher*, 43 F 3d 1412, 1424 n8 (11th Cir, 1995).

2.1.3.3 *Mounting Tensions in Haiti and the Use of Safe Havens in Third Countries*

At the same time as the settlement of HIV-positive Haitians from Guantánamo Bay was occurring, the Clinton administration was also searching for a political solution to the Haitian conflict.[102] Initially, the Clinton administration believed that the answer was one which could accommodate the military, the local economic elite and Aristide.[103]

The Clinton administration attempted to secure the cooperation of the military in reintroducing democracy in Haiti by offering the Haitian Army Chief Lt. General Raoul Cédras the opportunity to negotiate. Under pressure from the United Nations and the United States, on 3 July 1993, Aristide and Cédras signed a Governor's Island Agreement which outlined a strategy for re-democratisation of Haiti. The deal included Aristide's nomination as Prime Minister, the suspension of U.S. sanctions, the provision of international aid, amnesty for the perpetrators of the September 1991 coup and permission for Cédras to retain his position until Aristide resumed his presidency.[104]

Aristide was to return to Haiti on 30 October 1993. The military, however, chose to renege on the agreement and made it clear that they would not accept his presidency. By 15 January 1994, the military had failed to meet a single condition set down in the Governor's Island Agreement, including the reinstatement of Aristide.[105]

In late April 1994, the Clinton administration's policy towards Haiti hardened. The United States requested the United Nations Security Council's support for imposing a global trade embargo on Haiti together with financial sanctions, the freezing of overseas assets and travel bans against 600 military officers who supported the September 1991 coup or the autocratic regime.[106]

At the same time, President Clinton faced effective public advocacy against his continuation of the Kennebunkport Order. In March 1994,

[102] For an in-depth discussion of the Clinton White House's policy towards Haiti, see Morris Morley and Chris McGillion, 'Disobedient Generals and the Politics of Redemocratization: The Clinton Administration and Haiti' (1997) 112 *Political Science Quarterly* 363.

[103] Ibid., 368.

[104] Ibid.

[105] Ibid., 370.

[106] See Julia Preston, 'US Shifts on Haiti, Gets Tougher on Army', *Washington Post*, 29 April 1994 <www.highbeam.com/doc/1P2-888227.html>.

Aristide, who had not yet resumed his role as the President of Haiti, publicly denounced the policy of repatriating Haitians without status determinations, calling it 'racist' at a meeting of the Congressional Black Caucus in Miami.[107] A twenty-seven-day media-intensive hunger strike by Randall Robinson, protests in which members of Congress were arrested and the unwillingness of the Haitian military to cooperate in the democratisation of Haiti helped finally to convince President Clinton to overturn President George H.W. Bush's policy of denying Haitians status determinations and *non-refoulement* protection. Importantly, however, Clinton did not overturn Executive Order 12807 itself. Thus, the Clinton administration made changes to policies that governed the MIP without disturbing the legal basis on which the MIP rested.

On 8 May 1994, President Clinton announced a resumption of offshore processing for Haitians. Under the new arrangements, all Haitians fleeing their country were granted a status determination either on board Coast Guard vessels outside the U.S. territorial seas or in third countries. The administration declared that refugees who satisfied the tougher 'well-founded fear' of persecution test, rather than the previously used test of 'credible fear' of persecution, would be transferred to the U.S. mainland.

The Clinton administration signed a Memorandum of Understanding (MOU) with Jamaica and the United Kingdom for third-country status determination of Haitians interdicted under the MIP.[108] Under the MOU with Jamaica, a hospital ship was used for on-board processing of Haitians in Jamaican waters. The MOU with the United Kingdom allowed the United States to conduct third-country processing in the islands of Turks and Caicos. The Clinton administration also used Guantánamo Bay as a processing centre. Between May and July 1993, 30 per cent of all Haitians

[107] Associated Press, 'Aristide Says US Policy on Haiti Is Criminal, Racist', *Desert News* (Sale Lake City) 19 March 1994 <www.deseretnews.com/article/342492/ARISTIDE-SAYS-US-POLICY-ON-HAITI-IS-CRIMINAL-RACIST.html?pg=all>.

[108] Memorandum of Understanding Between the Government of the United States and the Government of Jamaica for the Establishment Within the Jamaican Territorial Sea and Internal Waters of a Facility to Process Nationals of Haiti Seeking Refuge Within or Entry to the United States of America, entered into force 2 June 1994, KAV 3901, Temp. State Dept. No 94–153, entered into force 18 June 1994, KAV 3906, Temp. State Dept. No 94–158; Memorandum of Understanding Between the Government of the United Kingdom, the Government of the Turks and Caicos Islands and the Government of the United States to Establish in the Turks and Caicos Islands a Processing Facility to Determine the Refugee Status of Boat People from Haiti, entered into force 18 June 1994, KAV 3906, Temp. State Dept. No 94–158.

who underwent status determinations in Guantánamo Bay had their refugee status recognised and were resettled in the U.S. mainland.[109]

However, faced with continuing numbers of Haitians fleeing their country, in July 1994, the Clinton administration changed the MIP again by ceasing status determinations and instead offering all Haitians a 'safe haven'.[110] Under the new arrangements, Haitians would be protected in third countries or in Guantánamo Bay but would never be permitted into the U.S. mainland. Panama agreed to allow the United States to send 10,000 Haitians to Panama but later rescinded its approval after facing international pressure. On 25 July 1994, Honduras announced that it would shelter up to 40,000 Haitians temporarily in exchange for increased U.S. aid.[111]

Furthermore, the surge of refugees from Haiti placed additional pressure on the United States to resolve the Haitian situation through military intervention.[112] President Clinton made his intention to invade Haiti clear in a televised address in the United States, in which he discussed politically motivated killings, torture and rape in Haiti and put the blame squarely on General Cédras and his accomplices.[113] President Clinton informed the public that all diplomatic efforts had been exhausted and warned the leaders of the Haitian military that they must relinquish power immediately.[114] An unopposed multinational force of 20,000 troops, led by the United States, landed in Haiti on 19 September 1994 to oversee the country's transition to democracy.[115] Aristide returned to Haiti on 15 October 1994 and was reinstated as President. Upon his return to power, Aristide terminated the 1981 interdiction agreement between Haiti and

109 Carlos Ortiz Miranda, 'Haiti and the United States during the 1980s and 1990s: Refugees, Immigration and Foreign Policy' (1995) 32 *San Diego Law Review* 673, 744.

110 Philip Martin, 'Economic Instruments to Affect Countries of Origin' in Rainer Münz and Myron Weiner (eds), *Migrants, Refugees, and Foreign Policy: U.S. and German Policies Toward Countries of Origin* (Berghahn Books, 1997), 258.

111 *Migration News*, Haitian Zig-Zags (1994) <http://migration.ucdavis.edu/mn/comments.php?id=383_0_2_0>.

112 Ann Devroy and Barton Gellman, 'Exodus from Haiti Strains US Policy', *Washington Post*, 2 July 1994, Al.

113 Morley and McGillion, n 102 in this chapter, 379.

114 Robert Pastor, 'The Clinton Administration and the Americas: The Postwar Rhythm and Blues' (1996) 38 *Journal of International Studies and World Affairs* 99, 105–06.

115 United Nations, *Haiti Background* (1994). <www.un.org/en/peacekeeping/missions/past/unmihbackgr2.html>.

the United States.[116] As explained in subsection 3.3.2, the termination of the agreement has important legal consequences under international law, for the United States is no longer authorised to interdict Haitian flagged sea vessels in the contiguous zone of neighbouring States, exclusive economic zone (EEZ, of the United States and other States) or the high seas without further sources of authority for interference with the vessel.

Following the return of Aristide to Haiti, the United States began a process of repatriating Haitians to Haiti from 'safe havens'. Some Haitians were offered incentives to return to their home country voluntarily by 5 January 1995.[117] By the middle of November 1994, the majority of Haitians had returned to Haiti from 'safe havens'; however, some Haitians refused the incentives. Haitians who refused 'voluntary repatriation' from Guantánamo Bay were forced to return to Haiti. The U.S. government relied on troops to carry out repatriations.[118]

The HRC and two named Haitians responded to the forced repatriations by moving for a temporary restraining order to stop the involuntary return of Haitians to Haiti. Oral hearings were held during the evening of 5 January 1995, the date set for the forced return of Haitians who had not volunteered to return to Haiti. In *HRC v Christopher*,[119] the request for injunctive relief was denied because the Court found that the plaintiffs did not have a substantial likelihood of success.[120]

The plaintiffs appealed the decision to the Eleventh Circuit on 9 January 1995. They asked for a summary reversal of the District Court's denial of injunctive relief. The Eleventh Circuit affirmed the decision of the District Court to refuse injunctive relief and found that '[u]nder the binding law of [the Eleventh Circuit] there is no statutory provision which prevents the President or the Attorney General from repatriating the Haitian

116 In April 1994, prior to being reinstated as President, Aristide had informed President Clinton that when he resumed his presidency of Haiti, he intended to abrogate the agreement. John Goshko, 'Aristide Renounces Treaty Allowing Return of Haitians", *Washington Post*, 7 April 1994 <www.highbeam.com/doc/1P2-884384.html>.

117 Paul Smith, 'Military Responses to the Global Migration Crisis: A Glimpse of Things to Come' (1999) 23 *Fletcher Forum of World Affairs* 77. The incentives included US $80 in cash and temporary employment in a U.S.-funded Haitian public works program.

118 Ibid., 86.

119 *Haitian Refugee Center, Inc. v Christopher*, (District Court for the Southern District of Florida/ No 95–0022–CIV–MOORE, 5 January 1995).

120 Ibid.

migrants'.[121] Thus, the Court found that providing a safe haven to Haitians in Guantánamo was a 'gratuitous humanitarian act which does not in any way create a liberty interest',[122] and therefore, Haitians in Guantánamo Bay did not have any procedural safeguards. This ruling meant that the forced return of Haitians from Guantánamo Bay could continue.

2.1.4 Interdiction of Haitians by the United States Post-1994

Following the return of Aristide to Haiti and the repatriation of Haitians from safe havens, the United States changed its policy towards Haitians interdicted under the MIP once again. Under the new incarnation, Haitians had to alert the Coast Guard to their protection needs. All Haitians with a credible fear of persecution were taken to Guantánamo Bay for further assessment of their status, and then resettled in a third country. All other Haitians were repatriated. The MIP has been largely unchanged since 1994. The United States continued to hold that

> [a]ny person of any nationality who is interdicted on the High Seas by the United States and indicates a need for protection will have such need evaluated, consistent with international standards, by the United States Government.[123]

However, as discussed in Section 5.2, status determinations for protection seekers interdicted by the United States under the MIP are not a matter of legal right under U.S. municipal law. Rather, they are part of a policy established by an unreviewable discretion of the Attorney General.

It should also be noted that on 15 November 2002, President George W. Bush issued Executive Order 13276.[124] The Order, as amended by Executive Order 13286,[125] authorises the Secretary of Homeland Security to maintain custody and conduct screening of any undocumented

[121] *Haitian Refugee Center, Inc. v Christopher* 43 F 3d 1431, 1433 (11th Cir, 1995).

[122] Ibid.

[123] Letter from Doris Meissner, Commissioner of INS, to Bill Frelick, Senior Policy Analyst, US Committee for Refugees (19 July 1996), cited in Karen Musalo, Lauren Gibson, Stephen Knight and J. Edward Taylor, *The Expedited Removal Study: Report on the First Three Years of Implementation of Expedited Removal*, Centre for Human Rights and International Justice University of California (Hastings College of Law, 2001).

[124] 67 *Federal Register* 69, 985 (2002).

[125] 68 *Federal Register* 10619 (2003).

non-citizens, intercepted in the Caribbean region, 'in Guantánamo Bay Naval Base or any other appropriate location'.[126] However, as shown earlier, Guantánamo Bay has been used under the MIP since 1991. As such, the Executive Order does not in fact change the impact of the MIP on protection seekers. Nevertheless, the Executive Order provides a legal basis for the utilisation of Guantánamo Bay under the MIP.

2.2 Cuba

Haitians are not the only nationality to be affected by the MIP and to be transferred to Guantánamo Bay if they are found to have a credible fear of persecution or torture. Cubans are also interdicted under the MIP and may be taken to Guantánamo Bay if they are found to have a credible fear of persecution or torture. However, Cubans were not subjected to the MIP until 1994, thirteen years after the program was introduced for Haitians. As with Haitians, the irregular sea movement of Cubans to the United States is best understood in the context of Cuba's modern history.

The United States' current policies regarding Cuban nationals can be traced back to 1952 when General Fulgencio Batista seized the presidency in Cuba after a coup.[127] The United States had great financial interest in Cuba at the time, and Batista enjoyed U.S. support.[128] The policies of Batista, however, alienated the Cuban people. In 1959, Fidel Castro overthrew the Batista government in a revolution. Batista was forced to flee Cuba on New Year's Day, 1959.[129] Fidel Castro was sworn in as Premier of Cuba on 16 February 1959 and became the President of Cuba on 2 December 1976.[130] The overthrow of the U.S. ally, Batista, by a communist leader led to tension between the United States and the new regime under Fidel Castro.

[126] Executive Order 13276, 67 *Federal Register* 69, 985 (2002), s 1(a)(i).

[127] Joseph Sweeney, 'Guantánamo and US Law' (2007) 30 *Fordham International Law Journal* 673, 677.

[128] Carmen Deere, 'Here Come the Yankees! The Rise and Decline of United States Colonies in Cuba 1898–1930' (1998) 78 *The Hispanic American Historical Review* 729.

[129] Sweeney, n 127 in this chapter, 697.

[130] Jessica Gibbs, *US Policy Towards Cuba: Since the Cold War* (Routledge, 2011) 10–25.

Public trials and executions of members of the old regime took place soon after Fidel Castro came to power in Cuba.[131] Between 1959 and 1961, approximately 125,000 Cubans fled the country for the United States.[132] Most of this movement occurred through commercial flights, which were still permitted at the time.[133] Initially the United States insisted that Cubans wishing to come to the United States follow all the usual visa requirements, including a police check to determine if the applicant had a criminal record. However, as U.S.-Cuban relations deteriorated, the United States adopted a more passive policy that was designed to let most Cubans enter the country.[134] As Galin observes, 'Cubans were once the most privileged immigrants; like Berlin Wall jumpers and Russian ballet dances, they were Cold War icons. For more than 30 years they served as evidence of America's moral superiority'.[135]

President Dwight Eisenhower believed the flow of Cuban refugees to the United States was temporary.[136] This may have accounted for the lack of detailed security checks on Cubans before their admission into the United States, lack of a formalised sponsorship program and lack of plans to distribute Cuban nationals through communities in the country. For this reason, the majority of early Cubans who came to the United States following the overthrow of the Batista regime settled in southern Florida.[137]

Cubans that were affiliated with the overthrown Fulgencio Batista were the first group to leave Cuba. They were followed by other Cubans who were not directly linked to the former government but held positions of wealth, privilege and power under the Batista regime. The final group of political exiles to flee between 1959 and 1961 were the disaffected followers

[131] Gil Loescher and John Scanlan, *Calculated Kindness: Refugees and America's Half-open Door, 1945 to the Present* (Free Press, 1986) 62.
[132] Karen Bockley, 'A Historical Overview of Refugee Legislation: The Deception of Foreign Policy in the Land of Promise' (1995) 21 *North Carolina Journal of International Law and Commercial Regulation* 253, 269.
[133] Roland Estevez, 'Modern Application of the Cuban Adjustment Act Of 1966 and Helms-Burton: Adding Insult to Injury' (2002) 30 *Hofstra Law Review* 1273, 1274.
[134] Loescher and Scanlan, n 131 in this chapter, 61.
[135] David Gavilan, 'Y Que Paso – And Then What Happened: The Plight of Cuban Detainees at Guantánamo Bay' (1996) 4 *Cardozo Journal of International and Comparative Law* 451, 451.
[136] Loescher and Scanlan, n 131 in this chapter, 64.
[137] John Scanlan and Gilburt Loescher, 'US Foreign Policy, 1959–80: Impact on Refugee Flow from Cuba' (1983) 467 *The Annals of the American Academy of Political and Social Science* 116, 117–18.

of Castro.[138] In the years following the Cuban revolution, undocumented Cubans began travelling to the U.S. mainland in small boats, but the U.S. Coast Guard made no attempt to interdict or repatriate them.[139] By the autumn of 1959, the U.S. Central Intelligence Agency (CIA) began helping in the ferrying of Cubans from Cuba to Florida.[140] Many of the Cubans brought to the United States by the CIA were counter-revolutionaries.[141]

Until January 1961, a Cuban national could go to the American consular offices in Cuba and apply for a visa that would allow a person to stay permanently in the United States and eventually become a citizen, or alternatively for a non-immigrant visa, which had an expiration date, such as a visa for a tourist, student or business person. Cubans who held a non-immigrant visa had to return to Cuba after the expiration date of their visa.[142] However, the United States did not insist that Cubans who overstayed their non-immigrant visa return home if they claimed they could not go to Cuba as long as Castro was in government.[143]

The United States broke diplomatic relations with Cuba on 3 January 1961 and closed its embassy in Havana on the same day. Cubans could no longer go to the U.S. embassy if they wished to enter the United States. Instead, a request to the Department of State was filed on behalf of a Cuban applicant by friends and relatives in the United States for a 'visa waiver'.[144] Under the visa waiver, the Attorney General waived the visa requirement for entry into the United States. The applicant would be informed by friends or family if they had been successful in their application and would make arrangements to come to the United States. Upon arriving, the Cuban national would apply for parole (entry) and refugee status.[145] All Cubans wishing to come to the United States were screened by the INS and the Department of State. Security checks were run for all who applied for visas and later for visa waivers (after 1961). After receiving

[138] Richard Fagen, Richard Brody and Thomas O'Leary, *Cubans in Exile: Disaffection and the Revolution* (Stanford University Press, 1968) Vol 7, 71.
[139] Loescher and Scanlan, n 131 in this chapter, 61.
[140] Ibid 63.
[141] Scanlan and Loescher, n 137 in this chapter, 117.
[142] Carl Bon-Tempo, *Americans at the Gate: The United States and Refugees During the Cold War* (Princeton University Press, 2008) 115.
[143] Loescher and Scanlan, n 131 in this chapter, 63.
[144] Bon-Tempo, n 142 in this chapter, 116.
[145] Ibid.

a visa or a waiver, the Cubans would submit to a health inspection before coming to the United States. A more complete health and security inspection took place once the Cuban reached the U.S. mainland.[146]

In 1961, President Kennedy took office. As Loescher and Scanlan point out, 'President Kennedy inherited from President Eisenhower … two correlative beliefs: that Castro could be overthrown with the help of Cubans in the US, and that once he was overthrown, these Cubans would … return home'.[147] In June 1962, the Kennedy administration secured passage of the *Migration and Refugee Assistance Act*.[148] The Act did not purport to change the law pertaining to the admission of non-citizens but made express provisions for ongoing assistance for 'refugees who are continuing to find their way out of Cuba'.[149]

Cuban-U.S. relations deteriorated even further in April 1961 when the United States unsuccessfully attempted to invade Cuba and overthrow the Castro government by using a trained force of Cuban exiles.[150] The invasion was named the 'Bay of Pigs' after the landing place of the Cuban exiles. The Cuban military defeated the exiles in a matter of days. The relationship between the United States and Cuba was further damaged after the Cuban Missile Crisis at the height of the Cold War.[151] On 15 October 1962, the United States identified secret missile bases being built in Cuba by the USSR. The United States responded by demanding that the Soviet Union remove the missile bases and ordering a naval quarantine of Cuba.[152] The USSR countered by ordering that tactical nuclear weapons be used if there was an invasion of Cuba by U.S. forces. On 28 October 1962, USSR supply ships were ordered away from Cuban waters and Soviet missiles were removed from Cuba's mainland, thereby averting a nuclear war.[153]

146 Loescher and Scanlan, n 131 in this chapter, 63.
147 Ibid 64.
148 Pub.L No 510, 87th Cong, 1st sess, (1962).
149 United States Senate, Report No 989, 87th Cong. 1st sess. (1962).
150 For a detailed account of the invasion, see Howard Jones, *The Bay of Pigs* (Oxford University Press, 2008).
151 The Cuban missile crisis has been the subject of numerous studies. For an introduction to the events around the Cuban Missile Crisis, see Priscilla Roberts, *Cuban Missile Crisis: The Essential Reference Guide* (ABC-CLIO, 2012). See also Don Munton and David Welch, *The Cuban Missile Crisis: A Concise History* (Oxford University Press, 2011).
152 Roberts, n 151 in this chapter, 172.
153 Ibid 228.

Following the Cuban Missile Crisis, commercial flights between Cuba and the United States were suspended and Castro tightened the restrictions on Cubans leaving Cuba. Some Cubans managed to come to the United States via third countries (such as Spain or Mexico) with U.S. visas. Other Cubans who escaped Cuba and came to Florida without authorisation were granted a visa waiver by the U.S. government and applied for admission. Certain individuals who had the permission of the Castro regime to depart (such as U.S. citizens or humanitarian cases) had their names given to the Swiss embassy. The Swiss embassy passed on the names to the United States for approval.[154]

The United States adopted a policy of economic denial towards Cuba from the beginning of 1962.[155] Many of the poor members of Cuban society benefited from expansions in education and medical programs under Castro. The standard of living of the middle class, however, deteriorated rapidly.[156] This led to a desire among many of the middle class to leave Cuba, and they joined political refugees fleeing the country. The United States believed that the departure of the educated middle class, with their technical expertise, would further hurt the Castro regime.[157]

In September 1965, overwhelmed by the number of people desiring to leave Cuba, Castro announced that any Cuban who had relatives living in the United States would be allowed to leave the island via the port of Camarioca, located on Cuba's northern shore.[158] The invitation to leave was not extended to political prisoners and draft-age men who may have sought refugee status as conscientious objectors.[159] It has been argued that Castro opened the border in order to expel those with close ties to the exile

[154] Bon-Tempo, n 142 in this chapter, 116.

[155] Scanlan and Loescher, n 137 in this chapter, 124. On 3 February 1962, President Kennedy issued Proclamation 3447, 27 *Federal Register* 1085 (1962), which placed a total embargo on Cuban-American trade. The United States placed sanctions on Cuba, and measures were taken to pressure the major industrial nations to cut all trade with Cuba. In July 1964, the Organisation of American States also imposed comprehensive diplomatic and trade sanctions on Cuba.

[156] James Olson and Judith Olson, *Cuban Americans: From Trauma to Triumph* (Twayne Publishers, 1995) 51.

[157] Scanlan and Loescher, n 137 in this chapter, 137.

[158] Kelly Greenhill, *Weapons of Mass Migration: Forced Displacement, Coercion, and Foreign Policy* (Cornell University Press, 2010).

[159] Gilburt Loescher, 'US Foreign Policy, 1959–80: Impact on Refugee Flow from Cuba' (1983) 467 *The Annals of the American Academy of Political and Social Science* 116, 125.

community because it enabled him to release the internal pressure from those who may have undermined his regime.[160] It has also been argued that the opening of the borders by Castro was an attempt to demonstrate to the United States that Cuba and not the United States controlled Florida's coastal borders.[161]

In response to the exodus that ensued, President Lyndon Johnson proclaimed that the United States would continue to welcome Cubans seeking freedom.[162] Two flights per day were resumed from Havana to Miami.[163] However, the Johnson administration became worried when the numbers of people leaving Cuba began to escalate.[164] The United States began a series of negotiations with the Castro regime that resulted in an MOU. Under the MOU, a formal procedure was established for the movement of Cubans to the United States. An airlift began in December 1965 (and continued until 1973) to bring Cubans to the United States. The aim of the resulting migration program, which came to be known as the freedom flights, was essentially to reunite families.[165] There were thus fewer refugees among the Cubans who left Cuba after 1965 than those who fled to the United States in the two years following the revolution.[166] However, Castro used the opportunity to export large numbers of dissidents and to redistribute their property.[167]

The question of integrating the large number of Cuban nationals led the U.S. Congress to clarify the legal status of newly arrived Cubans through the *Cuban Adjustment Act* (CAA).[168] The Act passed Congress on 2 November 1966 and attempted to ensure that Cubans were not in a state of 'citizenship limbo'.[169] The CAA, which continues to operate today, allows any Cuban national who has been living in the United States, under any circumstance

160 Miguel Gonzalez-Pando, *The Cuban Americans* (Greenwood Press, 1998) 44.
161 Ibid.
162 Kelly Greenhill, 'Engineered Migration and the Use of Refugees as Political Weapons: A Case Study of the 1994 Cuban "Balseros" Crisis' (2002) 40 *International Migration* 39, 48.
163 Ibid.
164 Ibid.
165 Statement of Robert Hurwitch, Deputy Assistant Secretary of State for Inter-American Affairs, 8 July 1970, cited in Scanlan and Loescher, n 137 in this chapter, 126.
166 Scanlan and Loescher, n 137 in this chapter, 125.
167 Ibid 127.
168 Pub.L. No 89–732, 80 Stat. 1161, as amended 8 USC § 1255 note (Supp, 1992).
169 Bon-Tempo, n 142 in this chapter, 127.

and for any reason, to apply to become a U.S. permanent resident after one year. Cubans are the only foreign nationals in the United States enjoying the privilege of the CAA. In 1996, the CAA was modified by the *Cuban Liberty and Democratic Solidarity Act* of 1996.[170] It now provides that the CAA will be repealed when democracy returns to Cuba.

2.2.1 Mariel Boat Lift

From 1973, when the 'freedom flights' were terminated, until 1980, the number of Cubans emigrating from Cuba decreased, as Cubans wishing to leave had to turn to clandestine methods of escape. Cuban migration to the United States was limited to a few thousand Cuban political prisoners, spouses of Cubans in the United States and children accompanying U.S. citizens.[171] Nevertheless, in March 1980, Castro threatened to unleash large-scale emigration from Cuba to the United States if the U.S. government did not stop giving asylum to Cubans who succeeded in reaching the country.[172] This warning was left unheeded by the Carter administration.[173]

One option available to Cubans wishing to leave Cuba was to take refuge in the embassies of Latin American countries. There was a well-established tradition that Latin American countries accepted refugees from their neighbouring nations.[174] These embassies were guarded by Cuban soldiers and, on 1 April 1980, a Cuban soldier guarding the Peruvian Embassy in Havana was killed trying to prevent a bus filled with Cubans seeking asylum from crashing through the gates of the embassy. Angered by this death, Castro responded by announcing that he would remove the security forces surrounding the embassy. The lack of security resulted in more than 10,000 Cubans attempting to seek asylum in Peru through the embassy. The sheer number of dissatisfied Cubans wishing to leave the country became a public relations nightmare for the Castro regime. Castro responded by blaming U.S. propaganda for misleading the Cuban people.[175] He invited Cuban exiles in the United States to come

[170] Pub L No 104–114, 110. Stat. 785, codified at 22 USC §§ 6021 to 6091.

[171] Scanlan and Loescher, n 137 in this chapter, 127.

[172] Mario Rivera, *Decision and Structure: US Refugee Policy in the Mariel Crisis* (University Press of America, 1991) 196.

[173] Greenhill, n 162 in this chapter, 48.

[174] Leycester Coltman, *The Real Fidel Castro* (Yale University Press, 2003) 251.

[175] Coltman, n 174 in this chapter, 251.

back to Cuba by sea and pick up not only the refugees who attempted to seek asylum at the Peruvian embassy but anyone who wanted to leave.[176] This led to yet another mass exodus from Cuba to the United States. The exodus was called the Mariel Boat Lift because the boats departed from Cuba's Mariel Harbour.

Like President Johnson before him, President Carter responded to the exodus from Cuba by welcoming the Cuban refugees. He proclaimed that the United States would continue to 'provide an open heart and open arms for the tens of thousands of refugees seeking freedom from Communist domination'.[177] Within a week of welcoming the Cubans into the country, however, President Carter was compelled to change the U.S. position. On 14 May 1980, the Carter administration ordered the boatlift to be stopped and a naval blockade was implemented. These measures were to no avail as almost 90,000 Cubans arrived in the United States in May 1980 alone.[178]

President Carter declared a state of emergency in South Florida and gave $10 million to local governments to assist with the crisis.[179] These attempts to ease pressure on South Florida's infrastructure finally culminated in the airlifting of newly arrived Cubans to military installations throughout the United States, including Fort Chaffee in Arkansas where Bill Clinton was governor – an event he was to remember and be influenced by in his future dealings, as president, with Cuban refugees.[180] The Carter administration also began threatening exiles with heavy fines and confiscation of their vessels if they continued to bring Cubans into the United States.[181]

The exodus was ended by mutual agreement between Cuba and the United States in October 1980. The Mariel Boat Lift had brought in between 120,000 and 125,000 Cubans to Florida.[182] Approximately 10,000–15,000 of the people leaving Cuba for the United States in 1980 were released from Cuban jails and mental health facilities and were

[176] Greenhill, n 162 in this chapter, 48.
[177] Felix Masud-Piloto, *From Welcomed Exiles to Illegal Immigrants: Cuban Migration to the US, 1959–1995* (Rowman & Littlefield Publishers, 1996) 83.
[178] Greenhill, n 162 in this chapter, 49.
[179] Rivera, n 172 in this chapter, 68.
[180] Greenhill, n 162 in this chapter, 49.
[181] Ibid.
[182] David Card, 'The Impact of the Mariel Boatlift on the Miami Labor Market' (1990) 43 *Industrial and Labor Relations Review* 245.

violent criminals or suffered from mental illness.[183] The Mariel Boat Lift was highly damaging politically to the standing of President Carter, who was accused of being too indecisive and ineffectual in his dealings with Cuba.[184] Most damaging of all was the fact that the crisis occurred during a presidential campaign. President Carter's challenger, Ronald Reagan, was able to take advantage of the refugee issue.[185]

2.2.2 The Extension of the Migrant Interdiction Program to Cuban Nationals

The Mariel Boat Lift in 1980 was not the last of the mass movements of Cuban nationals to the United States. Another major exodus from Cuba began on 5 August 1994, when thousands of Cubans attempted to set sail for the United States on rafts and boats in response to rumours that the Cuban authorities were permitting the departure of Cuban citizens from the country. The rumour was in fact incorrect, and those attempting to leave were confronted by Cuban officials who attempted to stop the exodus. The rafters and the police became involved in altercations which led to the death of two policemen and serious injury to a third. A riot in the commercial district of Havana followed. On 6 August 1994, Castro made an announcement that he was not opposed to letting those who wanted to leave Cuba emigrate. On 12 August 1994, Castro ordered the Cuban Coast Guard not to apprehend anyone leaving Cuba unless they attempted to do so on a stolen boat.[186] In response to the influx of Cuban nationals in 1994, the governor of Florida declared a state of emergency and openly urged President Clinton to take immediate action.[187]

President Clinton had seen firsthand as a governor in 1980 the political consequences of the Mariel Boat Lift. After the boatlift, popular

[183] Mathew Pingeton, 'United States Immigration Policy; Detaining Cuban Refugees Taken from the Sea' (1998) 8 *Journal of Transnational Law & Policy* 329, 330.

[184] See David Engstrom, *Presidential Decision Making Adrift: The Carter Administration and the Mariel Boatlift* (Rowman & Littlefield Publishers, 1997).

[185] Greenhill, n 162 in this chapter, 51.

[186] Human Rights Watch, *Cuba: Repression, the Exodus of August 1994, and the US Response* (1994) <http://www.hrw.org/reports/pdfs/c/cuba/cuba940.pdf>.

[187] Jonathan Wachs 'Recent Development: The Need to Define the International Legal Status of Cubans Detained at Guantánamo' (1996) 11 *The American University Journal of International Law & Policy* 79.

sentiment in the United States regarding Cuban emigration changed.[188] Furthermore, by 1994, the fall of the Soviet Union as a superpower and the end of the Cold War had made Cuban refugees less potent as a statement against communism. Fearing another crisis similar to the Mariel Boat Lift and the consequent loss of political standing as occurred in Carter's presidency, President Clinton announced that Cubans interdicted outside the territorial sea of the United States would not be permitted to reach the U.S. mainland. Thus, unlike his predecessors, President Clinton was prepared to fundamentally change U.S. policy towards Cubans and extend the MIP to Cuban nationals.

On 19 August 1994, President Clinton announced that interdicted Cubans would be taken to the Guantánamo Bay naval base to join the 15,000 Haitians already there at that time.[189] The use of the naval base for Cubans wishing to come to the U.S. mainland thus reversed the long-standing policy of welcoming Cubans into the United States.[190] As Guantánamo became overcrowded, the United States once again looked to its neighbours for assistance to share the perceived burden. By September 1994, Cubans were also given refuge in safe havens in Panama where four temporary camps and other facilities were set up with the capacity to accommodate 2,500 Cubans interdicted by the United States.[191]

Advocates responded to the extension of the MIP to Cuban nationals through litigation. On 24 October 1994, the Cuban American Bar Association, Cuban Legal Alliance, Inc., Due Process Inc., Cuban protection seekers and two U.S. permanent residents who were relatives of detained protection seekers in Guantánamo Bay filed a suit for declaratory and injunctive relief in the U.S. District Court for the Southern District of Florida.[192] The case was about the rights of the approximately 32,000 Cubans detained at Guantánamo Bay,

188 Scanlan and Loescher, n 137 in this chapter, 127.

189 Maria Sartori 'Cuban Migration Dilemma: An Examination of the United States Policy of Temporary Protection of Offshore Save Havens' (2001) 15 *Georgetown Immigration Law Journal* 319.

190 Ibid.

191 Thomas Jones, 'A Human Rights Tragedy: The Cuban and Haitian Refugee Crises Revisited' (1995) 9 *Georgetown Immigration Law Journal* 479, 493; Smith, n 117 in this chapter.

192 *Cuban American Bar Association v Christopher*, No 94–2183 (Class Action Complaints) (SD Fla, 1994).

in the Republic of Panama and 'in other locations under the exclusive jurisdiction and control of the United States'.[193]

A temporary restraining order was issued by Judge Atkins of the District Court on 25 October 1994. The District Court ruled that the United States was obliged to provide the legal organisations access to their clients in Guantánamo Bay and forbade the involuntary repatriation of the refugees to Cuba prior to the visit by the legal team. The Court distinguished the case from *Sale I* on the grounds that the earlier case involved interdictees outside the territorial sea of the United States and not in Guantánamo Bay. The Court also distinguished *Baker III*, arguing that the Baker litigation involved interdictees on Coast Guard vessels and not refugees in Guantánamo Bay.

The United States filed an appeal in the Eleventh Circuit on 1 December 1994. In *Cuban-American Bar Association v Christopher* (*Christopher*),[194] the Court of Appeals for the Eleventh Circuit found for the U.S. government. The Court held that Cuba was not U.S. territory and, therefore, denied that non-citizens in Guantánamo Bay had any rights under U.S. statute, international law or the U.S. Constitution. The Court held that *Baker III* could not be distinguished in the case before it because *Baker III* applied not only to Haitians interdicted at sea but also those transported to Guantánamo Bay.[195] The Eleventh Circuit vacated all District Court orders and remanded the case. The Court concluded that 'although the human crisis is compelling, there is no solution to be found in a judicial remedy'.[196] The decision of the Eleventh Circuit in *Christopher* is seminal because, as discussed in Section 5.2, it is the authority for the proposition that the First and Fifth Amendments of the U.S. Constitution do not extend to Guantánamo Bay.

On 12 June 2008, the Supreme Court recognised the constitutional prohibition against the suspension of the writ of *habeas corpus* in Guantánamo Bay, in *Boumediene v Bush* (*Boumediene*).[197] Prior to the *Boumediene* decision, *Christopher* was one of three cases (including *Johnson v Eisentrager*[198]

[193] Ibid.
[194] 43 F 3d 1412, 1417 (11th Cir, 1995).
[195] *Cuban American Bar Association v Christopher*, 43 F 3d 1412, 1425 (11th Cir, 1995).
[196] Ibid.
[197] 553 US 723 (2008).
[198] 339 US 763 (1950).

and *United States v Verdugo-Urquidez*[199]) relied on by the U.S. executive to deny all constitutional protections to non-citizens in Guantánamo Bay. Although, as discussed in Section 5.2, *Boumediene* has cast a question mark over the denial of constitutional protections in Guantánamo Bay, *Christopher* has not been overturned and continues to be used to deny interdictees rights under the First and Fifth Amendments of the U.S. Constitution in Guantánamo Bay.

2.2.3 Return of Cubans to Cuba and the 'Wet Foot/Dry Foot' Policy

Following the repatriation of Haitians from Guantánamo Bay in late 1994,[200] it became clear to the U.S. executive that Guantánamo Bay was not a satisfactory long-term solution to the problem of Cubans seeking to enter the U.S. mainland. As Wachs points out,

> United States citizens, neighbouring governments, and the international community condemned the United States for its treatment of the Cuban refugees at Guantánamo. These factors, combined with political and economic conditions in Cuba that may initiate a new wave of Cuban refugees, prompted the Clinton administration to re-evaluate its Guantánamo detention policy.[201]

A publication by the Joint Working Group of Non-Governmental Civil, Political and Human Rights Organizations in the United States provided a detailed, analytical critique of the U.S. policy of detaining Cubans in Guantánamo Bay, and gained some public attention.[202] Further, a visit to Guantánamo Bay by Senator Bob Graham and Representative Porter Goss, who returned to warn the Clinton administration of their belief that there could be riots inside the detention camps, also influenced public attitude towards the situation.[203]

199 494 US 259 (1990).
200 See subsection 2.1.4.
201 Wachs, n 187 in this chapter, 85.
202 Joint Working Group of Non-Governmental Civil, Political, and Human Rights Organizations in the U.S and Morton Sklar (eds), *The Status of Human Rights in the United States: An Analysis of the Initial US Government Report to the Human Rights Committee of the United Nations Under the International Covenant on Civil and Political Rights* (S.N., 1995).
203 Ann Devroy and Daniel Williams, 'Serious Alarm Bells Led to Talks with Cuba: Congressmen Warned of Exodus, Riots at Camp' *Washington Post*, 5 May 1995, A4.

In response, the Clinton administration agreed to the resettlement of all Cubans in Guantánamo Bay at the time in the U.S. mainland.[204] However, the Clinton administration also entered negotiations with Cuba to curb the flow of Cuban nationals. On 9 September 1994, an agreement was signed between Cuba and the United States in New York. The U.S.-Cuba Joint Communiqué on migration provided that the United States would accept 20,000 immigrants a year from Cuba in exchange for Cuban government efforts to prevent citizens from leaving Cuban shores.[205] The communiqué stated:

> The United States and the Republic of Cuba recognize their common interest in preventing unsafe departures from Cuba which risk loss of human life. The United States underscored its recent decisions to discourage unsafe voyages. Pursuant to those decisions, migrants rescued at sea attempting to enter the United States will not be permitted to enter the United States, but instead will be taken to safe haven facilities outside the United States. Further, the United States has discontinued its practice of granting parole to all Cuban migrants who reach U.S. territory in irregular ways. The Republic of Cuba will take effective measures in every way it possibly can to prevent unsafe departures using mainly persuasive methods.[206]

A Joint Statement between Cuba and the United States was entered into on 2 May 1995.[207] The Joint Statement established the current policy of repatriating interdicted Cubans to their homeland (if they are not found to be in need of protection from *refoulement*).[208] It contained a promise from the Cuban government that repatriated Cuban nationals would not be punished for attempting to escape Cuba.[209]

[204] Wachs, n 187 in this chapter.

[205] *US-Cuba Joint Communiqué On Migration*, US Department of State Dispatch, 9 December 1994, Vol. 5, Issue 37, 603.

[206] Ibid.

[207] *Joint Statement on Migration*, U.S. Department of State Dispatch, 8 May 1995, Vol. 6, Issue 19, 397.

[208] Cubans held at Guantánamo Bay at the time were repatriated at a rate of 500 per week. Jonathan, Friedman et al., *Maritime Interception: History, Practice and Emerging Issue*, Yale Law School, Allard K. Lowenstein International Human Rights Clinic (Unpublished, 2002) 17. Copy on file with author.

[209] The agreement also established in-country processing of Cuban nationals wishing to come to the United States through the U.S. interest section in Havana. On the history of the U.S. Interest Section in Havana, see Frank Magill and John Loos, *Great Events from History: 1956–1996* (Salem Press, 1997) 1199.

The two agreements, combined with the CAA, created what came to be known as the 'wet foot / dry foot' policy.[210] Cubans who are interdicted at sea and are not identified as having protection needs are returned to Cuba. Cubans who express fear of persecution during an interdiction operation will be processed in Guantánamo Bay and will be resettled in a third country if they are refugees or at risk of torture in Cuba. Importantly, it is U.S. policy that no Cubans interdicted at sea are permitted to enter the U.S. mainland (except in the rare case of medical evacuations).[211] In contrast, any Cubans who avoid interdiction and make it to the U.S. mainland are, as a matter of policy, paroled into the country[212] and permitted to apply for an adjustment of status after one year under the CAA. There is therefore a great disparity between the privileges afforded to Cubans who have 'dry feet' – that is, those who reach the United States – and Cubans with 'wet feet' – that is, those who are interdicted at sea. As such, although the privileged status of Cuban nationals has been diminished by their inclusion under the MIP, it has not been removed completely. Furthermore, as discussed in Section 5.1, Cubans are provided greater rights during interdiction operations than are other nationals.

On 19 February 2008, Fidel Castro formally resigned as Cuba's president. He was succeeded by his brother Raul. The change in leadership in Cuba has not affected the policy of interdicting Cuban nationals under the MIP. Nor has the election of Barak Obama to the U.S. presidency affected the interdiction practices. Like the administrations of George H.W. Bush, Clinton and George W. Bush, the Obama administration's continuing commitment to the inclusion of Cubans under the MIP shows an enduring shift in U.S. policy away from treating Cubans as valuable political tools in the Cold War, although, as stated earlier, the remnants of this privileged status continue to this day. The extension of the MIP to Cuban nationals also signalled a new attitude towards irregular movement of persons by sea into the U.S. mainland. By including Cuban nationals

[210] Bon-Tempo, n 142 in this chapter, 200.

[211] Despite this policy, a very limited number of Cuban nationals interdicted at sea and processed in Guantánamo Bay have been admitted into the United States. See note 15 in Chapter 1.

[212] Ruth Wasem, Congressional Research Service, 'Cuban Migration to the United States: Policy and Trends' (2 June 2009) <http://www.fas.org/sgp/crs/row/R40566.pdf>. See also Heather Reynolds, 'Irreconcilable Regulations: Why the Sun Has Set on the Cuban Adjustment Act in Florida' (2011) 63 *Florida Law Review* 1014, 1020.

under the MIP, the United States has made clear its fixed commitment to tackling the perceived problem of irregular boat arrivals, regardless of the nationality of the interdictees.

2.3 The Migrant Interdiction Program and Other Nationalities

As the history of the MIP demonstrates, the program was created as a response to the irregular movement of Haitians and Cubans via maritime routes. Haitians and Cubans are, respectively, the largest and second-largest groups interdicted by the U.S. Coast Guard, with 119,665 Haitian nationals and 72,771 Cuban nationals interdicted between the years 1982 and 2014.[213] There are several other population groups that are also interdicted by the United States under the MIP. However, discussion of non-Haitian and non-Cuban interdictees is limited in this book. This is because with the exception of two small groups of Chinese nationals transferred to Guantánamo Bay in 1996 and 1997, discussed later in this chapter, there is no evidence that any other groups have ever been transferred to Guantanamo Bay under the MIP. Furthermore, the transfer of the two groups of Chinese nationals was an ad hoc event in contrast to the systematic manner in which Haitians and Cubans identified as having a credible fear of persecution or torture are transferred to Guantánamo Bay under the MIP.

Dominican nationals are the third-largest group interdicted by the U.S. Coast Guard, with 36,939 Dominicans interdicted between 1982 and 2014.[214] Dominicans 'typically travel through the Mona Passage to Puerto Rico in a variety of vessels but most commonly in small wooden boats that can carry as few as 10 or as many as 250' people.[215] There is no evidence that any Dominican national has been transferred to Guantánamo Bay for further status determination under the MIP.

[213] The statistic refers to U.S. fiscal years, which are calculated from 1 October to 30 September: U.S. Coast Guard, *Statistics: Alien Migrant Interdiction* <http://www.uscg.mil/hq/cg5/cg531/AMIO/FlowStats/currentstats.asp>.

[214] Ibid.

[215] Hearing before the Subcommittee on Coast Guard and Maritime Transportation of the Committee on Transportation and Infrastructure, House of Representatives, 111th Congress, 1st sess. 11 March 2009, 12. See also Gary Palmer, 'Guarding the Coast: Alien Migrant Interdiction Operations at Sea' (1996) 29 *Connecticut Law Review* 1565, 1581.

The United States entered into a Maritime Migration Law Enforcement agreement with the Dominican Republic on 20 May 2003.[216] The agreement permits the United States to carry out interdiction operations in Dominican waters and to interdict Dominican flagged vessels, under certain conditions.[217] The agreement also facilitates easier repatriation of Dominicans following interdiction. The signing of the agreement had an immediate impact, resulting in a sharp rise in the number of Dominicans interdicted by the United States.[218] In 2004, the United States interdicted 5,014 Dominicans, in contrast with 1,748 Dominicans interdicted in 2003 (the year the agreement was signed) and 177 Dominicans interdicted in 2002.[219] A further 3,612 Dominicans were interdicted under the MIP in 2005 and 3,011 in 2006.[220] The number of Dominicans interdicted began to drop significantly in 2007 to 1,469 people and remained at less than 1,000 persons annually in the years 2008 to 2014.[221] The U.S. Coast Guard has attributed the drop in the number of Dominicans interdicted in part to the effectiveness of the bilateral agreement with the Dominican Republic resulting in a reduced number of Dominicans attempting to enter the United States without prior authorisation via maritime routes.[222]

A further bilateral agreement that has impacted the MIP is the comprehensive interdiction agreement signed with the Bahamas on 29 June 2004.[223] The United States has close ongoing bilateral cooperation with the Bahamas on interdiction issues. Cooperation with the Bahamas is important for the United States in conducting the MIP because the

216 *Agreement between the Government of the United States of America and the Government of the Dominican Republic Concerning Maritime Migration Law Enforcement*, signed at Washington May 20, 2003.

217 For more in-depth analysis of the agreement, see subsection 3.3.2. See also Douglas Guilfoyle, *Shipping Interdiction and the Law of the Sea* (Cambridge University Press, 2009) 195–97.

218 See Hearing before the Subcommittee on Coast Guard and Maritime Transportation of the Committee on Transportation and Infrastructure, House of Representatives, 111th Congress, 1st sess. 11 March 2009, 12.

219 The statistics refers to U.S. fiscal years. U.S. Coast Guard, n 212 in this chapter.

220 Ibid.

221 Ibid.

222 John Marcario, 'Immigration Assist: The Coast Guard is Making Fewer Migrant Interdictions at Sea as Tougher Laws, Partnerships Take Hold' (2012) *Seapower* 44.

223 *Agreement between the Government of the United States of America and the Government of the Bahamas Concerning Cooperation in Maritime Law Enforcement*, signed at Nassau 29 June 2004; entered into force 29 June 2004. (U.S.-Bahamas agreement). For more in-depth analysis of the agreement, see subsection 3.3.2.

Bahamas has traditionally served as a transit country in the region, particularly for Haitians wishing to enter the United States.[224] Nationals of the Bahamas have been interdicted under the MIP.[225] However, the numbers of Bahamians interdicted is very small and there is no evidence that any Bahamian national has been transferred to Guantánamo Bay under the MIP.[226] The U.S.-Bahamas interdiction agreement has therefore been used predominantly to interdict Haitians (and, to a lesser extent, people of other nationalities, such as Cubans) on Bahamian flagged vessels or in Bahamian territory.

The fourth-largest group interdicted by the United States under the MIP are Ecuadorians, with 8,266 Ecuadorians interdicted in the 1982–2014 period.[227] Almost all (8,249 persons) were interdicted between 1999 and 2008.[228] Only two Ecuadorians were interdicted prior to 1999[229] and only fifteen have reportedly been interdicted under the MIP in the 2009–2014 period.[230] The dramatic increase in the interdiction of Ecuadorians at sea after 1999 was in part a response to the closing of certain land routes out of Ecuador.[231] To escape detection, Ecuadorians began travelling to Guatemala, Nicaragua or Mexico by sea before continuing on to the United States.[232] The opening up of new sea routes for Ecuadorians was accompanied by increased U.S. interdiction activity in the eastern Pacific.[233] The United States signed an interdiction agreement with Ecuador in 2006 that facilitates communication between the U.S. Coast Guard and the

[224] U.S. Coast Guard, n 1 in this chapter; Elizabeth Thomas-Hope, World Institute for Development Economics. *Irregular migration and asylum seekers in the Caribbean*. No. 2003/48 (2003) 7.

[225] See, for example, U.S. Embassy, IIP Digital, 'Migrants intercepted in two vessels in Windward Passage' <http://iipdigital.ait.org.tw/st/english/texttrans/2002/11/20021114123706smiller@pd.state.govo.4453089.html>.

[226] The numbers of Bahamians interdicted are too small to be listed separately in the statistics released on migrant interdictions by the U.S. Coast Guard. See U.S. Coast Guard, n 212 in this chapter.

[227] The statistic refers to U.S. fiscal years. Ibid.

[228] Ibid.

[229] The two Ecuadorians were interdicted in the 1996 U.S. fiscal year. Ibid.

[230] Ibid.

[231] Nancy Hiemstra, 'The US and Ecuador: Is Intervention on the Table?' (2012) 12 *NACLA Report on the Americas* 20.

[232] Alison Mountz, and Nancy Hiemstra, 'Spatial Strategies for Rebordering Human Migration at Sea' in Thomas Wilson and Hastings Donnan (eds), *A Companion to Border Studies* (Wiley-Blackwell, 2012) 461.

[233] Hiemstra n 230 in this chapter, 20. See also Nancy Hiemstra, *The View from Ecuador: Security, Insecurity, and Chaotic Geographies of U.S. Migrant Detention and Deportation* (PhD Dissertation, Syracuse University, 2011) 91.

Ecuadorian Coast Guard.[234] The agreement allows for the exchange of information on suspect vessels and expedited authorisation for the interdiction of vessels. No Ecuadorian is reported to have been transferred to Guantánamo Bay under the MIP.

The fifth-largest group interdicted by the United States under the MIP are Chinese nationals, with 5,946 Chinese interdicted under the MIP between 1982 and 2014. The vast majority of those (5,496) were interdicted between 1991 and 2000.[235] The U.S. Coast Guard identified irregular migration of Chinese nationals as their 'most challenging maritime' problem in the 1990s.[236] It is estimated that 15,000 to 20,000 Chinese nationals entered the western hemisphere by sea annually in the 1990s with the ultimate aim of entering the United States without prior authorisation.[237] The irregular movement of Chinese nationals affected all coastal areas of the United States, including its territories of Guam, Puerto Rico and the U.S. Virgin Islands.[238] In 1993, President Clinton issued Presidential Decision Directive 9[239] in response to 'Asian criminal syndicate smuggling of Chinese nationals illegally into the US by air, sea and across land borders'.[240] Under the Directive, the United States is to

> deal with the problem at its source, in transit, at our borders and within the U.S. [The United States] will attempt to *interdict and hold smuggled aliens as far as possible* from the U.S. border and to repatriate them when appropriate.[241]

[234] *Operational Procedures for Boarding and Inspecting Vessels Suspected of Illicit Traffic in Narcotic Drugs and Psychotropic Substances and of Smuggling Migrants by Sea*, signed at Quito, 30 August 2006. See subsection 3.3.2.

[235] The statistic refers to U.S. fiscal years. U.S. Coast Guard, n 212 in this chapter.

[236] Statement of Captain Anthony Tangeman, Department of Transportation US Coast Guard, on Coast Guard Migrant Interdiction Operations, Hearing before the Subcommittee on Immigration and Claims Committee on the Judiciary, House of Representatives, 106th Cong, 18 May 1999 <http://testimony.ost.dot.gov/test/pasttest/99test/Tangeman1.htm>.

[237] Ibid.

[238] Ibid. In the late 1990s, several thousand Chinese nationals from interdicted vessels (not in the Caribbean Region but the Pacific) were detained for processing on Guam. See Lory Rosenberg, 'International Association of Refugee Law Judges Conference: The Courts and Interception: The United States' Interdiction Experience and Its Impact on Refugees and Asylum Seekers' (2003) 17 *Georgetown Immigration Law Journal* 199.

[239] Presidential Decision Directive 9, 'Alien Smuggling', White House, 18 June 1993.

[240] Ibid.

[241] Emphasis added.

Only two groups of Chinese nationals are known to have been transferred to Guantánamo Bay under the MIP, both in the mid 90s. On 2 October 1996, the U.S. Coast Guard interdicted a ship that held 83 passengers and 26 crew members of Chinese nationality.[242] The ship was interdicted approximately 210 km northeast of Bermuda. The passengers on board had been on the ship for three months and many were severely dehydrated.[243] The interdicted ship was filled with garbage and had no electricity.[244] The government of Bermuda reluctantly allowed the ship to be anchored in Bermuda on the condition that it would be removed as soon as possible. The Chinese nationals were then taken to Guantanamo Bay and were later repatriated to China.[245]

In February 1997, forty-three Chinese nationals were transferred to Guantanamo Bay. They had been on board a Guyanese flagged fishing vessel, which had been interdicted by the U.S. Coast Guard off the coast of Cuba. The interdicted Chinese had been on the boat for several months. All forty-three men and women were returned to Guyana.[246]

The number of Chinese interdicted by the Coast Guard under the MIP has dramatically decreased from its peak in the 1990s.[247] According to the U.S. Coast Guard, the reduction in numbers is due in part to the success of the MIP and the increased use of alternative routes through Mexico and Central America by Chinese nationals attempting to enter the United States without prior authorisation.[248] Chinese with the financial resources are also more likely to arrive in the United States irregularly by air (either directly from China or from several transit points) because of the relative safety and comfort of air travel in contrast with sea travel.[249]

[242] Palmer, n 214 in this chapter, 1581.

[243] Ibid 1582.

[244] Ibid.

[245] Ibid.

[246] See U.S. Navy on the World Wide Web, 'GTMO Hospital Supports Operation Present Haven' (1997) <https://archive.org/stream/Med97010/med97010#page/n0/mode/2up/search/present+haven>.

[247] Fifty-three Chinese were interdicted in 2001, 80 in 2002, 15 in 2003, 68 in 2004, 32 in 2005, 31 in 2005, 73 in 2007, 1 in 2008, 35 in 2009, 0 in 2010, 11 in 2011, 23 in 2012, 5 in 2013 and 0 in 2014. The statistic refers to U.S. fiscal years. US Coast Guard, n 212 in this chapter,.

[248] Statement of Captain Anthony Tangeman, Department of Transportation US Coast Guard, on Coast Guard Migrant Interdiction Operations, Hearing before the Subcommittee on Immigration and Claims Committee on the Judiciary, House of Representatives, 106th Cong, 18 May 1999 <http://testimony.ost.dot.gov/test/pasttest/99test/Tangeman1.htm>.

[249] Sheldon Zhang and Ko-Lin Chin, 'Enter The Dragon: Inside Chinese Human Smuggling Organizations' (2002) 40 *Criminology* 737, 738–39. Clandestine air travel into the United

2.4 Conclusion

The MIP continues to be an important feature of the United States' border protection policies, and there are no signs that the United States is considering ending its interdiction program. There is also no indication from the Obama administration that the United States will stop transferring interdictees with protection claims to Guantánamo Bay.[250] In fact, President Obama has never discussed or acknowledged publicly the use of Guantánamo Bay under the MIP. This is despite a stated intention by the Obama administration to close down the detention facility in Guantanamo Bay used in the 'war on terror'.[251] In further evidence of the United States' continuing commitment to utilising Guantanamo Bay under the MIP, the U.S. military and security agencies conduct biannual drills in Guantánamo Bay to prepare soldiers, sailors and officials from the Department of Homeland Security (DHS) in the event of an attempted mass migration of people in the Caribbean region, of the kind seen in the 1990s.[252] There are reports that guardsmen have conducted topographical surveys and earth-moving estimates on unused land in Guantánamo Bay for a facility that will accommodate a larger number of people.[253] The United States may therefore be looking to expand its use of Guantánamo Bay under the MIP.

As shown in this chapter, attempts to challenge the MIP in the U.S. courts have been largely unsuccessful in the past. This is because the MIP is compliant with U.S. municipal law, an issue that will be further explored in subsequent chapters. However, advocates have had some success using

States has become more difficult since the terrorist attacks in New York in 2001: Guilfoyle, *Shipping Interdiction and the Law of the Sea* (Cambridge University Press, 2009) 183.

250 Azadeh Dastyari and Libbey Effeny, 'Immigration Detention in Guantánamo Bay: (Not Going Anywhere Anytime Soon)' (2012) 6 *Shima* 49.

251 On 22 January 2009, two days after his first inauguration, President Obama mandated the closing of the Guantánamo Bay detention facility 'as soon as practicable, and no later than one year from the date of this order'. Executive Order 13492, 74 *Federal Register* 4897 (2009). At the time of writing, the detention facility used in the 'war on terror' in Guantánamo Bay remained open.

252 Carol Rosenberg, 'U.S. Rehearses Mass-Migration Scenarios at Guantánamo Base' *Miami Herald*, 4 May 2013 <http://www.miamiherald.com/2013/02/10/3227065/us-rehearses-mass-migration-scenarios.html>.

253 Mathew Wilson, 'Missouri Guard Engineers to Conduct Annual Training in Guantanamo Bay' *Sedalia News Journal*, 14 February 2013 <http://www.army.mil/article/96444/Missouri_Guard_engineers_to_conduct_annual_training_in_Guantanamo_Bay/>.

public campaigns to assist individuals interdicted by the United States. This includes successful campaigns that led to the resettlement of HIV-positive Haitians in the U.S. mainland (which was combined with litigation in *Sale II*); the temporary suspension of the repatriation of Haitian nationals in March 1994; and the resettlement of Cuban nationals remaining in Guantánamo Bay at the time of the signing of the Joint Statement between Cuba and the United States in May 1995. Unfortunately, all of these victories were temporary and only affected a small subset of individuals under the MIP, because the changes in each case were pursuant to modifications in policy rather than municipal law. As such, advocates may have more success by turning their attention to ensuring that U.S. municipal law is compliant with the United States' international obligations under international human rights and refugee law – an issue discussed in greater detail in Chapters 5, 6 and 7 of this book.

3

Authority for the Exercise of Jurisdiction under the Municipal Law of the United States and the International Law of the Sea

Under the MIP, the U.S. Coast Guard board foreign flagged and stateless vessels, search the foreign vessels, transfer interdictees from the boarded vessels to Coast Guard cutters[1] and seize and destroy interdicted vessels that are unseaworthy.[2] Interdictees are then either returned to their point of origin or taken to Guantánamo Bay for further status determination.[3]

This chapter examines the authority on which the United States relies for the exercise of jurisdiction under the MIP. The chapter consists of three sections. First, this chapter discusses the location of interdiction operations under the MIP. Second, this chapter provides an examination of the authority for the operation of the MIP under U.S. municipal law. This includes a consideration of the relevant Presidential Proclamation, Executive Orders and statutory provisions. Third, this chapter analyses the authority on which the United States relies under the international law of the sea for the operation of the MIP.

Whilst the exercise of municipal law extraterritorially is not controversial if it does not infringe on the sovereign rights of other States, the enforcement of a State's municipal law, outside a State's territory, requires

1 'Cutters' are 'any [Coast Guard] vessel 19.8 metres (65 feet) in length or greater, having adequate accommodations for crew to live onboard'. U.S. Coast Guard, *The Maritime Counter Drug and Alien Migrant Interdiction Operations Manual*, COMDTINST M16247.4/NWP 3-07-4. 46 USC, 13.

2 Ibid.

3 It should also be noted that a small number of individuals interdicted are brought to the U.S. mainland to be prosecuted for a range of offences related to the transfer of certain non-citizens into the United States, discussed in subsection 3.2.1. Some of these individuals may in fact be U.S. citizens: U.S. Coast Guard, Operations Law Group, *Guide to the Law of Boarding Operations* (U.S. Coast Guard, 2008).

additional sources of authority under international law. This chapter shows that the international law of the sea authorises the U.S. interdiction of vessels in its contiguous zone, vessels flagged to a State with which the United States has a relevant agreement and stateless vessels. However, the current practice of turning rescue operations into interdictions or the destruction of unseaworthy vessels flagged to another State with which the United States does not have a relevant agreement are not authorised under the international law of the sea.

It should be noted from the outset that the power granted to the U.S. executive under municipal and international law to carry out migrant interdiction operations, in certain circumstances, is not without its limitations. The United States owes certain obligations to individuals it interdicts, under international human rights and refugee law. These obligations are discussed in greater detail in Chapter 4 and subsequent chapters.

3.1 Location of Interdiction Operations

Coastal States have varying degrees of control and authority over three offshore zones under the *United Nations Convention on the Law of the Sea* (UNCLOS).[4] The United States has signed the UNCLOS but has not ratified the treaty.[5] Nevertheless, the United States is bound, and accepts that it is bound, by the provisions of UNCLOS discussed in this book as codification of existing customary international law.[6]

The first zone under the control of a coastal State is the territorial sea which extends up to 12 nautical miles from the baselines (usually the mean low-water mark) of a coastal State.[7] President Reagan brought

4 Opened for signature 10 December 1982, 1833 UNTS 3 (entered into force 14 November 1994).

5 The United States signed the UNCLOS on 7 October 1994. It chose not to ratify the UNCLOS in the 1980s because of objection to parts dealing with deep seabed mineral resources beyond national jurisdictions: See, for example, President Ronald Reagan, Statement on United States Ocean Policy, 19 Weekly Comp. Pres. Doc. 383 (10 March 1983). However, much of the United States' objections regarding UNCLOS have now been addressed by the *Agreement Relating to the Implementation of Part XI of the United Nations Convention on the Law of the Sea of 10 December 1982*, registration 16 November 1994, 1836 UNTS 3 (entered into force provisionally on 16 November 1994 and definitively on 28 July 1996). The contention provisions are not relevant to the MIP and the issues discussed in this book.

6 See Gary Palmer, 'Guarding the Coast: Alien Migrant Interdiction Operations at Sea' (1996) 29 *Connecticut Law Review* 1565, 1568.

7 UNCLOS, Art 3.

U.S. municipal law in line with international law by extending the territorial sea of the United States to 12 nautical miles from the baseline of the U.S. mainland in 1988.[8] The second zone over which a coastal State has some control is the contiguous zone. The contiguous zone extends up to 24 nautical miles from the baseline where the territorial sea is measured.[9] President Clinton extended the contiguous zone of the United States to the limits permitted by international law in 1999.[10] The third zone over which a coastal State has some authority is the EEZ, which does not extend beyond 200 nautical miles from the baselines from which the breadth of the territorial sea is measured.[11] The United States claimed an EEZ in 1983.[12] Article 86 of UNCLOS states that beyond the EEZ lie the high seas.

The interdictions discussed in this book occur 'beyond the territorial sea of the United States'.[13] The United States has repeatedly stated that its interdiction operations take place on the high seas.[14] However, it is more accurate to state that interdictions are carried out in 'international waters', that is, in waters that include the contiguous zone and EEZ of the United States and neighbouring countries, in addition to the high seas. This is because the United States, Cuba,[15]

[8] Presidential Proclamation 592854, *Federal Register* 777 (1988).

[9] UNCLOS, Art 33.

[10] Proclamation 7219, 64 *Federal Register* 48701 (1999).

[11] UNCLOS, Art 57.

[12] This was again under President Reagan. Proclamation 5030, 48 *Federal Register* 10605 (1983).

[13] The interdiction operations discussed in this book are pursuant to Presidential Proclamation 4865, 46 *Federal Register* 48, 107, (1981) and Executive Order 12807, 57 *Federal Register* 12133 (1992), which limit the MIP to 'beyond the territorial sea of the United States'. See a more detailed discussion in Section 3.1.

[14] See, for example, U.S. Coast Guard, n 8 in this chapter; Lt Rachel Canty, 'Limits of the Coast Guard Authority to Board Foreign Flag Vessels on the High Seas', Unclassified Report, Naval War College (29 April 1997); U.S. Coast Guard, *Maritime Law Enforcement Manual* <www.uscg.mil/hq/cg5/cg531/AMIO/FOIA_Docs.pdf>, D.8; Testimony of Rear Admiral Vincent Atkins, U.S. Coast Guard, before the House Subcommittee on Homeland Security, on Department of Homeland Security Air and Marine Operations and Investments, 19 April 2010. <www.dhs.gov/ynews/testimony/testimony_1271690315007.shtm>.

[15] Decree Law No 2 of 24 February 1977. Entered into force 26 September 1977. See also Robert Smith, *Exclusive Economic Zone Claims: An Analysis and Primary Documents* (Martinus Nijhoff Publishers, 1986), 109. As the EEZs of Cuba and the United States overlap, an agreement was reached between the two governments delimiting a maritime boundary in the Straits of Florida and eastern Gulf of Mexico. *Maritime Boundary Agreement between the United States of America and the Republic of Cuba* (1977) Senate Treaty Document EX. H, 96–1. In accordance with Article V of the agreement, the United States and Cuba agreed to 'apply the

Haiti[16] and the Dominican Republic[17] have all claimed an EEZ. Interdictions are also likely to be occurring in the contiguous zones of Cuba, Haiti, the Dominican Republic or the United States.[18]

Whether the United States interdicts vessels in the EEZ or the high seas is, however, immaterial for the purposes of the relevant international law of the sea. Article 58(2) of UNCLOS provides that Articles 88–115 of the UNCLOS, which outline certain rights and duties on the high seas, are applicable to the EEZ as long as they are compatible with rights outlined specifically for the EEZ (these include rights over natural resources, fishing and other resource-related activities). Therefore, any provision of UNCLOS relating to the high seas discussed in this book are also relevant to the EEZ of the United States and the EEZ of any other State such as Haiti, Cuba, Dominican Republic or the Bahamas.

As with the mischaracterisation of the EEZ as the high seas, the mischaracterisation of the contiguous zone of other States as the high seas has little legal consequence for the United States in relation to its exercise of jurisdiction under the MIP. Article 55 of UNCLOS provides that the contiguous zone constitutes a section of the EEZ.[19] Except for express rights and obligation provided for under UNCLOS,[20] the contiguous zone, as

terms of this Agreement provisionally from 1 January 1978, for a period of two years'. The agreement was never ratified by the U.S. Senate, but every two years the two governments have been exchanging diplomatic notes to continue provisional application of the agreement. See David Colson, Robert Smith and the American Society of International Law, *International Maritime Boundaries* (The American Society of International Law, 1995).

16 Article V, Decree No 38, entered into force 8 April 1977 *Le Moniteur* No 38.

17 Dominican Republic: Law No 573, entered into force 1 April 1977.

18 The inaccurate references by the United States to the MIP taking place exclusively on the high seas may have come about because in 1981, when the MIP began, the applicable definition of the 'high seas' was that under the *Convention on the High Seas*, opened for signature 29 April 1958, 13 UST 2312 (entered into force 30 September 1962). Article 1 of the Convention on the High Seas categorises the high seas as all bodies of water that are not 'included in the territorial sea or in the internal waters of a State'. The UNCLOS definition did not come into force until 1994.

19 The Contiguous Zone is not the territorial sea of a State. This is clarified under Article 33(1) of UNCLOS. For commentary on the placement of the Contiguous Zone within the EEZ, see Robin Churchill and Vaughan Lowe, *Law of the Sea* (Manchester University Press, 3rd ed., 1999) 138.

20 These are relating to the enforcement of 'customs, fiscal, immigration or sanitary' laws pursuant to Article 33 of UNCLOS discussed in subsection 3.2.1. There is no reason to believe that current U.S. interdiction practices are in conflict with attempts by States in the region to enforce such municipal law.

with the EEZ, 'is juridically part of the high seas'.[21] As such, any references to the permissible exercise of jurisdiction by the United States in the high seas discussed in this book, are equally applicable to the exercise of jurisdiction by the United States in the contiguous zone of other States.

3.2 Municipal Law of the United States

U.S. migrant interdiction operations in international waters are in part governed under U.S. municipal law by a Presidential Proclamation and Executive Orders. As explained in Chapter 2, President Reagan suspended the 'entry of undocumented aliens from the high seas' under Proclamation 4865.[22] This was followed by Executive Order 12324,[23] which authorised the Secretary of State to enter into relevant agreements with appropriate foreign governments 'for the purpose of preventing illegal migration to the United States by sea'.[24] Executive Order 12324 also required the Secretary of Transportation to instruct the Coast Guard to enforce 'the suspension of the entry of undocumented aliens and the interdiction of any defined vessels carrying such aliens.'[25]

Executive Order 12324 was revoked and replaced on 24 May 1992[26] by President George H. W. Bush's Executive Order 12807 (Kennebunkport Order).[27] The Kennebunkport Order authorises the Secretary of Defence, the Attorney General, the Secretary of State and the Secretary of the Department in which the Coast Guard is operating to 'issue appropriate instruction to the Coast Guard in order to enforce the suspension of the entry of undocumented aliens by sea and the interdiction of any defined vessel carrying such aliens'.[28] The Kennebunkport Order also controversially states:

> The international legal obligations of the United States under the United Nations Protocol Relating to the Status of Refugees … to

[21] Ivan Shearer, 'Problems of Jurisdiction and Law Enforcement Against Delinquent Vessels' (1986) 35 *International & Comparative Law Quarterly* 320, 330.

[22] 46 Federal Register 48,107 (1981).

[23] 46 *Federal Register* 48,109 (1981).

[24] Ibid § 1.

[25] Ibid § 2(a).

[26] Section 4 of Executive Order 12807 states: 'Executive Order 12324 is hereby revoked and replaced by this order'.

[27] 57 *Federal Register* 23,133 (1992).

[28] Ibid § 2(a). Under §2(b), the instructions are to apply to '(1) Vessels of the United States…; (2) Vessels without nationality or vessels assimilated to vessels without nationality…; (3) Vessels

> apply Article 33 of the United Nations Convention Relating to the Status of Refugees do not extend to persons located outside the territory of the United States.[29]

The Kennebunkport Order was supplemented, but not revoked, by Executive Order 13276,[30] issued by President George W. Bush on 15 November 2002. Section 3(a) of Executive Order 13276 confirms that nothing in the order 'shall be construed to impair or otherwise affect the authorities and responsibilities set forth in' the Kennebunkport Order. Executive Order 13276 authorised the Attorney General to

> *maintain custody*, at any location he deems appropriate, of any undocumented aliens he has reason to believe are seeking to enter the United States and who are interdicted or intercepted in the Caribbean region. In this regard, the Attorney General shall provide and operate a facility, or facilities, to house and provide for the needs of any such aliens. Such a facility may be located at *Guantánamo Bay Naval Base* or any other appropriate location.[31]

Executive Order 13276 is the current authority relied on by the U.S. executive for the transfer and holding of interdictees in Guantánamo Bay. It is also the current authority for status determinations in Guantánamo Bay under municipal law.[32] Under the Executive Order, the Secretary of State provides for the custody, care, safety, transportation, resettlement and other needs of interdictees,[33] and the Secretary of Defense assists with the housing and care of any interdictees in Guantánamo Bay.[34] The operation and maintenance of facilities in Guantánamo Bay, under the Executive Order, was the responsibility of the Attorney General. However, the responsibility for border protection was transferred from the

of foreign nations with whom [the United States has] arrangements authorizing the United States to stop and board such vessels'.

29 Executive Order 12807, 57 *Federal Register* 23,133 (1992). The United States' denial of its *non-refoulement* obligations to refugees outside its municipally defined territory is discussed in greater detail in subsection 4.2.1.

30 Executive Order 13276, 67 *Federal Register* 69,985 (2002).

31 Ibid § 1(a)(i). Emphasis added.

32 This is analysed further in Section 5.2.

33 Ibid § 1(b).

34 Ibid § 1(c).

Attorney General to the DHS in 2003.[35] Executive Order 13286,[36] signed on 28 February 2003, reflects this change and amends the Kennebunkport Order and Executive Order 13276 by replacing the words 'the Attorney General' with the words 'the Secretary of Homeland Security'.

Thus the Kennebunkport Order and Executive Order 13276, as amended by Executive Order 13286, set forth the current duties and authorities of the Secretary of Homeland Security, Secretary of State and Secretary of Defence with respect to interdictees during migrant interdiction operations, including status determinations in Guantánamo Bay.

3.2.1 Statutory Authority

The Kennebunkport Order (as amended by Executive Order 13286) only authorises the Secretary of the Department in which the Coast Guard is operating to 'issue appropriate instruction to the Coast Guard in order to enforce the suspension of the entry of undocumented aliens by sea and the interdiction of any defined vessel carrying such aliens'.[37] It does not expressly address boarding and seizure of vessels outside U.S. territorial waters. In the absence of more clear authority under the Kennebunkport Order, the Coast Guard's authority for the boarding and seizure of vessels is derived from statute.

The Coast Guard is 'the United States' primary maritime law enforcement agency, … tasked with enforcing immigration law at sea'.[38] 14 USC § 89(a) provides:

> The Coast Guard may make inquiries, examinations, inspections, searches, seizures, and arrests *upon the High Seas* and waters over which the United States has jurisdiction, for the prevention, detection, and suppression of *violations of laws of the United States*. For such purposes, commissioned, warrant, and petty officers may at any time go *onboard of any vessel subject to the jurisdiction, or to the operation of any law*, of the United States, address inquiries to those

35 See Charles Wise, 'Organizing for Homeland Security' (2002) 62 *Public Administration Review* 131. The Department of Homeland Security was created by the *Homeland Security Act* of 2002 Pub.L. 107–296, 116 Stat. 745 following the terrorist attacks in New York on 11 September 2001.

36 68 *Federal Register* 10619 (2003).

37 See n 29 in this chapter, § 2(a).

38 U.S. Coast Guard, *Alien Migrant Interdiction* (2014) <www.uscg.mil/hq/cg5/cg531/AMIO/amio.asp>.

> onboard, examine the ship's documents and papers, and examine, inspect, and search the vessel and use all necessary force to compel compliance.[39]

Therefore, 14 USC § 89(a) establishes the statutory authority for the Coast Guard to board sea vessels beyond U.S. territorial waters. However, 14 USC § 89(a) is not in itself sufficient authority for the boarding and seizure of sea vessels, as it permits only enquiries, searches, examination and inspection of sea vessels (including the use of all necessary force to compel compliance)[40] for the 'prevention, detection, and suppression of violations of laws of the United States'. That is, the actions of the Coast Guard in boarding a vessel must be related to the violation of another law.[41]

Boarding, search and seizure of sea vessels during migrant interdiction operations may, however, be related to the 'detection'[42] of violations of section 274 of the INA,[43] codified under 8 USC § 1324, which concerns and creates criminal penalties for individuals who bring in and harbour certain aliens.[44] Of most interest for present purposes is 8 USC § 1324(a)1(A)(i)[45] which creates an offence for any person who

> *knowing that a person is an alien, brings to or attempts to bring* to the United States in any manner whatsoever such person *at a place other than a designated port of entry* or place other than as designated by the Commissioner, regardless of whether such alien has received prior official authorization to come to, enter, or reside in the United

39 Emphasis added.

40 All U.S. Coast Guard personnel carry firearms when boarding vessels, pursuant to 46 USC § 70117 (1). Further information on use of force against non-compliant vessels can be found in U.S. Coast Guard, n 1 in this chapter.

41 Coast Guard authority for seizure of property can be found under 46 USC § 70117, but this too requires the seizure to be provided by law, as 46 USC § 70117 (2)(B) states that 'subject to guidelines approved by the Secretary, members of the Coast Guard may, "seize property as otherwise provided by law.

42 14 USC § 89(a).

43 Pub L No 82–414, 66 Stat. 163.

44 Note this is similar to the concept of 'people smuggling'; see *Protocol against the Smuggling of Migrants by Land, Sea and Air*, opened for signature 15 November 2000, 2241 UNTS 507 (entered into force 28 January 2004), Art 3, which defines the smuggling of migrants as 'the procurement, in order to obtain, directly or indirectly, a financial or other material benefit, of the illegal entry of a person into a State Party of which the person is not a national or a permanent resident'. However, 8 USC § 1324 (a); INA § 274(a) is not limited to situations where there has been a direct or indirect financial or other material benefit.

45 INA § 274 (a)1(A)(i).

> States and regardless of any future official action which may be taken with respect to such alien.[46]

Also relevant is 8 USC § 1324(a)(2),[47] which creates an offence for any person who

> *knowing or in reckless disregard* of the fact that an alien has not received prior official authorization to come to, enter, or reside in the United States, *brings to or attempts to bring* to the United States in any manner whatsoever, such alien, regardless of any official action which may later be taken with respect to such alien shall, for each alien in respect to whom a violation of this paragraph occur.[48]

It is, therefore, not necessary for a person transporting individuals into the United States to know that the people they are transporting have not received prior official authorisation to come to the United States for a breach of 8 USC § 1324(a)(2) to occur. It is enough that the person engaged in the movement of non-citizens exercised 'reckless disregard'.[49] It is conceivable that many persons involved in attempting to bring interdictees to the United States would breach 8 USC § 1324(a)(2) by having 'reckless disregard' of the high probability that the people they are transporting do not have legal authority to enter the United States. Individuals wishing to make the dangerous journey by sea on such vessels are likely not to have authority to enter the United States. If the people wishing to come to the United States had authority to enter, it is likely they would choose a safer and less covert means of travelling.

It is important that both 8 USC § 1324(a)1(A)(i) and 8 USC § 1324(a)(2) create an offence even if the individual concerned has not in fact brought an alien to the United States at a place other than a designated port of entry or brought an alien to the United States without authorisation. That is, in addition to prohibiting the actions, both sections also prohibit any

[46] Emphasis added.

[47] INA § 274(a)(2).

[48] Emphasis added.

[49] That is, consciously disregarded a substantial and unjustifiable risk that the person did not have legal authority to come into the United States, which was a gross deviation from the standard of care that a reasonable person would exercise in the situation. *Matter of Median*, 151 & N Dec. 611, 613–614 (BIA, 1976).

attempt to perform such actions.[50] Given that the interdictions discussed in this book occur before an alien can enter the municipally defined territory of the United States, interdictees in the MIP who are prevented from bringing aliens into the United States can nevertheless be prosecuted under 8 USC § 1324(a)1(A)(i) and 8 USC § 1324(a)(2).

An issue with the enforcement of 8 USC § 1324(a)1(A)(i) and 8 USC § 1324(a)(2) during interdiction operations is whether the provisions apply extraterritorially, to international waters. The U.S. Court of Appeals for the District of Columbia in *United States v Degado-Garcia* (*Degado-Garcia*)[51] found that 8 USC § 1324(a) (which encompasses both 8 USC § 274(a)(1)(A)(i) and 8 USC § 1324(a)(2)) does apply extraterritorially. The Court acknowledged in its decision the existence of a presumption against extraterritorial application of U.S. statutes; however, it found that 'contextual factors' could provide the requisite evidence necessary to overcome this presumption.[52] The Court held that the focus of 8 USC § 1324(a) was international rather than domestic, since it was concerned with border protection, which is best understood as an issue of national security and foreign policy.[53] The Court also reasoned that the nature of the offences in question made them likely to be committed extraterritorially. Since many incomplete attempts to bring a non-citizen to the United States will occur outside of U.S. territory, an offender will usually be outside of the United States when attempting to bring someone into the country.[54]

Authority for seizure and forfeiture of sea vessels is found under 8 USC § 1324(b)(1),[55] which provides

> Any conveyance, including any vessel, vehicle or aircraft that has been or is being used in the commission of a violation of subsection (a) of this section, the gross proceeds of such violation and any property traceable to such conveyance or proceeds, shall be seized and subject to forfeiture.

[50] See discussion *United States v Aslam*, 936 F 2d 751, 755 (2nd Cir, 1991).
[51] 374 F 3d 1137 (DC Cir, 2004).
[52] *United States v Degado-Garcia*, 374 F 3d 1137, 1340–41 (DC Cir, 2004).
[53] Ibid 1345.
[54] Ibid 1347.
[55] INA § 274(b)(1).

8 USC § 1324(b)(2)[56] states that seizures and forfeitures under 8 USC § 1324(b) are governed by 18 USC § 981, which relates to civil forfeiture. That is, 'authorities must simply satisfy a requirement of probable cause that the property was used in an illicit activity or was purchased with funds from illicit activity in order to subject the property to forfeiture'.[57] No criminal arrest or conviction is required for property to become forfeited.[58] Finally, it follows that if 8 USC § 1324(a) applies extraterritorially, 8 USC § 1324(b) also applies extraterritorially because it is intricately linked with 8 USC § 1324(a).

No warrant or court process is required before the U.S. executive may seize or forfeit property under 18 USC § 981 if the seizure does not enjoy protections under the Fourth Amendment of the U.S. Constitution.[59] The Coast Guard is not bound by the Fourth Amendment when conducting interdiction operations in international waters. This is because the Fourth Amendment was found not to apply extraterritorially in *United States v Verdugo-Urquidez* (*Verdugo-Urquidez*).[60] *Verdugo-Urquidez* was a decision of the U.S. Supreme Court, involving a citizen and resident of Mexico charged with criminal narcotics violation and murder. A warrant for the arrest of Mr Verdugo was issued by the U.S. District Court for the Southern District Court of California. U.S. government officials contacted Mexican authorities, who arrested Mr Verdugo in Mexico and handed him to U.S. authorities. The U.S. Drug Enforcement Administration and Mexican officials searched Mr Verdugo's Mexican residence after his arrest without approval from any other U.S. authorities. In the course of that search they seized evidence that Mr Verdugo subsequently sought to exclude, on the grounds that it violated his rights under the Fourth Amendment of the U.S. Constitution. The U.S. Supreme Court found that the Fourth Amendment of the U.S. Constitution does not apply to searches conducted abroad by U.S. agents in relation to an alien who

56 INA § 274(b)(2).

57 Nkechi Taifa, 'Civil Forfeiture vs. Civil Liberties' (1994) 95 *New York Law School Law Review* 95, 98.

58 '[F]orfeiture is a civil, remedial measure brought against the offending property rather than a criminal penalty against the person acquitted': *United States v* $228,536, 895 F 2d 908, 916 (2nd Cir, 1990).

59 18 USC (b)(2)(B)(ii). The Fourth Amendment, when applicable, limits interference with persons or property.

60 494 US 259 (1990).

lacks sufficient connection to the United States.[61] The application of *Verdugo-Urquidez* to foreign vessels outside U.S. territorial waters was confirmed in *United States v Davis*,[62] where the U.S. Court of Appeals for the Ninth Circuit found that

> [A]lthough *Verdugo–Urquidez* only held that the Fourth Amendment does not apply to searches and seizures of non resident aliens in foreign countries, the analysis and language adopted by the Court creates no exception for searches of non resident aliens on the high seas.[63]

The applicability of the U.S. Constitution to the MIP is discussed further in Section 5.2. For present purposes, it suffices to note that the United States is not constrained by the Fourth Amendment of the U.S. Constitution in carrying out interdiction operations in international waters, and that the U.S. executive enforces U.S. municipal law when conducting operations under the MIP.

3.3 The International Law of the Sea and the Exercise of Enforcement Jurisdiction during Migrant Interdiction Operations

The authority derived from municipal law for the actions of the U.S. executive during interdiction operations does not, however, automatically lead to authority, under international law, for interference with foreign flagged or stateless vessels in international waters. There is a presumption against the enforcement of U.S. municipal laws, or the exercise of enforcement jurisdiction, outside U.S. territory. The United States exercises enforcement jurisdiction when it boards foreign flagged and stateless vessels, searches the vessels, transfers interdictees to its own vessels and destroys unseaworthy vessels.

International law places strict limits on interdicting States because interdiction practices limit the freedom of navigation.[64] Article 92 of UNCLOS

[61] *United States v Verdugo-Urquidez*, 494 US 259, 274–75 (1990).

[62] 905 F 2d 245 (9th Cir, 1990).

[63] Ibid., 251.

[64] Alemayehu Mariam, 'International Law and the Pre-emptive Use of State Interdiction Authority on the High Seas: The Case of Suspected Illegal Haitian Immigrants Seeking Entry into the US' (1987) 12 *Maryland Journal of International Law and Trade* 211, 223.

provides that a vessel flagged to a State is within the flagged State's jurisdiction. As observed by the U.S. Supreme Court in *Lauritzen v Larsen*, '[e]ach State under international law may determine for itself the conditions on which it will grant its nationality ... thereby accepting responsibility for [a vessel] and acquiring authority over it'.[65] However, international law does permit the exercise of jurisdiction by a State over a foreign flagged vessel in certain circumstances. For example, interference for the purposes of enforcing immigration laws is permitted if the vessel being interdicted is in the interdicting State's contiguous zone. Interference is also permitted if the interdicting State has an agreement with the State whose flag the foreign vessel lawfully flies, permitting the interdicting State to exercise jurisdiction over the vessel. Furthermore, the international law of the sea permits the exercise of jurisdiction in cases where a vessel is stateless. The sources of authority for the exercise of enforcement jurisdiction by the United States during interdiction operations is discussed and analysed below.

3.3.1 The U.S. Contiguous Zone

Article 33(1) of UNCLOS authorises the exercise of enforcement jurisdiction by the United States in its own contiguous zone as part of its MIP. It provides

> In a zone contiguous to its territorial sea, described as the Contiguous Zone, the coastal State may exercise the control necessary to: (a) Prevent infringement of its customs, fiscal, immigration or sanitary laws and regulations within its territory or territorial sea[.]

As explained earlier in the chapter, 8 USC § 1324(a)1(A)(i) and 8 USC § 1324(a)(2) prohibit the bringing in and harbouring of certain aliens into the U.S. mainland, which includes *attempts* to do the same, and vessels used for such purposes may be seized under 8 USC § 1324(b). Thus, the United States is empowered to exercise the jurisdiction necessary over persons and vessels in its contiguous zone to prevent infringement of its immigration laws, which includes boarding of vessels, search of boarded vessels and transfer of interdictees from boarded vessels onto Coast Guard cutters

[65] *Lauritzen v Larsen*, 345 US 571, 584 (1953).

if necessary under Article 33(1)(a) of UNCLOS. It should be noted that during interdiction operations, the United States destroys only vessels that it claims are unseaworthy, so it does not destroy vessels it has interdicted simply because they are in its contiguous zone.

UNCLOS does not provide the United States with an express source of authority to exercise its enforcement jurisdiction beyond its contiguous zone. An additional source of authority, such as a treaty providing authority for the exercise of jurisdiction over a foreign flagged vessel or the statelessness of an interdicted vessel, is required before a State may enforce its municipal law outside its territorial waters and contiguous zone.

3.3.2 Treaty Providing for Jurisdiction

Under Article 110 of UNCLOS, the United States is prohibited from exercising jurisdiction over vessels flagged to a foreign State on the high seas (and therefore in the EEZ and the contiguous zone of foreign States). However, Article 110 of UNCLOS provides an exception to the prohibition on the exercise of jurisdiction if the 'act of interference derive[s] from powers conferred by treaty'.

The United States has two agreements with Cuba that, it will be argued, allow the United States to exercise its enforcement jurisdiction over Cuban flagged vessels during migrant interdiction operations pursuant to the exception provided by Article 110 of UNCLOS: the *U.S.-Cuba Joint Communiqué on Migration* (Communiqué),[66] and the *Joint Statement on Migration* (Joint Statement).[67]

The agreements between the United States and Cuba do not expressly provide the United States with authority to interdict Cuban flagged vessels. However, the Communiqué provides that the United States and Cuba 'pledged their cooperation to take prompt and effective action to prevent the transport of persons to the United States illegally'.[68] The Joint Statement further provides

[66] U.S. Department of State Dispatch, 9 December 1994, Vol. 5, Issue 37, 603.

[67] U.S. Department of State Dispatch, 8 May 1995, Vol. 6, Issue 19, 397. See earlier discussion in subsection 2.2.3.

[68] *U.S.-Cuba Joint Communiqué on Migration*, U.S. Department of State Dispatch, 9 December 1994, Vol. 5, Issue 37, 603, [2].

> Effective immediately, *Cuban migrants intercepted at sea* by the United States and attempting to enter the United States will be taken to Cuba ... the United States and the Republic of Cuba will cooperate jointly in this effort. All actions taken will be consistent with the parties' international obligations.[69]

The authority for the exercise of enforcement jurisdiction under the Communiqué is very broad. It is arguable that interdiction of Cuban flagged vessels at sea is effective action that prevents the transport of persons to the United States without prior authorisation. The authority for interdictions under the Communiqué is supported by the Joint Statement, where it is stated that 'Cuban migrants intercepted at sea by the United States ... will be taken to Cuba'.[70] That is, under the Joint Statement, Cuba does not object to the interception of Cuban nationals at sea. Therefore, read together, the Communiqué provides the authority for interference with Cuban flagged vessels at sea and this authority for interception is confirmed in the Joint Statement. Furthermore, despite meeting with the United States frequently to discuss the implementation of the Communiqué and the Joint Statement, Cuba has not at any time objected to the interdiction of its flagged vessels by the United States. In fact, Cuba's willingness to enter into a further agreement with the United States in May 1995 under the Joint Statement, after the United States had begun the interception of Cuban vessels under the Communiqué in September 1994, indicates that Cuba consented to the continuing interdiction of its flagged vessels by the United States.

A more difficult question is whether Cuba consents to the destruction of Cuban flagged vessels during interdiction operations if they are unseaworthy. It may be argued by the United States that the ordinary meaning of the terms of the Communiqué in their context and in light of their object and purpose permit the destruction of unseaworthy vessels.[71] The

69 *Joint Statement on Migration*, U.S. Department of State Dispatch, 8 May 1995, Vol. 6, Issue 19, 397, [3]. Emphasis added.

70 Ibid.

71 Article 31(1) of the *Vienna Convention on the Law of Treaties*, opened for signature 23 May 1969, 1155 UNTS 331 (entered into force 27 January 1980) (VCLT), provides that, as a general rule of interpretation, '[a] treaty shall be interpreted in good faith in accordance with the ordinary meaning to be given to the terms of the treaty in their context and in the light of its object and purpose'. The United States has not ratified the VCLT but accepts that the VCLT reflects customary international law governing treaty interpretation. See discussion in Section 4.1.

Communiqué provides that the United States 'and the Republic of Cuba recognize their common interest in preventing unsafe departures from Cuba which risk loss of human life'.[72]

The above-quoted statement is reiterated in the Joint Statement, which provides that 'the United States and the Republic of Cuba reaffirm their common interest in preventing unsafe departure from Cuba'.[73] The Joint Statement also provides that the Joint Statement and the Communiqué 'seek to address *safety* and humanitarian concerns, and to ensure that migration between the countries is *safe*'.[74] Therefore, ensuring maritime safety is one of the objects and purposes of the agreements. The destruction of unseaworthy and unsafe vessels is consistent with the object and purposes of this agreement, as unseaworthy and unsafe vessels put lives at risk. Furthermore, as with interdictions more generally, Cuba has not at any time objected to the destruction of unseaworthy vessels flagged to it. Cuba also entered into the Joint Statement of September 1994, knowing that the United States was engaged in the destruction of unseaworthy vessels flagged to Cuba, without objecting to this practice. It can thus be concluded that under the agreements, Cuba consents to the destruction of Cuban flagged vessels that are unseaworthy.

The United States also has bilateral agreements with the Dominican Republic[75] and the Bahamas.[76] These agreements affect all individuals (including Haitians and Cubans) intending to travel to the United States without prior authorisation on Dominican or Bahamian flagged vessels or within the territory of the Dominican Republic or the Bahamas.

The agreement with the Dominican Republic permits the United States to 'board, address inquiries, inspect the documents of and search'.[77] Dominican flagged vessels suspected of engaging in the unsafe transport

[72] *U.S.-Cuba Joint Communiqué on Migration*, U.S. Department of State Dispatch, 9 December 1994, Vol. 5, Issue 37, 603, [1].

[73] *Joint Statement on Migration*, U.S. Department of State Dispatch, 8 May 1995, Vol. 6, Issue 19, 397, [2].

[74] Ibid [1]. Emphasis added.

[75] *Agreement between the Government of the United States of America and the Government of the Dominican Republic Concerning Maritime Migration Law Enforcement*, signed at Washington May 20, 2003; entered into force 20 May 2003. (U.S.-Dominican Agreement). See Section 2.3.

[76] *Agreement between the Government of the United States of America and the Government of the Bahamas Concerning Cooperation in Maritime Law Enforcement*, signed at Nassau 29 June 2004; entered into force 29 June 2004. (U.S.-Bahamas Agreement). See Section 2.3.

[77] U.S.-Dominican Agreement, Art 8 (1).

or 'smuggling'[78] of migrants outside the territorial sea of any State. The United States is also permitted to detain suspect vessels in case of evidence of unsafe transport or smuggling of migrants.[79] The U.S.-Dominican agreement further provides that the government of the Dominican Republic

> does not object to the U.S. Coast Guard destroying any vessel subject to the jurisdiction of the Dominican Republic and detained pursuant to this Agreement that the U.S. Coast Guard deems to be unseaworthy and/or a hazard to navigation.[80]

In addition, the U.S.-Dominican agreement states that a representative of the Dominican Republic may serve as a ship-rider on U.S. government vessels to authorise the pursuit of vessels suspected of engaging in unsafe transport or smuggling of migrants into Dominican territorial waters and authorise the United States to conduct 'maritime migration law enforcement patrols in Dominican waters'.[81] The United States is also permitted to pursue a vessel suspected of unsafe transport or smuggling of migrants into Dominican waters in order to investigate, board, search and, if warranted, detain a vessel, even if there is no Dominican ship-rider on board that particular U.S. government vessel, if a ship-rider or a Dominican law enforcement vessel is not immediately available.[82] A U.S. official may serve as a ship-rider on Dominican vessels to 'enforce, seaward of the territorial sea of the Dominican Republic, the laws, including appropriate Executive Orders, of the United States'.[83]

The U.S.-Bahamas agreement also provides for Bahamian ship-riders to serve aboard U.S. government vessels. The presence of a Bahamian ship-rider permits the United States to board and search suspect vessels within Bahamian territorial waters,[84] and to board and search Bahamian flagged vessels in waters outside the territory of any State and within 200 nautical miles from the Bahamas.[85] In both cases, the United States must

[78] 'Smuggling of migrants' is defined under the U.S.-Dominican Agreement as 'the procurement or attempted procurement of the illegal entry of a person into a State of which the person is not a national or a permanent resident'. U.S.-Dominican Agreement, Art 1.

[79] U.S.-Dominican Agreement, Art 8(2).

[80] U.S.-Dominican Agreement, Art 9(4).

[81] U.S.-Dominican Agreement, Art 4.

[82] U.S.-Dominican Agreement, Art 5(2)(a).

[83] U.S.-Dominican Agreement, Art 4(3)(c).

[84] U.S.-Bahamas Agreement, Art 5(a).

[85] U.S.-Bahamas Agreement, Art 5(b).

carry out 'the disposition instructions of Bahamian law enforcement authorities'.[86]

In the absence of a Bahamian ship-rider, the United States may request authorisation to 'board and search'[87] vessels claiming Bahamian nationality suspected of the unsafe transport or smuggling of migrants outside the territorial waters of the Bahamas. The U.S.-Bahamas agreement requires a requested party to 'make best efforts to respond to requests ... as expeditiously as possible'.[88]

Furthermore, the United States is permitted, under the U.S.-Bahamas agreement, to 'stop, board, search and detain non-Bahamian flag vessels'[89] (including vessels that make no claim to nationality)[90] in the territorial waters of the Bahamas even without the presence of a Bahamian ship-rider, but must seek instructions from the government of the Bahamas for any further action.[91] With regard to the destruction of unseaworthy vessels, the U.S.-Bahamas agreement provides that 'either party may destroy any vessel subject to its jurisdiction that it deems to be unseaworthy and/or a hazard to navigation.'[92]

In addition to its agreements with the Dominican Republic and the Bahamas, the United States has an agreement with Ecuador that outlines operational procedures for boarding and inspecting vessels suspected of engaging in the irregular movement of people to the United States.[93] The agreement with Ecuador does not provide an independent source of authority for the exercise of jurisdiction by the United States on Ecuadorian flagged vessels. The agreement merely facilitates better communication between the two nations and standardises operational procedures for the interdiction of vessels flagged to either party to the agreement.[94]

86 U.S.-Bahamas Agreement, Art 5(a) and Art 5(b).
87 U.S.-Bahamas Agreement, Art 8(2)(b)(i).
88 U.S.-Bahamas Agreement, Art 8(3).
89 U.S.-Bahamas Agreement, Art 6(2)(b).
90 U.S.-Bahamas Agreement, Art 6(2)(c).
91 Ibid. An exception is provided for U.S. flagged vessels interdicted in Bahamian waters.
92 U.S.-Bahamas Agreement, Art 10(6).
93 *Operational Procedures for Boarding and Inspecting Vessels Suspected of Illicit Traffic in Narcotic Drugs and Psychotropic Substances and of Smuggling Migrants by Sea*, signed at Quito, 30 August 2006. (U.S.-Ecuador Agreement).
94 See, for example, U.S.-Ecuador Agreement, Art 8, which outlines the procedures for requesting verification of a suspect vessel's registry and the manner in which requests should be made to board and search a vessel.

The United States does not have an agreement that authorises its exercise of enforcement jurisdiction over Haitian nationals and Haitian flagged vessels. As explained in Chapter 2, the United States, under the Reagan administration, negotiated an agreement with Haiti under the regime of Jean-Claude 'Baby Doc' Duvalier, to establish a cooperative interdiction program.[95] However, this agreement was terminated in October 1994 after the Haitian President Aristide invoked the termination provision of the agreement.[96] Therefore, the United States is not authorised to carry out migrant interdictions of Haitian flagged vessels outside the territorial sea or its own contiguous zone, without an additional source of authority. In fact, the United States does interdict many Haitian flagged vessels on the high seas, and it justifies it by claiming to rescue individuals from unseaworthy vessels.[97] In addition, many Haitians seek to reach the United States by travelling aboard stateless vessels, to which we now turn. It should be noted that other nationals can also be interdicted on stateless vessels, and the analysis provided here applies to the interdiction of all persons aboard stateless vessels regardless of nationality.

3.3.3 Stateless Vessels

International law requires all vessels to have a nationality, so as to ensure that each vessel will be subject to some system of laws.[98] The International Law Commission has asserted that

> [t]he absence of any authority over ships sailing the High Seas would lead to chaos. One of the essential adjuncts to the principle of the freedom of the seas is that a ship must fly the flag of a single State.[99]

95 *Agreement Effected by Exchange of Notes Regarding Migrants and Interdiction*, 23 September, 1981, U.S.-Haiti, 33 U.S.T. 3559, TIAS. No. 10, 241.

96 Steven Greenhouse, 'Aristide to End Accord That Allows US to Seize Refugee Boats' *New York Times*, 8 April 1994, A6. See also Migration News, *Aristide to Cancel US Return Policy* <migration.ucdavis.edu/mn/more.php?id=302_0_2_0>.

97 See later discussion in subsection 3.3.4.

98 UNCLOS, Art 92. See Edward Anderson III, 'The Nationality of Ships and Flags of Convenience: Economics, Politics, and Alternatives' (1996) 21 *Tulane Maritime Law Journal* 139, 140.

99 International Law Commission. 'Report of the International Law Commission Covering the Work of Its Eighth Session (April 23–July 4, 1956)' [1956] II *Yearbook of the International Law Commission* 253, 279.

The nationality of a vessel is linked to the flag it is permitted to fly. Article 91 of UNCLOS provides that

> Every State shall fix the conditions for the grant of its nationality to ships, for the registration of ships in its territory, and for the right to fly its flag. Ships have the nationality of the State whose flag they are entitled to fly. There must exist a genuine link between the State and the ship.

A vessel that is deprived of the right to sail under a particular flag, does not have a recognised flag, or flies two or more flags (using them for convenience)[100] is stateless.[101] As a result of being stateless and lacking a nationality, a vessel suffers certain disabilities. Most notably, the stateless vessel will lack protection from a flag State.

The authority for the boarding and search of a stateless vessel is clear. Article 110 of UNCLOS provides that a warship or 'any other duly authorised ship or aircraft clearly marked and identifiable as being on government service' may board a ship without nationality on the high seas (and thus also within the EEZ or the contiguous zone of foreign States).[102] Coast Guard vessels such as cutters are duly authorised ships marked and identifiable as being in government service. Thus, the Coast Guard is authorised to

> proceed to verify the ship's right to fly its flag. To this end, it may send a boat under the command of an officer to the suspected ship. If suspicion remains after the documents have been checked, it may proceed to a further examination onboard the ship, which must be carried out with all possible consideration.[103]

However, a right to board does not automatically equate to a right to exercise enforcement jurisdiction over interdictees on a stateless vessel, which

[100] UNCLOS, Art 92. See also *Convention on the High Seas*, opened for signature 29 April 1958, 13 UST 2312 (entered into force 30 September 1962), Art 6(2). See further Churchill and Lowe, n 19 in this chapter, 213–14.

[101] A vessel is not necessarily stateless if it lacks registration, for a State may not require or even permit registration of certain vessels (for example, vessels of a particular size) but nevertheless recognise that the vessels have its nationality if they are owned by its nationals. See Churchill and Lowe, n 19 in this chapter, 213.

[102] UNCLOS, Art 110(1)(d).

[103] UNCLOS, Art 110(2).

includes transferring them to Coast Guard cutters. Determining whether or not the U.S. Coast Guard has authority under international law to enforce U.S. municipal law and transfer interdictees to its own vessels is more challenging and requires consideration of two opposing views.

The first view is that boarding States can assimilate a stateless vessel and subject it to their laws, including transferring interdictees to their own vessels.[104] This view is held by a number of countries, including the United States.[105] The United States reasons that if a vessel does not lawfully fly the flag of any one country, it cannot enjoy the protection of any nation and is thus subject to the jurisdiction of all nations. This view was reiterated by the U.S. Court of Appeals for the Eleventh Circuit, which found in *United States v Marino-Garcia*[106] that

> International law permits any nation to subject stateless vessels on the high seas to its jurisdiction. Such jurisdiction neither violates the law of nations nor results in impermissible interference with another sovereign nation's affairs. Jurisdiction exists solely as a consequence of the vessel's status as stateless.[107]

[104] This position is supported by a number of scholars. See, for example, Douglas Guilfoyle, *Shipping Interdiction and the Law of the Sea* (Cambridge University Press, 2009) 341–42; Myles McDougal, 'The Maintenance of Public Order at Sea and the Nationality of Ships' (1960) 59 *American Journal of International Law* 25, 27; Gillian Triggs, *International Law: Contemporary Principles and Practices* (LexisNexis Butterworths, 2nd ed., 2011) 407; Anastasia Stratē, Maria Gavouneli and Nikolaos Skourtos, *Unresolved Issues and New Challenges to the Law of the Sea: Time Before and Time After* (Martinus Nijhoff Publishers, 2006).

[105] UK legislation reflects this view. For example, Section 19(1) of the *Criminal Justice (International Cooperation) Act 1990* brings stateless vessels within the ambit of UK jurisdiction. Italy also shares the view that stateless vessels are subject to the jurisdiction of the boarding State. In the 2001 case of *Pamuk e Altri*, Tribunale de Crotone, 27 September 2001, the Italian government was found to be acting lawfully by an Italian court when asserting its municipal law on the high seas by arresting interdictees bound for the coast of Italy, because the interdictees were on a stateless vessel.

[106] 679 F 2d 1373 (11th Circ. 1982).

[107] *United States v Marino-Garcia* 679 F 2d 1373, 1383 (11th Circ. 1982). Furthermore, in *United States v Rendon*, 354 F 3d 1320, 1325 (11th Cir, 2003), the Court of Appeals for the 11th Circuit found that the United States was permitted under international law to prosecute drug offenders that were interdicted on stateless ships on the high seas. The U.S. Commander's Handbook states that 'stateless vessels may be boarded upon being encountered in international waters by a warship or other government vessel and subjected to all appropriate law enforcement actions': Department of the Navy Office of the Chief of Naval Operations and Headquarters, U.S. Marine Corps, *Department of Homeland Security and U.S. Coast Guard, United States Commander's Handbook on the Law of Naval Operations* (2007) [3.11.2.3].

This position is consistent with the idea that stateless vessels exist in a vacuum of law that may be filled by the exercise of jurisdiction by the interdicting State, thus avoiding the outbreak of chaos if vessels are left with no nationality.[108]

The second position is that statelessness does not in itself permit a State to enforce its laws against a stateless vessel without an additional jurisdictional nexus.[109] Article 110 of UNCLOS does not permit a State to do anything other than visit and board a stateless vessel to determine whether or not it is stateless. If further exercise of jurisdiction over a stateless vessel was envisioned by UNCLOS, it could have been specified. For example, UNCLOS does specify under Article 105 that pirate ships can be seized on the high seas or in any other place outside the jurisdiction of any State, and any State is permitted to arrest the persons involved and confiscate the property on board the pirate ship. The contrast between the authority provided in Article 105 of UNCLOS for the exercise of jurisdiction over pirate ships and the silence of Article 110 of UNCLOS on the exercise of jurisdiction over stateless vessels suggests that a boarding State cannot assert jurisdiction over a stateless vessel without another independent source of authority. Furthermore, whilst it is true that a stateless vessel does not enjoy the protection of any State, this does not mean that a stateless vessel is open to the exercise of jurisdiction by any State that may board it under Article 110 of UNCLOS. It means only that no State may complain of any violation of international law by another State against a stateless vessel. That is, the statelessness of the vessel does not itself create an authority for jurisdiction; however, should jurisdiction be exercised without authority, no State will be in a position to protect the stateless vessel. Normatively, there is a difference between a stateless vessel's lack of protection against the assertion of a State's municipal law and any right that a State may have to enforce its law.

If we examine the second view closely, we can see that it is based on the idea of the high seas (and consequently also of the EEZ and the contiguous zone) as being subject to the authority of no nation except in the

[108] International Law Commission, n 99 in this chapter, 279.

[109] Churchill and Lowe, n 19 in this chapter, 214. See also Efthymios Papastavridis, *The Interception of Vessels on the High Seas: Contemporary Challenges to the Legal Order of the Oceans* (Hart Publishing, 2013) 264–67.

case of explicit authority. This is in contrast with the first view of the high seas (and consequently also of the EEZ and the contiguous zone) as being subject to the jurisdiction of all nations except in the case of explicit immunity. The second view denies a source of authority for the exercise of jurisdiction over a stateless vessel other than boarding and determining the statelessness of the vessel, and is compelling in the abstract. However, it does not address the vacuum that would be created if stateless vessels were not subject to the jurisdiction of any State, and boarding States could do little more than confirm the statelessness or otherwise of a vessel.

Therefore, the first position is preferable, namely that in the absence of immunity from the exercise of jurisdiction, a stateless vessel is subject to the exercise of jurisdiction by an interdicting State.[110] The difference between the express activities permitted under Article 105 and Article 110 of UNCLOS can be accounted for by way of the fact that pirate ships may enjoy the protection of a flag State – that is, they may not be stateless. As such, greater authority is needed to pierce the immunity of the flag State from intervention under Article 105 than is necessary for the exercise of jurisdiction over a stateless vessel that enjoys no immunity from intervention. Article 110 authorises a State to board a stateless vessel and determine its status; however, even in the absence of this express authority, States would be permitted to exercise jurisdiction over stateless vessels.

It should also be noted that the *Protocol against the Smuggling of Migrants by Land, Sea and Air* (Smuggling Protocol),[111] provides under Article 8(7) that

> A State Party that has reasonable grounds to suspect that a vessel is engaged in the smuggling of migrants by sea and is without nationality or may be assimilated to a vessel without nationality may board and search the vessel. If evidence confirming the suspicion is found, that State Party *shall take appropriate measures in accordance with relevant domestic and international law*.[112]

The United States is a party to the Smuggling Protocol, which is the sole multilateral treaty 'for the right to visit on the high seas for counter-migration purposes'.[113] The Protocol reiterates the authority provided under Article

[110] As Guilfoyle argues, this is the more coherent position: Guilfoyle, n 104 in this chapter, 342.
[111] Opened for signature 15 November 2000, 2241 UNTS 507 (entered into force 28 January 2004).
[112] Smuggling Protocol, Art 8(7). Emphasis added.
[113] Efthymios Papastavridis, 'Interception of Human Beings on the High Seas: A Contemporary Analysis Under International Law' (2009) 36 *Syracuse Journal of International Law and*

110 of UNCLOS that States may board and search stateless vessels, and goes further to require that States take measures against the 'smuggling of migrants' by sea. However, as Guilfoyle has noted, the reference to relevant international law, under Article 8(7) of the Smuggling Protocol, does not clarify the ambiguity in international law concerning permissible enforcement jurisdiction over stateless vessels.[114]

Another related issue to consider on the point of State protection over its nationals is that whilst no State can object to breaches of international law with regard to stateless vessels, the same cannot be said for individuals on board a stateless vessel who have a nationality. An individual does not become stateless simply by virtue of being on board a stateless vessel. That is, as Churchill and Lowe point out, individuals on board a stateless vessel may enjoy the protection of the country of their nationality, which may complain of violations of international law by another State against its citizens.[115]

Finally, the last question that needs to be answered is whether or not the United States is permitted to destroy unseaworthy vessels as part of its interdiction of stateless vessels. As determined earlier in the chapter, when exercising jurisdiction over a stateless vessel, the United States substitutes its flag for that of the stateless vessel and thus is authorised as the flag State under Article 94(3) to 'take such measures for ships flying its flag as are necessary to ensure safety at sea', which arguably includes the destruction of unseaworthy vessels. Thus, the United States does enjoy authority under international law to subject interdictees on stateless vessels to all aspects of its current interdiction operations.

3.3.4 Rescue

The final means by which the United States attempts to justify its exercise of enforcement jurisdiction on vessels flagged to a State with which it

Commerce 145, 187. The United States signed the Smuggling Protocol on 13 December 2000 and ratified it on 3 November 2005. Cuba has not signed or ratified the Smuggling Protocol, and although Haiti signed the Smuggling Protocol on 13 December 2000, it has not ratified it at the time of this writing.

114 Guilfoyle, n 104 in this chapter, 183.

115 Churchill and Lowe, n 19 in this chapter, 214. Guilfoyle notes that in his interview with practitioners he came across no example in which States had exercised diplomatic protection in such cases. See Ibid 18.

does not have a treaty and located outside its territorial waters or its contiguous zone is by reference to the duty to rescue vessels in distress. The U.S. Coast Guard seeks out vessels in distress and brings individuals rescued aboard Coast Guard cutters. The rescued individuals (rescuees) are then provided with food, water and medical attention.[116] An Emergency Medical Technician (EMT) is also on board most Coast Guard cutters.[117] If the condition of an individual is deemed to be serious and adequate care cannot be provided aboard the Coast Guard vessel, the individual is taken to the hospital of nearest convenience, which may be in the United States. The decision to carry out a medical evacuation is based strictly on medical necessity. Members of the immediate family of medically evacuated individuals are brought to the medical treatment site where the individual needing medical care is treated. The Coast Guard reports that once it has achieved its aim of getting people on a distressed vessel out of danger, it may turn the rescue operation into a migrant interdiction – that is, it may exercise its enforcement jurisdiction.[118]

UNCLOS not only permits rescue but obliges every State, under Article 98, to require the master of a ship flying its flag to assist any person at sea in danger of being lost and 'to proceed with all possible speed to the rescue of persons in distress if informed of their need of assistance, insofar as such action may be reasonably expected of him'.[119] The formulation of Article

[116] See U.S. Coast Guard, *Migrant Interdiction: Safety of Life at Sea* (2011) <http://coastguard.dodlive.mil/2011/03/migrant-interdiction-safety-of-life-at-sea>. This should be contrasted with many commercial ships that are not equipped to care for large numbers of rescued persons. For example, the *MV Tampa*, which had rescued 438 Afghan asylum seekers from a distressed fishing vessel in international waters near Australia in 2001, was not in a position to provide the rescued asylum seekers with food, water and medical attention. In fact, Captain Rinnan alerted Australian officials to the scarcity of food and water on board the *Tampa* and requested medical supplies. See Penelope Mathew, 'Australian Refugee Protection in the Wake of the *Tampa*' (2002) 96 *American Journal of International Law* 661 and Mary Crock, Ben Saul and Azadeh Dastyari, *FutureSeekersII* (Federation Press, 2006) 114.

[117] The EMT is not a doctor, however the EMT will make a determination as to the seriousness of a medical condition of any interdicted individual. Interview with Commander Chris Carter, Head of U.S. Coast Guard Alien Migrant Interdiction Section (22 March 2001), cited in Jonathan Friedman et al., *Maritime Interception: History, Practice and Emerging Issue*, Yale Law School, Allard K. Lowenstein International Human Rights Clinic (Unpublished, 2002) 26. Copy on file with the author.

[118] See U.S. Coast Guard, *Maritime Safety* (2008) <www.uscg.mil/top/missions/M_Safety.asp>. The relevant webpage had been removed at 23 February 2012.

[119] It should be noted that the master of a ship is only obligated to provide assistance 'in so far as he can do so without serious danger to the ship, crew or the passengers'. UNCLOS, Art 8(7).

98 of UNCLOS is based on Article 12(a)(1) of the *Convention on the High Seas*.[120] Thus, as the United States is a party to the *Convention on the High Seas*, it is bound not only by UNCLOS as customary international law but also by a similar provision in a treaty that it is a party to.[121]

UNCLOS also provides under Article 94(4) that the flag State of a vessel has a duty to ensure 'that the master, officers and, to the extent appropriate, the crew are fully conversant with and required to observe the applicable international regulations concerning the safety of life at sea'. Article 94(5) of UNCLOS clarifies Article 94(4) of UNCLOS by pointing out that the applicable international regulations concerning the safety of life at sea are the 'generally accepted international regulations, procedures and practices'.

Two treaty instruments in particular contain the international obligation to render assistance to a person in distress, and are accepted instruments of the sort envisioned by UNCLOS. The first is the *International Convention on Salvage*,[122] which under Article 10 states that 'every master is bound, so far as he can do so without serious danger to his vessel, and persons thereon, to render assistance to any person in danger of being lost at sea'. The second treaty and the most recent repetition of the duty to rescue is the *International Convention for the Safety of Life at Sea* (SOLAS),[123] which is 'arguably the most important international convention regarding maritime safety'.[124] The United States has signed and ratified the SOLAS.[125] SOLAS provides greater specificity for the procedure to rescue and under Regulation V/33(a)[126] states:

120 Opened for signature 29 April 1958, 13 UST 2312 (entered into force 30 September 1962).

121 The United States became a party to the *Convention on the High Seas* in April 1961. The *Convention on the High Seas* is superseded by the UNCLOS for parties that are parties to both Conventions. However, as the United States is not party to the UNCLOS and views it only as a codification of customary international law, the *Convention on the High Seas* has not been superseded by the UNCLOS for it.

122 Opened for signature 1 July 1989, 1953 UNTS 33479 (entered into force 14 July 1996). The United States signed the *International Convention on Salvage* on 27 March 1992. The convention entered into force for the United States on 14 July 1996.

123 Opened for signature 1 November 1974, 164 UNTS 113 (entered into force 25 May 1980).

124 Fredrick Kenney and Vasilos Tasikas, '*Tampa* Incident: IMO Perspectives and Responses on the Treatment of Persons Rescued at Sea, (2003) 12 *Pacific Rim Law & Policy Journal* 143, 149. For a discussion of the historical underpinnings of the duty to rescue see Ernst Willheim, '*MV Tampa*: The Australian Response' (2003) 15 *International Journal of Refugee* 159.

125 The United States signed the SOLAS on 7 September 1978; the Convention entered into force for the United States on 25 May 1980.

126 Formerly regulation v/10 but renumbered to v/33 in amendments adopted in 2000.

> The master of a ship at sea which is in a position to be able to provide assistance, on receiving a signal from any source that persons are in distress at sea, is bound to proceed with all speed to their assistance, if possible informing them or the search and rescue service, that the ship is doing so. If the ship receiving the distress alert is unable or, in the special circumstances of the case, considers it unreasonable or unnecessary to proceed to their assistance, the master must enter in the log-book the reason for failing to proceed to the assistance of the persons in distress and, taking into account the recommendations of the Organization, inform the appropriate search and rescue service accordingly.

In addition to the duty to render assistance to those in distress at sea, international law also contains a duty to search and rescue. The *International Convention on Maritime Search and Rescue* (SAR)[127] states that parties to the Convention

> shall, as they are able to do so individually or in co-operation with other States and, as appropriate, with the Organization, participate in the development of search and rescue services to ensure that assistance is rendered to any person in distress at sea. On receiving information that any person is, or appears to be, in distress at sea, the responsible authorities of a Party shall take urgent steps to ensure that the necessary assistance is provided.[128]

Rescue is defined under the SAR as 'an operation to retrieve persons in distress, provide for their initial medical or other needs, and deliver them to a place of safety'.[129] Distress is defined as '[a] situation wherein there is reasonable certainty that a person, a vessel or other craft is threatened by grave and imminent danger and requires immediate assistance'.[130] The United States has signed and ratified the SAR.[131] Thus it is clear that if the United States is in fact rescuing vessels in international waters, it is not only permitted but obliged to do so under the international law of the

[127] Opened for signature 27 April 1979, 1405 UNTS 97 (entered into force 22 June 1985).
[128] Ibid annex, ch 2, para 2.1.1.
[129] Ibid annex, ch 1, para 1.3.2.
[130] Ibid annex, ch 1, para 1.3.13.
[131] The United States signed the SAR on 12 August 1980; the Convention entered into force for the United States on 22 June 1985.

sea, as both the duty to render assistance and to provide search and rescue services are well established under international law.[132]

3.3.4.1 Interdiction or Rescue?

Whilst the United States must rescue vessels in 'grave and imminent danger'[133] that require 'immediate assistance',[134] it cannot justify as a rescue mission an interdiction operation concerned with the enforcement of domestic immigration laws if the vessel concerned is not threatened by 'grave and imminent danger' and does not require immediate assistance. There has been concern that some States, including the United States, are cloaking interdiction operations, which are an exercise of their enforcement jurisdiction, as 'rescue' operations.[135] Legomsky argues that 'interdiction is ... frequently depicted [by the U.S.] as a rescue mission, designed to save lives, by deterring passengers from taking to sea in flimsy vessels in the first place'.[136] Nothing in the international law of the sea supports the privilege to deter in the interest of maritime safety.

[132] A number of General Assembly resolutions also condemn and deplore the failure to rescue asylum seekers distressed at sea. See, for example, *Report of the United Nations High Commissioner for Refugees*, UN GAOR, 38th sess, 100th mtg, UN Doc A/Res/38/121 (16 December 1983), [3]; *Report of the United Nations High Commissioner for Refugees*, UN GAOR, 39th sess, 101st mtg, UN Doc A/RES/39/140 (14 December 1984), [3]; *Report of the United Nations High Commissioner for Refugees*, UN GAOR, 40th sess, 116th mtg, UN Doc A/RES/40/118 (13 December 1985), [3]; *Office of the United Nations High Commissioner for Refugees*, UN GAOR, 41st sess, 97th mtg, A/RES/41/124 (4 December 1986), [4].

[133] *International Convention on Maritime Search and Rescue*, 27 April 1979, TIAS No 11,093, 1405 UNTS 97, Ch 1.3.13.

[134] Ibid.

[135] In May 2006, the United Nations High Commissioner for Refugees (UNHCR) convened a meeting with representatives of States bordering the Mediterranean Sea and relevant intergovernmental organisations to discuss rescue and interception in the Mediterranean basin. At the meeting, concerns were raised over the practice whereby several States were classifying some interception measures as rescue-at-sea operations, in order to use SAR operational capacity for such activities. See UNHCR, State Representative Meeting, *Rescue at Sea and Maritime Interception in the Mediterranean*, Madrid, Spain, 23–24 May 2006, Chairman Summary <www.unhcr.org/4963237a11.pdf>. For a discussion of the meeting, see Barbara Miltner, 'Irregular Maritime Migration: Refugee Protection Issues in Rescue and Interception' (2006) 30 *Fordham International Law Journal* 75, 111.

[136] Stephen Legomsky, 'The USA and the Caribbean Interdiction Program' (2006) 18 *International Journal of Refugee Law* 677, 685.

Frelick has also argued that the United States likes

> to put a humanitarian gloss on interdiction by calling it "rescue at sea." Of course, it isn't. The United States "rescues" boats that are not in distress and detains their occupants, even against their will. In all cases, without exception, the boats are sunk, destroying the property of the boat owners.[137]

If Frelick's contention is true and the United States is in fact rescuing boats that are not in distress, then the United States would have no legal authority for its actions. The situation, however, appears to be more complex.

The Coast Guard does not refer to rescue operations as interdictions. The Coast Guard Manual directs that

> unless the persons onboard are in immediate and life threatening danger, assistance should not be provided to a foreign vessel not subject to the jurisdiction of the United States without the consent of the master or approval from the flag State.[138]

However, the Coast Guard Manual also provides that 'categorizing a situation as a [rescue] case does not preclude subsequent enforcement action'.[139] The Coast Guard maintains that it only 'rescues' individuals in need of rescue and only after a vessel has been rescued does a rescue operation turn into an interdiction operation. That is, only after a rescue has been completed will the Coast Guard enforce U.S. municipal law in the form of an interdiction. The Coast Guard's position raises two questions. First, is it true that the U.S. Coast Guard is in fact rescuing only vessels in grave and imminent danger? Second, is the United States permitted to turn a rescue operation into an interdiction operation once it has completed the rescue?

The Coast Guard holds that the vessels 'rescued' are unseaworthy, overloaded, lacking basic safety equipment, unsanitary and often operated by inexperienced sailors.[140] The sea vessels interdicted by the United States

137 Bill Frelick, 'Haitian Boat Interdiction and Return: First Asylum and First Principles of Refugee Protection' (1993) 26 *Cornell International Law Journal* 675, 687.

138 U.S. Coast Guard, *Maritime Law Enforcement Manual* <www.uscg.mil/hq/cg5/cg531/AMIO/FOIA_Docs.pdf>, D.2.c.

139 U.S. Coast Guard, *Model Maritime Operations Guide, Maritime Security* <www.uscg.mil/INTERNATIONAL/affairs/MMOG/English/Chapter2.htm>, C.1.c(2).

140 Ibid.

are often vessels that were once registered in the country of origin and then scrapped because they are no longer safe. They are then restored and have their markings removed by salvagers.[141] Haitian vessels in particular are reportedly in poor condition. Palmer notes that 'Haitian migrant vessels are typically crude, handmade, wooden-hulled vessels … [that are] powered by unreliable engines prone to mechanical failure'.[142] The UNHCR has also noted the use of 'unseaworthy vessels'[143] by Haitians, stating that it is 'very concerned by the loss of life [they] are seeing in maritime incidents in the Caribbean among people trying to escape difficult conditions in Haiti'.[144]

It is feasible that vessels engaged in the transport of persons to the United States without prior authority would be in poor condition and even be unseaworthy. The transport of people who do not have prior authorisation is a risky activity and, if done for profit, it is imaginable that cost-cutting measures would be taken that would endanger the lives of those on board. Therefore, there does not appear to be a strong reason to doubt the claim of the United States that the vessels it purports to rescue are indeed unseaworthy, in grave and imminent danger and in need of immediate assistance.

We turn now to the question of whether or not the United States is permitted to turn a rescue operation into an interdiction operation once it has completed the rescue – that is, whether it is permitted to subject individuals it rescues to its municipal laws. Answering this question requires an examination of the jurisdictional nexus between States involved in search and rescue operations on the one hand and the individuals rescued on the other.[145]

In *Hirsi Jamaa and Others v Italy* (*Hirsi Jamaa*),[146] the European Court of Human Rights considered the exercise of jurisdiction by Italy when

[141] See Friedman et al., n 117 in this chapter, 22.

[142] See n 6 in this chapter, 1572.

[143] UNHCR, *Briefing Notes: More People Are Risking Lives In The Caribbean To Reach Safety* (13 July 2012) <www.unhcr.org/cgibin/texis/vtx/search?page=search&docid=4ffff6becf&query=Caribbean>.

[144] Ibid.

[145] Efthymios Papastavridis, 'Enforcement Jurisdiction in the Mediterranean Sea: Illicit Activities and the Rule of Law on the High Seas' (2010) *The International Journal of Marine and Coastal Law* 569, 587.

[146] European Court of Human Rights, Grand Chamber, Application No 27765/09, 23 February 2012 [178].

interdicting Somali and Eritrean nationals at sea. In that case, Italy argued that 'the vessels carrying the applicants had been intercepted in the context of the rescue on the high seas'.[147] As such, Italy contended that it did not exercise 'jurisdiction' over the individuals rescued by handing them over to Libya. The European Court of Human Rights disagreed, stating that 'Italy cannot circumvent its "jurisdiction", under the *European Convention for the Protection of Human Rights and Fundamental Freedoms*, by describing the events at issue as rescue operations on the High Seas'.[148] That is, the European Court of Human Rights has clarified that a rescue operation is an exercise of jurisdiction by a State. However, this should not be confused with an authority under international law for the unlimited exercise of enforcement jurisdiction during interdiction operations. The Court in *Hirsi Jamaa* did not clarify the extent of the permissible exercise of jurisdiction and control by a State party engaged in a rescue.

A rescuing State is constrained in its exercise of jurisdiction over rescues and cannot rely on the authority provided for the carrying out of a rescue operation to engage in further exercises of jurisdiction. Both SOLAS[149] and the SAR Convention[150] require States parties to ensure that 'survivors assisted are disembarked from the assisting ship and delivered to a place of safety' as soon as reasonably practicable. It is this disembarkation and delivery that mark the completion of the rescue. While a rescue operation is ongoing, a State cannot rely on its authority to rescue, and the jurisdiction that this entails, for further exercises of its jurisdiction under an interdiction program. Once a rescue mission is complete, however, a State may rely on other sources of authority such as the presence of the rescuees on its flagged vessels (where by virtue of Article 92 of UNCLOS the State has independent authority to exercise jurisdiction and control). Locating the precise moment when a rescue has been completed is, therefore, crucial

[147] Ibid [65].

[148] The Court went on to state that '[i]n particular, the Court cannot subscribe to the Government's argument that Italy was not responsible for the fate of the applicants on account of the allegedly minimal control exercised by the authorities over the parties concerned at the material time'. *Hirsi Jamaa and Others v Italy* (European Court of Human Rights, Grand Chamber, Application No 27765/09, 23 February 2012), [79].

[149] *International Convention for the Safety of Life at Sea*, opened for signature 1 November 1974, 164 UNTS 113 (entered into force 25 May 1980), ch V, Reg 33-1-1.

[150] See n 133 this chapter, Ch III, Para 3.1.9.

to determining when a State is freed from the limitations on its exercise of jurisdiction and can thus turn a rescue operation into an interdiction operation.

Unfortunately, a 'place of safety', which marks the end of a rescue operation, is not defined under the international law of the sea.[151] As Barnes notes, there are significant gaps in the regulation of migration at sea which are filled by soft law norms. Such norms 'do not restructure State obligations ... but promote cooperation between the affected parties'.[152] SOLAS and SAR do provide that in disembarking rescuees at a place of safety, States must take into account 'the particular circumstances of the case and guidelines developed by Organizations'.[153] A relevant set of guidelines is the *Guidelines on the Treatment of Persons Rescued at Sea* (Rescue Guidelines),[154] which provide that a place of safety is where

> the survivors' safety of life is no longer threatened and where their basic human needs (such as food, shelter and medical needs) can be met. Further, it is a place from which transportation arrangements can be made for the survivors' next or final destination.[155]

A place of safety need not be on land. The Rescue Guidelines state

> A place of safety may be on land, or it may be aboard a rescue unit or *other suitable vessel or facility at sea* that can serve as a place of safety until the survivors are disembarked to their next destination.[156]

However, significantly, the Rescue Guidelines also state

> An assisting ship should not be considered a place of safety based solely on the fact that the survivors are no longer in immediate danger once aboard the ship. An assisting ship may not have appropriate facilities and equipment to sustain additional persons on board

[151] Miltner, n 135 in this chapter, 87.

[152] Richard Barnes, 'The International Law of the Sea and Migration Control' in Bernard Ryan and Valsamis Mitsilegas (eds) *Extraterritorial Immigration Control: Legal Challenges* (Martinus Nijhoff Publishers, 2010) 103, 149.

[153] See n 149 and 150 in this chapter.

[154] International Maritime Organization, *Resolution MSC.167(78), Guidelines on the Treatment of Persons Rescued at Sea*, 20 May 2004. The Rescue Guidelines is the sort of instrument envisioned by SOLAS and the SAR Convention to provide guidance on what can constitute a place of safety.

[155] Ibid [6.12].

[156] Ibid [6.14]. Emphasis added.

> without endangering its own safety or to properly care for the survivors. Even if the ship is capable of safely accommodating the survivors and may serve as a temporary place of safety, it should be relieved of this responsibility as soon as alternative arrangements can be made.[157]

That is, despite the provision of food, water and any necessary medical treatment on board Coast Guard cutters, rescue operations should not be seen to have come to an end when individuals rescued are brought onto a Coast Guard cutter. At best, the Coast Guard vessel used in the rescue is a 'temporary place of safety'.[158] It may be conceivable that commercial ships engaged in rescue should be relieved of their responsibility to rescuees by disembarking them on the vessels of a State at sea (and thus minimise inconvenience to the commercial vessel). However, the U.S. Coast Guard does not disembark the rescuees on another vessel. It therefore follows that the U.S. practice of turning rescue operations into interdiction operations on board the rescuing vessel is not permitted, because the United States is impeded in its attempts to subject rescuees to its municipal laws by its obligation to complete the rescue operations and disembark the rescuees at a place of safety.

Another related question is where rescued individuals should be disembarked.[159] Goodwin-Gill points out that '[i]nternational law is silent as to disembarkation, or follow up for those who have been rescued';[160] and as the Expert Meeting on International Cooperation to Share Burdens

[157] Ibid [6.13].

[158] See UNHCR, Rescue At Sea. A Guide to Principles and Practice as Applied to Migrants and Refugees <http://www.unhcr.org/publ/PUBL/450037d34.pdf>, 7.

[159] UNHCR notes that 'States should avoid the categorisation of interception operations as search and rescue operations, because this can lead to confusion with respect to disembarkation responsibilities'. See UNHCR, Report of the Office of the United Nations High Commissioner for Refugees, *The Treatment of Persons Rescued at Sea: Conclusions and Recommendations from Recent Meetings and Expert Round Tables Convened by the Office of the United Nations High Commissioner for Refugees*, 11 April 2008, A/AC.259/17 <www.unhcr.org/refworld/docid/49997aeb27.html> [20].

[160] Guy Goodwin-Gill, 'Refugees and Responsibility in the Twenty-First Century: More Lessons Learned From the South Pacific' (2003) 12 *Pacific Law and Policy Journal* 23, 35–36. Goodwin-Gill argues that the lack of definitive rules on disembarkation disadvantage the rescued but allows for a 'more nuanced approach to complex situations [and] may in fact promote coherent and principled solutions, at least in a world in which States are prepared to co-operate'. See also Lori Nessel, 'Externalized Borders and the Invisible Refugee' (2009) 40 *Columbia Human Rights Law Review* 625, 632–33.

and Responsibilities has noted, there is an 'absence of a system to allocate responsibility for disembarkation'.[161] This gap in the international law of the sea and international refugee law as to the appropriate place of disembarkation has also been recognised by the UNHCR.[162] According to UNHCR's Model Framework for Cooperation Following Rescue at Sea Operations Involving Refugees and Asylum Seekers to Encourage Cooperation Between States in Rescue Operations (Model Framework),[163] when choosing a point of disembarkation states should be mindful of

> [p]ractical considerations (eg. Maritime safety; geographical proximity; the extent to which the rescuing vessel will be required to deviate from its intended voyage; the needs of rescued persons; facilities at the proposed site of disembarkation, including *access to fair and efficient asylum procedures*); applicable SAR and SOLAS provisions; [and] *the principle of non-refoulement*[.][164]

The Rescue Guidelines also provide for

> [t]he need to avoid disembarkation in territories where the lives and freedoms of those alleging a well-founded fear of persecution would be threatened is a consideration in the case of asylum-seekers and refugees recovered at sea.[165]

The United States' *non-refoulement* obligations are discussed in Chapter 5, but for present purposes it suffices to note that a place where a refugee has

[161] UNHCR, Expert Meeting on International Cooperation to Share Burdens and Responsibilities, *Expert Meeting on International Cooperation to Share Burdens and Responsibilities*, Amman, Jordan, 27 and 28 June 2011 Summary Conclusions <www.unhcr.org/refworld/docid/4e9fed232.html> [12].

[162] UNHCR, Expert Roundtable, *Rescue-at-Sea: Specific Aspects Relating to the Protection of Asylum-Seekers and Refugees*, Lisbon, Portugal, 25–26 March 2002, Summary of Discussions <www.unhcr.org/refworld/docid/3cd14e3b4.html> [9]. See also Guy Goodwin-Gill and Jane McAdam, *The Refugee in International Law* (Oxford University Press, 3rd ed., 2007) 281.

[163] UNHCR, 'Expert Meeting on Refugees and Asylum-Seekers in Distress at Sea – how best to respond? Djibouti, 8–10 November 2011' (2012) 2 *International Journal of Refugee Law* 485. The United States has not adopted the Model Framework, but it is nevertheless a helpful guide as to the most appropriate place for disembarkation of rescuees.

[164] Ibid 494. Emphasis added.

[165] International Maritime Organization, *Resolution MSC.167(78), Guidelines on the Treatment of Persons Rescued at Sea*, 20 May 2004, [6.1.7]. For commentary, see Violeta Moreno Lax, 'The EU Regime on Interdiction, Search and Rescue, and Disembarkation: The Frontex Guidelines for Intervention at Sea' (2010) 25 *The International Journal of Marine and Coastal Law* 621.

a well-founded fear of persecution does not constitute a place of safety. Likewise, disembarkation of rescuees in a place where the rescuee may be at risk of death, torture, or cruel, inhuman or degrading treatment or punishment does not constitute a place of safety and should not end the rescue obligation. That is, the United States is limited in the range of places a person owed a *non-refoulement* obligation can be disembarked.[166]

It may be possible for the United States to claim that its obligation to disembark rescuees to a place of safety is discharged when individuals who are not owed a *non-refoulement* obligation are repatriated. However, as discussed in Chapter 5, the United States does not carry out fair and effective status determinations at sea to identify individuals in need of *non-refoulement* protection. As such, the United States does not have adequate procedures in place, on board Coast Guard cutters, to differentiate between persons who may be disembarked safely in their point of origin and those who cannot. As is also discussed further in Chapter 5, the U.S. mainland is the most appropriate place for the conduct of status determinations to ensure that the United States will not inadvertently engage in *refoulement* and disembark protected persons at an unsafe place. Therefore, rescuees should be disembarked in the U.S. mainland to ensure that they have access to fair and effective status determination procedures.

Furthermore, the Coast Guard often destroys unseaworthy vessels from which individuals are rescued. Not only does the United States not enjoy an authority to turn a rescue operation into an interdiction operation on board Coast Guard cutters in international waters; there is also no authority under international law that permits the United States to destroy unseaworthy vessels outside its territory that are not in its contiguous zone or flagged to a State with which it has an agreement authorising the destruction of vessels. If the United States has clear grounds to believe that proper jurisdiction and control with respect to a ship have not been exercised, all it is permitted to do under Article 94(5) of UNCLOS is to 'report the facts to the flag State. Upon receiving such a report, the flag State shall investigate the matter and, if appropriate, take any action necessary to remedy

166 Violeta Moreno Lax, 'Seeking Asylum in the Mediterranean: Against a Fragmentary Reading of EU Member States' Obligations Accruing at Sea' (2011) 33 (2) *International Journal of Refugee Law* 174, 218.

the situation'. As such, the United States acts illegally when it destroys unseaworthy vessels that are flagged to another State during rescue operations outside its territorial waters or its contiguous zone, unless it has an agreement with the flag State authorising such action.

3.4 Conclusion

This chapter has shown that the United States enjoys some authority under municipal and international law to carry out its MIP. Interdiction operations derive authority from Executive Orders and a Presidential Proclamation as well as statute under municipal law. The United States is authorised to exercise jurisdiction in the form of migrant interdiction operations under the international law of the sea when a vessel is located in U.S. territorial waters or the U.S. contiguous zone; when the United States has an agreement allowing for interdiction with the flag State of a vessel; and in cases where a vessel is stateless. However, the United States is not authorised to turn rescue operations into interdictions on board its vessels or to destroy vessels not flagged to a State with which it has an appropriate treaty, which are seized in rescue operations outside its territorial sea or contiguous zone.

As discussed at the beginning of this chapter, the power granted to the U.S. executive under municipal and international law to carry out migrant interdiction operations, in certain circumstances, is not without its limitations. The United States must ensure that returning a person to their point of origin does not violate any other treaty law obligations. The next chapter discusses the obligations owed to interdictees under international human rights and refugee law.

4

The United States' Obligations under International Human Rights and Refugee Law

In the previous chapter, this book explored the legal authority under U.S. municipal law and the international law of the sea for the exercise of jurisdiction by the United States as part of its MIP. The authority granted to the U.S. executive under municipal law and the international law of the sea to carry out migrant interdiction operations, in certain circumstances, is not without its limitations. The United States owes certain obligations to interdictees under international human rights and refugee law. In particular, the United States is bound by obligations under the Refugee Protocol, the *Convention Against Torture and Other Cruel, Inhuman or Degrading Treatment or Punishment* (CAT),[1] the *International Covenant on Civil and Political Rights* (ICCPR)[2] and the *International Convention on the Elimination of All Forms of Racial Discrimination* (CERD).[3]

The United States argues that it is not bound by a number of international human rights and refugee law treaty obligations when it exercises jurisdiction outside its municipally defined territory. Therefore, as the MIP takes place in international waters and in Guantánamo Bay, the United States believes that its interdiction operations need not be constrained by human rights and refugee law obligations.[4] This chapter contests the validity of the U.S. position and argues for the applicability of U.S. treaty obligations wherever the United States exercises jurisdiction, including in international waters and in Guantánamo Bay.

1 Opened for signature 4 February 1985, 1465 UNTS 85 (entered into force 26 June 1987).
2 Opened for signature 19 December 1966, 999 UNTS 171 (entered into force 23 March 1976).
3 Opened for signature 21 December 1965, 660 UNTS 195 (entered into force 4 January 1969).
4 As explained in Section 4.3, one exception to this is the CAT. The United States has acknowledged that the CAT may apply in both Guantánamo Bay and on board U.S. vessels.

This chapter consists of two parts. The first part provides an analysis of the relevant international human rights and refugee law treaties signed and ratified by the United States, and the territorial scope of their application. The second part of this chapter is an examination of the lack of effective mechanisms within the international and municipal legal regimes for the enforcement of the United States' human rights and refugee law treaty obligations in its operation of the MIP. Despite enjoying protections under international human rights and refugee law, there are three reasons why interdictees cannot turn to either the international or municipal legal regimes to enforce the United States' obligations to them under international human rights and refugee law treaties. First, there are no effective enforcement mechanisms under international law that are available to interdictees. Second, the treaty obligations discussed in this chapter are not directly incorporated into U.S. municipal law and thus cannot be the cause of action in U.S. courts without implementing legislation. Third, the United States has not implemented all of its treaty obligations, and when implementing legislation does exist, it has been found (or is likely to be found) to not limit the exercise of jurisdiction by the U.S. executive in the operation of the MIP.

4.1 International Covenant on Civil and Political Rights and Its Scope of Application

The first treaty under discussion in this chapter is the ICCPR, which the United States signed on 5 October 1977 and ratified on 8 June 1992.[5] Importantly for our discussion of the MIP, which takes place outside the municipally defined territory of the United States, the ICCPR applies wherever a State exercises jurisdiction, including outside its territorial boundaries. Article 2(1) of the ICCPR states

> Each State Party to the present Covenant undertakes to respect and to ensure to all individuals *within its territory and subject to its jurisdiction* the rights recognized in the present Covenant, without distinction of any kind, such as race, colour, sex, language, religion, political or other opinion, national or social origin, property, birth or other status.[6]

[5] The ICCPR entered into force for the United States on 8 September 1992.

[6] Emphasis added.

The interpretation of the term 'and' in Article 2(1) of the ICCPR is very important. The interpretation espoused by the United States is that an individual must be both 'within the territory' *and* 'subject to [the] jurisdiction' of a party to the ICCPR before he or she can enjoy the protection of the ICCPR. In its appearance before the Human Rights Committee (HR Committee) in 2006 to report on its implementation of the ICCPR the United States argued that

> [I]t is the long-standing view of the United States that the [ICCPR] by its very terms does not apply outside of the territory of a State Party … [A]pplying the basic rules for the interpretation of treaties described in the Vienna Convention on the Law of Treaties leads to the conclusion that the language in Article 2, Paragraph 1, establishes that States Parties are required to respect and ensure the rights in the Covenant only to individuals who are BOTH within the territory of a State Party and subject to its jurisdiction. First, this interpretation is confirmed by the ordinary meaning of the treaty text. Article 2, Paragraph 1, of the Covenant states explicitly that State Parties are required to respect and ensure the rights in the Covenant to all individuals, and I quote, "within its territory and subject to its jurisdiction."[7]

The Obama administration continues to deny the extraterritorial application of the ICCPR.[8] This is despite legal advice in 2010, from the then Legal Advisor to the Department of State, that the ICCPR imposes obligations on a State party's extraterritorial conduct.[9]

The better view of Article 2(1) is that the Article applies to all individuals within the territory of a State party, and all individuals subject to the

[7] U.S. Department of State, Opening Statement by Matthew Waxman on the Report Concerning the International Covenant on Civil and Political Rights (ICCPR) (17 July 2006) <http://2001–2009.state.gov/g/drl/rls/70392.htm>.

[8] In April 2014, the HR Committee communicated its regret that the United States 'continues to maintain its position that the Covenant does not apply with respect to individuals under its jurisdiction but outside its territory, despite the contrary interpretation of article 2(1) supported by the Committee's established jurisprudence, the jurisprudence of the International Court of Justice and State practice'. Human Rights Committee, *Concluding Observations on the Fourth Periodic Report of the United States of America*, UN Doc CCPR/C/USA/CO/4, (23 April 2014), [4].

[9] Harold Hongju Koh, 'Memorandum Opinion on the Geographic Scope of the International Covenant on Civil and Political Rights' 19 October 2010 <www.documentcloud.org/documents/1053853-state-department-iccpr-memo.html>.

jurisdiction of a State party.[10] This is the position of the International Court of Justice (ICJ), which has found that the ICCPR applies wherever a State party exercises jurisdiction. In *Legal Consequences of the Construction of a Wall in the Occupied Palestinian Territory* (*Israeli Wall*)[11] the ICJ stated

> The scope of application of the International Covenant on Civil and Political Rights is defined by Article 2, paragraph 1 … The Court would observe that, while the jurisdiction of States is primarily territorial, it may sometimes be exercised outside the national territory. Considering the object and purpose of the International Covenant on Civil and Political Rights, it would seem natural that, even when such is the case, State parties to the Covenant should be bound to comply with its provisions.[12]

The ICJ reiterated its findings in *Democratic Republic of Congo v Uganda*[13] where it stated that 'international human rights instruments are applicable "in respect of acts done by a State in the exercise of its jurisdiction outside its own territory"'.[14]

The HR Committee has also been clear in its view that the ICCPR applies where a State party exercises jurisdiction, even outside the State party's territory.[15] In General Comment No 31 the HR Committee stated

[10] This is the position of a number of prominent scholars. See, for example, Nigel Rodley, 'The Extraterritorial Reach and Applicability in Armed Conflict of the International Covenant on Civil and Political Rights: A Rejoinder to Dennis and Surena' (2009) 5 *European Human Rights Law Review* 628; Thomas Buergenthal, 'To Respect and to Ensure: State Obligations and Permissible Derogations' in Louis Henkin (ed), *The International Bill of Human Rights: The Covenant on Civil and Political Rights* (Columbia University Press, 1981) 72; Sigrun Skogly, 'Extraterritoriality – Universal Human Rights without Universal Obligations?' in Sarah Joseph and Adam McBeth, *Research Handbook on International Human Rights Law* (Edward Elgar Pub, 2010) 92–93.

[11] *Legal Consequences of the Construction of a Wall in the Occupied Palestinian Territory* (Advisory Opinion) [2004] ICJ Rep 136.

[12] Ibid [108]–[109].

[13] *Armed Activities on the Territory of the Congo* (Democratic Republic of Congo v Uganda) (Judgment, Merits) [2005] ICJ Rep 168, [216].

[14] Ibid [216].

[15] The HR Committee first suggested that the ICCPR could apply outside the territorial boundaries of a State party in three communications concerning the exercise of jurisdiction by Uruguay over Uruguayan citizens in foreign territory in the 1980s: *Casariego v Uruguay*, UN Doc.CCPR/C/13/D/56/1979 (29 July 1981); *Burgos v Uruguay*, UN Doc.CCPR/C/13/D/52/1979 (29 July 1981); and *Montero v Uruguay*, UN Doc.CCPR/C/18/D/106/1981 (31 March 1983).

> The enjoyment of Covenant rights is not limited to citizens of State Parties but must also be available to all individuals, regardless of nationality or statelessness, such as asylum seekers, refugees, migrant workers and other persons, who may find themselves in the territory or subject to the jurisdiction of the State Party. This principle also applies to those within the power or effective control of the forces of a State Party acting outside its territory, regardless of the circumstances in which such power or effective control was obtained.[16]

It should be noted that in determining the reach of an analogous human rights treaty, the *Convention for the Protection of Human Rights and Fundamental Freedoms* (ECHR),[17] the European Court of Human Rights, in 2001, considered the extraterritorial application of the ICCPR in *Banković v Belgium* (*Banković*)[18] and found that

> [A]s early as 1950 the drafters [of Article 2 § 1 the ICCPR] had definitively and specifically confined its territorial scope and it is difficult to suggest that exceptional recognition by the Human Rights Committee of certain instances of extra-territorial jurisdiction (and the applicants give one example only) displaces in any way the territorial jurisdiction expressly conferred by that Article of the CCPR 1966.[19]

Banković concerned an extraterritorial air campaign against the Federal Republic of Yugoslavia in 1999 by NATO forces,[20] which resulted in sixteen deaths. The Court concluded that the exercise of military force over an individual was insufficient to constitute a link between the victim and the respondent State under the given circumstances. Thus, the rejection of the extraterritorial reach of the ICCPR in *Banković* was in the context of the Court's rejection of the extraterritorial reach of the ECHR and is not an authoritative determination of the application of the ICCPR.

[16] Human Rights Committee, *General Comment No 31 Nature of the General Legal Obligation Imposed on State Parties to the Covenant*, 80th sess, 12 UN Doc CCPR/C/21/Rev1/Add.13 (26 May 2004), [10].

[17] Opened for signature 4 November 1950, 213 UNTS 222 (entered into force 3 September 1953).

[18] (2001) XII Eur Court HR 333.

[19] Ibid [78].

[20] NATO is the North Atlantic Treaty Organization, an intergovernmental military alliance established by the *North Atlantic Treaty*, opened for signature 4 April 1949, 34 UNTS 243 (entered into force 24 August 1949).

Importantly, *Banković* predates the ICJ's decision in *Israeli Wall*, which has put the extraterritorial reach of the ICCPR beyond doubt as a matter of international law. The decision also predates the HR Committee's explicit statement regarding the extraterritorial reach of Article 2(1) of the ICCPR in General Comment No 31. Approximately ten years after its decision in *Banković*, the European Court of Human Rights found in *Al-Skeini v United Kingdom* (*Al-Skeini*)[21] that the ECHR is applicable 'whenever the State through its agents exercises control and authority over an individual, and thus jurisdiction'.[22] As such, the British military was found to be bound by its obligations under the ECHR with regard to the deaths of Iraqi civilians detained in a British military prison in Iraq. In *Al-Skeini*, the Court also recognised the ICJ's finding in *Israeli Wall* and *Congo v Uganda* that 'international human rights instruments [including the ICCPR, are] capable of having an [extraterritorial] application'.[23] Finally, in *Hirsi Jamaa and Others v Italy* (*Hirsi Jamaa*),[24] the European Court of Human Rights found that the ECHR could also apply extraterritorially in Italy's exercise of extraterritorial jurisdiction during interdiction operations in international waters.[25] It can thus be seen that the European Court's understanding of the extraterritorial application of human rights obligations in *Banković* has been further clarified and extended by subsequent decisions such as *Al-Skeini* and *Hirsi Jamaa*.[26]

4.2 Protocol Relating to the Status of Refugees and Its Scope of Application

In addition to the ICCPR, the Refugee Protocol provides further international protection to refugees interdicted by the United States under

[21] (2011) 53 EHRR 18.

[22] Ibid [136].

[23] Ibid [98].

[24] (European Court of Human Rights, Grand Chamber, Application No 27765/09, 23 February 2012), [178].

[25] Judge Pinto De Albuquerque referred to the extraterritorial application of the ICCPR in his concurring decision: Ibid 63 n2; 69 n25.

[26] On the European Court of Human Rights' expanding understanding of extraterritorial jurisdiction, see Angelika Neuberger, 'The Concept of "Jurisdiction" in the Jurisprudence of the European Court of Human Rights' (2012) 1 *Current Legal Problems* 1. See also Federico Sperotto, 'Ten Years After Bankovic' (2012) 12 *Global Jurist* 1; Violeta Moreno-Lax, '*Hirsi Jamaa and Others v Italy* or the Strasbourg Court Versus Extraterritorial Migration Control' (2012) 1 *Human Rights Law Review* 1.

the MIP. The United States became a party to the Refugee Protocol on 1 November 1968.[27] The United States is thus obliged to abide by Articles 2 to 34 inclusive of the Refugee Convention.

The title of the U.S. 'Migrant Interdiction Program' or references by the United States to 'Alien Migrant Interdictions'[28] is misleading for it implies that *all* individuals interdicted by the United States are migrants and have left their home countries of their own volition for economic or social reasons.[29] This is an incorrect characterisation. Many individuals are interdicted by the United States attempting to enter purely for economic and social reasons. However, among the people interdicted are also individuals seeking protection because they are fleeing death, torture, or cruel, inhuman, degrading treatment or punishment in their home countries.[30]

Most significantly, among the individuals interdicted by the United States as part of its MIP are refugees whose status is defined under Article 1(A) the Refugee Convention as amended by the Refugee Protocol.[31] The United States owes a duty of *non-refoulement* to refugees under Article 33(1) of the Refugee Convention. In considering who constitutes a 'refugee' it is important to remember that

> A person is a refugee within the meaning of the 1951 Convention as soon as he fulfils the criteria contained in the definition. This would necessarily occur prior to the time at which his refugee status is formally determined. Recognition of his refugee status does not therefore make him a refugee but declares him to be one. He does not become a refugee because of recognition, but is recognized because he is a refugee.[32]

[27] The Refugee Protocol came into force for the United States on 1 November 1968.

[28] See, for example, White House, ExpectMore.gov, *The Coast Guard Migrant Interdiction Program* <www.whitehouse.gov/sites/default/files/omb/assets/OMB/expectmore/summary/10002406.2004.html>; U.S. Coast Guard, *Alien Migrant Interdiction* <www.uscg.mil/hq/cg5/cg531/AMIO/amio.asp>.

[29] Diana Wong, 'Semantics of Migration' (1989) 4 *Journal of Social Issues in Southeast Asia* 275, 281.

[30] As analysed in subsection 5.3.1 and Section 5.3, respectively, the United States owes such individuals protection from *refoulement* under the ICCPR and the CAT.

[31] Article 1(2) of the Refugee Protocol removed the temporal limits in the definition of a 'refugee under Article 1(A) of the Refugee Convention. Article 1(3) of the Refugee Protocol removed the geographical limits in the definition of Refugee under Article 1(A) of the Refugee Convention.

[32] United Nations High Commissioner for Refugees (UNHCR), *Handbook and Guidelines on Procedures and Criteria for Determining Refugee Status Under the 1951 Convention and the*

Therefore, rights owed to a refugee under international refugee law are owed regardless of whether or not the United States has in fact assessed the status of an individual and found him or her to require protection. Yet Coast Guard personnel are directed not to refer to any individuals they interdict as refugees and are only permitted to use the term 'migrants'.[33] Furthermore, refugees whose status is confirmed pursuant to a status determination procedure in Guantánamo Bay are also not given the correct title of 'refugee' by the United States, but are labelled as 'protected migrants'.[34] The United States' refusal to refer to refugees under the MIP by their correct legal title is highly problematic and highlights its unwillingness to accept its international obligations to refugees outside its municipally defined territory. However, the use of an incorrect title does not remove the United States' obligations under international refugee law.

4.2.1 The United States' Rejection of the Extraterritorial Application of Article 33(1) of the Refugee Convention

Refugees acquire rights under the Refugee Convention in accordance with their level of attachment to a State party.[35] Certain rights under the Refugee Convention, such as the right to *non-refoulement* (Article 33(1)) and the right to non-discrimination (Article 3), are applicable to all refugees subject to a State's jurisdiction regardless of where jurisdiction is exercised. This is because the provisions providing for the relevant rights do not contain any territorial limits in their scope of application.[36]

The United States, however, has expressly denied the extraterritorial application of Article 33(1) of the Refugee Convention.[37] On 25 June 1996, the U.S. delegation at the meeting of the UNHCR Executive

1967 *Protocol Relating to the Status of Refugees* (1992, reissued 2011), [28]. As Hathaway and Foster point out, 'the declaratory nature of refugee status is not simply good policy but follows, inextricably from the way in which rights accrue under the Refugee Convention': James Hathaway and Michelle Foster, *The Law of Refugee Status* (Cambridge University Press, 2nd ed., 2014) 26.

33 U.S. Coast Guard, *Maritime Law Enforcement Manual* <www.uscg.mil/hq/cg5/cg531/AMIO/FOIA_Docs.pdf>, D.8.

34 See the opening section of Chapter 6.

35 James Hathaway and Michelle Foster, n 32 in this chapter, 26.

36 Articles 3 is discussed in Section 5.4. Article 34 is discussed in subsection 6.4.3.

37 The U.S. executive has not made any public statements regarding its position on the extraterritorial application of Article 3 of the Refugee Convention. The content of the *non-refoulement*

Committee of the High Commissioner's Programme (ExCom) criticised a draft Conclusion that reaffirmed

> [t]he fundamental importance of the observance of the principle of *non-refoulement* both at the border and from within the territory of a State … of persons who may be subjected to persecution, torture or inhuman treatment if returned to their country of origin or another country where they are not protected against *refoulement*, irrespective of whether or not they have been formally recognised as refugees.[38]

The United States argued that the UNHCR should adopt a definition of *non-refoulement* that restricts its scope of application to the territory of a State party.[39]

On 7 October 1996, there was a softening in U.S. policy. Assistant Secretary of State Oakley addressed the UNHCR ExCom, stating

> We must seek to maintain and to strengthen the humanitarian principle that refugees must not be returned to persecution or torture, either from within the territory of a receiving State or from its border.[40]

However, the United States contended that *non-refoulement* at the border was a 'humanitarian principle' rather than a legal principle.[41] During 1997 and 1998, the United States did not object to language regarding *non-refoulement* that it had previously found objectionable. This included UNHCR ExCom Conclusion No 85, which stated that ExCom

> [s]trongly deplores the continuing incidence and often tragic humanitarian consequences of *refoulement* in all its forms,

obligation under Article 33(1) of the Refugee Convention is discussed in Section 5.3. It suffices to note here that Article 33(1) prohibits the return or *refoulement* of a refugees to within borders of territories where a refugee's 'life or freedom would be threatened on account of his [or her] race, religion, nationality, membership of a particular social group or political opinion'.

38 UNHCR Draft Conclusion on International Protection, 2 September 1996 cited in Bill Frelick, '"Abundantly Clear": *Refoulement*' (2004) 19 *Georgetown Immigration Law Journal* 245, 254.

39 U.S. Mission to International Organizations, 'Statement of the United States Delegation to the Standing Committee of the Executive Committee of the Program of the UN High Commissioner for Refugees' (Geneva, 25 June 1996). For an analysis of this response see Frelick, n 38 in this chapter, 254–55.

40 Phyllis Oakley, Assistant Secretary for Population, Refugees, and Migration United States, 'The Pursuit and Implementation of Durable Solutions' (Geneva, 7 October 1996).

41 Ibid. See also Frelick, n 38 in this chapter, 258.

> including through summary removals, occasionally *en masse*, and reiterates in this regard the need to admit refugees to the territory of States, which includes no rejection at frontiers without access to fair and effective procedures for determining their status and protection needs.[42]

It also did not object to UNHCR ExCom Conclusion No 81, which held ExCom

> [r]ecognises the fundamental importance of the principle of *non-refoulement*, which prohibits expulsion and return of refugees in any manner whatsoever to the frontiers of territories where their lives or freedom would be threatened on account of their race, religion, nationality, membership of a particular social group or political opinion, whether or not they have formally been granted refugee status, or of persons in respect of whom there are substantial grounds for believing that they would be in danger of being subjected to torture, as set forth in the 1984 Convention against Torture and Other Cruel, Inhuman or Degrading Treatment or Punishment.[43]

In October 2003, the UNHCR ExCom articulated its clearest assertion that the principle of *non-refoulement* applies extraterritorially in interception measures. UNHCR ExCom Conclusion No 97 on Protection Safeguards in Interception Measures recommended that

> Interception measures should not result in asylum-seekers and refugees being denied access to international protection, or result in those in need of international protection being returned, directly or indirectly, to the frontiers of territories where their life or freedom would be threatened on account of a Convention ground, or where the person has other grounds for protection based on international law. Intercepted persons found to be in need of international protection should have access to durable solutions.[44]

[42] Executive Committee of the High Commissioner's Programme (UNHCR ExCom) *Conclusion No 85: Conclusion on International Protection*, 49th sess, UN Doc A/53/12/Add.1 (9 October 1998), [q].

[43] UNHCR ExCom, *Conclusion No 81: General Conclusion on International Protection*, 48th sess, UN Doc A/52/12/Add.1 (17 October 1997), [i].

[44] UNHCR ExCom, *Conclusion No 97: Conclusion on Protection Safeguards in Interception Measures*, 58th sess, UN Doc A/58/12/Add.1 (10 October 2003), [a].

UNHCR ExCom Conclusion number 97 also recommended that:

> State authorities and agents acting on behalf of the intercepting State should take, consistent with their obligations under international law, all appropriate steps in the implementation of interception measures to preserve and protect the right to life and the right not to be subjected to torture or other cruel, inhuman or degrading treatment or punishment of persons intercepted.[45]

The Conclusion further noted the needs of vulnerable groups, including women and children, and called for all intercepted persons to be treated in a humane manner.[46] The United States did not object to the language of the UNHCR ExCom Conclusion.

The movement of the United States towards an acknowledgement of its *non-refoulement* obligations in its interdiction practices, however, came to an abrupt end on 25 February 2004, when President George W. Bush publicly stated

> I have made it abundantly clear to the Coast Guard that we will turn back any refugee that attempts to reach our shores. That message needs to be very clear as well to the Haitian people.[47]

Up to that point, no U.S. president had ever openly called interdicted Haitians refugees who were being returned to political instability 'refugees'. Presidents Reagan, George H.W. Bush and Clinton had all referred to returned interdicted Haitians as 'migrants', and as mentioned earlier, the Coast Guard has continued to refer to all interdictees, including refugees, as 'migrants'. However, as Frelick points out, President George W. Bush's use of the term 'refugee' in describing the Haitians fleeing Haiti was not a mistake. There was no correction or clarification of the quote cited above. In fact, on 29 April 2004, the Department of State's web page repeated the President's quote as a statement of U.S. policy.[48]

45 Ibid (ii).

46 Ibid.

47 The White House, *President Bush Welcomes Georgian President Saakashvili to White House* (25 February 2004) <http://georgewbushwhitehouse.archives.gov/news/releases/2004/02/20040225-1.html>.

48 Ibid. See also Frelick, n 38 in this chapter, 247.

In 2007, the UNHCR in an Advisory Opinion held that

> [T]he obligation under Article 33(1) of the 1951 Convention not to send a refugee or asylum-seeker to a country where he or she may be at risk of persecution is not subject to territorial restrictions; it applies wherever the State in question exercises jurisdiction.[49]

The United States responded by making clear its continuing position that 'Article 33 of the 1951 Refugee Convention applies only in respect of aliens within the territory of the Contracting States'.[50] As the policy adopted by President George W. Bush in 2004 has not been amended or overturned by President Obama, the United States remains committed to the denial of the extraterritorial application of Article 33(1) of the Refugee Convention.

4.2.1.1 Sale I and the Supreme Court's Rejection of the Extraterritorial Scope of the Refugee Convention's Non-Refoulement Obligation

The United States did not provide a detailed justification to UNHCR ExCom regarding its denial of the extraterritorial reach of Article 33(1) of the Refugee Convention on the occasions reported in the preceding section. However, the U.S. Supreme Court, in *Sale v Haitian Centers Council* (*Sale I*),[51] provided a detailed analysis of this position in its finding that Article 33(1) of the Refugee Convention does not bind the U.S. executive when it exercises jurisdiction over interdictees in waters outside the U.S. territorial sea.[52]

In *Sale I*, the Supreme Court relied on a narrow interpretation of *refoulement* defining the terms 'return (*refouler*)' as the 'exclusion of aliens who are merely on the threshold of initial entry',[53] to find that Article 33(1) of the Refugee Convention did not apply outside the territorial limits of

49 UNHCR, *Advisory Opinion on the Extraterritorial Application of Non-Refoulement Obligations under the 1951 Convention Relating to the Status of Refugees and its 1967 Protocol* (26 January 2007) <www.unhcr.org/refworld/docid/45f17a1a4.html>.

50 U.S. Mission to the United Nations and other international organisations in Geneva, Observations of the United States on the Advisory Opinion of the UN High Commissioner for Refugees on Extraterritorial Application of *Non-Refoulement* Obligations under the 1951 Convention Relating to the Status of Refugees and its 1967 Protocol (Geneva, 28 December 2007), 9.

51 509 US 155 (1993).

52 For a discussion of the historical and political events leading up to the case, see subsection 2.1.3.

53 *Sale v Haitian Centers Council, Inc.*, 509 US 155, 156 (1993).

States. To reach this meaning, the Supreme Court analysed the French word '*refouler*' and found that it was not an exact synonym for the word 'return' because the two French-English dictionaries the Court consulted did not mention the word 'return' as a possible meaning for the word '*refouler*'. The Supreme Court found instead that the term '*refouler*' was translated into English as 'repulse', 'repel', 'drive back' and 'expel'. The Court concluded therefore that the term 'return' when followed by the term '*refouler*'

> means a defensive act of resistance or exclusion at a border, rather than an act of transporting someone to a particular destination. In the context of [the Refugee] Convention, to "return' means to "repulse" rather than "reinstate".[54]

The narrow reading of the term *refoulement* in *Sale I* fails to interpret the Refugee Convention 'in good faith in accordance with the ordinary meaning to be given to the terms of the treaty in their context and in the light of its object and purpose' as required under Article 31 of the *Vienna Convention on the Law of Treaties* (VCLT).[55] As Justice Blackmun argues in the dissenting judgment in *Sale I*, the ordinary meaning of Article 33(1) of the Refugee Convention is that:

> "No contracting State shall expel or [repulse, drive back, or repel] a refugee in any manner whatsoever to the frontiers of territories where his life or freedom would be threatened ..." That, of course, is exactly what the Government is doing [when it returns refugees to their home countries during interdiction operations].[56]

54 Ibid 157.

55 Opened for signature 23 May 1969, 1155 UNTS 331 (entered into force 27 January 1980). The United States signed the VCLT on 24 April 1970 but has not ratified the treaty. Nevertheless, the VCLT is widely recognised as reflecting customary international law governing treaty interpretation, including by the United States: U.S. Department of State, *Vienna Convention on the Law of Treaties* <www.state.gov/s/l/treaty/faqs/70139.htm>. The VCLT post-dates the Refugee Convention. However as the United States is bound by customary international law obligations reflected in provisions of VCLT, the VCLT can nevertheless assist in the interpretation of the Refugee Convention as a reference to the customary international law which pre-dated the VCLT and the Refugee Convention. See for example *Minister for Immigration and Multicultural Affairs v Savvin* (2000) 98 FCR 168, [14].

56 See n 53 in this chapter. See also James Hathaway, *The Rights of Refugees Under International Law* (Cambridge University Press, 2005) 337–38.

Furthermore, Article 33(1) of the Refugee Convention is concerned with where a refugee is returned to rather than with where a refugee is found.[57] As Goodwin-Gill and McAdam explain, the essential purpose of the principle of *non-refoulement* 'is the prohibition of return *in any manner whatsoever* of refugees to countries where they may face persecution'.[58] As such, Article 33(1) regulates *refoulement* by State parties regardless of where such *refoulement* occurs. A reading of Article 33(1) that limits its scope of application to the territory of a State party creates a protection vacuum whereby a State may avoid its *non-refoulement* obligations by proactively exercising jurisdiction outside its territory. As Justice Blackburn points out in his dissenting judgment in *Sale I*, such a reading is inconsistent with the 'aim of the provision … to protect refugees against persecution'.[59]

In rejecting the extraterritorial application of Article 33(1) of the Refugee Convention, the Supreme Court also examined Article 33(2) of the Refugee Convention in *Sale I*. The Court found that under Article 33(2) of the Refugee Convention, a refugee is not protected from *refoulement* if he or she is a danger to the country in which he or she is located. That is, Article 33(2) only applies in the territory of a State. As such, the Court reasoned that if Article 33(1) did apply in waters outside the U.S. territorial sea, Article 33(2) would

> create an absurd anomaly: dangerous aliens on the high seas would be entitled to the benefits of 33.1 while those residing in the country that sought to expel them would not. It is more reasonable to assume that the coverage of 33.2 was limited to those already in the country because it was understood that 33.1 obligated the signatory State only with respect to aliens within its territory.[60]

As Legomsky contends, a reading that Article 33(1) of the Refugee Convention applies extraterritorially when Article 33(2) of the Refugee

[57] Hathaway argues that the 'duty under Art.33 is to avoid certain *consequences* … whatever the nature of the actions which lead to that result': Hathaway, n 56 in this chapter, 318. Emphasis in the original. See also Thomas Gammeltoft-Hansen, *Access to Asylum: International Refugee Law and the Globalisation of Migration Control* (Cambridge University Press, 2011) 46–47, 57–58.

[58] Guy Goodwin-Gill and Jane McAdam, *The Refugee in International Law* (Oxford University Press, 3rd ed., 2007) 248. Emphasis in the original.

[59] See n 53 in this chapter.

[60] Ibid 180.

Convention does not apply extraterritorially does not create an anomaly. The drafters of the Refugee Convention did not require a State party to host a refugee who is a danger to the State. It does not follow, however, that the drafters were thus happy to permit a State to interdict individuals before they reached its borders and return them to harm.[61] As Judge Pinto De Albuquerque of the European Court of Human Rights in his concurring decision of *Hirsi Jamaa* has also stated

> Article 33 § 2 merely provides for an exception to the rule formulated in Article 33 § 1. The scope of application of a rule beneficial to refugees should not be limited by a territorial reference foreseen in the exception to the rule. Such a "spill-over effect" of the detrimental exception to a favourable rule is unacceptable.[62]

Finally, in rejecting the extraterritorial application of Article 33(1) of the Refugee Convention, the Supreme Court further turned to the *travaux préparatoires* of the Refugee Convention and found that Article 33(1) was not intended to apply outside the territory of a State party. The Court relied on statements made by the Swiss delegate to the negotiating conference of plenipotentiaries held in Geneva, Switzerland, on 11 July 1951, in which the delegate stated

> In the Swiss Government's view, the term "expulsion" applied to a refugee who had already been admitted to the territory of a country. The term '*refoulement*', on the other hand, had a vaguer meaning; *it could not, however, be applied to a refugee who had not yet entered the territory of a country* … the States represented at the Conference should take a definite position with regard to the meaning to be attached to the word 'return'. The Swiss Government considered that in the present instance *the word applied solely to refugees who had already entered a country, but were not yet resident there*.[63]

61 Stephen Legomsky, 'The USA and the Caribbean Interdiction Program' (2006) 18 *International Journal of Refugee Law* 677, 689. See also Hathaway, n 56 in this chapter, 336.

62 *Hirsi Jamaa and Others v Italy* (European Court of Human Rights, Grand Chamber, Application No 27765/09, 23 February 2012) 71 (Judge Pinto De Albuquerque).

63 Conference of Plenipotentiaries on the Status of Refugees and Stateless Persons, Summary Record of the Sixteenth Meeting, U.N. Doc. A/CONF.2/SR.16, p. 6 (11 July 1951). Cited in *Sale v Haitian Centers Council, Inc.*, 509 US 155, 184 (1993). Emphasis in the original.

The Supreme Court noted that no one expressed disagreement with the position of the Swiss delegate, and that the Netherlands recalled the Swiss delegate's position two weeks later when the Article in question was debated again and asked that his support for the Swiss position be placed on the record.[64] However, as UNHCR points out, formal amendments to the Refugee Convention to which delegates consented were either 'agreed to' or 'adopted'. The placing of a view on the record was a tacit acknowledgement that the view did not attract enough support to change the language of the Convention.[65] Furthermore, as UNHCR has shown, it is arguable that the drafters of the Convention understood the term '*refoulement*' to apply extraterritorially.[66] The UNHCR makes reference to a statement from the U.S. delegate, Louis Henkin, to the Committee drafting the Convention in which he stated

> Whether it was a question of closing the frontier to a refugee who asked admittance, or of turning him back after he had crossed the frontier, or even of expelling him after he had been admitted to residence in the territory … whatever the case might be … he must not be turned back to a country where his life or freedom could be threatened.[67]

It should be noted that Article 31(3)(b) of the VCLT provides that 'any subsequent practice in the application of the treaty which establishes the agreement of the parties regarding its interpretation' should be taken into account in interpreting the treaty provision. The bilateral interdiction agreements signed by the United States with the Bahamas and the Dominican Republic both contain an Article which states

> No person found on board a suspect vessel shall be involuntarily returned to a country in which: that person has a well-founded fear of persecution on account of race, religion nationality, membership in a particular social group, or political opinion, except on grounds

64 See n 54 in this chapter.

65 UNHCR, 'The Haitian Interdiction Case 1993 Brief amicus curiae' (1994) 6 *International Journal of Refugee Law* 85, 101.

66 Ibid 87.

67 United Nations Ad Hoc Committee on Statelessness and Related Problems, *Summary Record of the Twentieth Meeting* 11–12, [54]–[55]. <www.unhcr.org/refworld/docid/3ae68c1c0.html>.

recognized as precluding protection as a refugee under the Refugee Protocol.[68]

Neither agreement limits the *non-refoulement* obligation under the bilateral treaty to the territory of a signatory State. The U.S.-Bahamas and U.S.-Dominican Republic agreements, therefore, mandate that the parties to the agreement respect the *non-refoulement* of refugees regardless of where they are interdicted (including extraterritorially).

As shown in Chapter 2, the United States has also been inconsistent in denying the extraterritorial scope of application of Article 33(1) of the Refugee Convention. The United States respected the legal obligation of *non-refoulement* under Executive Order 12324,[69] which was the governing legal authority for the operation of the MIP between September 1981 and the issuance of the Executive Order 12807 (Kennebunkport Order)[70] in May 1992. Furthermore, the United States has offered *non-refoulement* protection to certain refugees under the MIP as a matter of policy. In addition, as shown earlier, the United States has occasionally wavered in its objection to UNHCR ExCom Conclusions that affirm the extraterritorial scope of Article 33(1) of the Refugee Convention. Thus, as the UNHCR has pointed out, the United States' own prior practice suggests an understanding that Article 33(1) is to be applied extraterritorially.[71]

There is some jurisprudence from Australian courts in support of the Supreme Court's finding in *Sale I* that Article 33(1) of the Refugee Convention is not binding extraterritorially.[72] However, as pointed out by

68 *Agreement between the Government of the United States of America and the Government of the Dominican Republic Concerning Maritime Migration Law Enforcement*, signed at Washington 20 May 2003; entered into force 20 May 2003, Art 10; *Agreement between the Government of the United States of America and the Government of the Bahamas Concerning Cooperation in Maritime Law Enforcement*, signed at Nassau 29 June 2004; entered into force 29 June 2004, Art 11 (the agreement with the Bahamas also references the Refugee Convention).

69 Executive Order 12324, 46 *Federal Register* 48, 109, 48, 210 (1981).

70 57 *Federal Register* 23, 133 (1992).

71 UNHCR, n 65 in this chapter, 93–94. See also Goodwin-Gill and McAdam, n 58 in this chapter, 224 and Gammeltoft-Hansen, n 57 in this chapter, 78.

72 See, for example, *Minister for Immigration and Multicultural Affairs v Ibrahim* (2000) 204 CLR 1, [136] where Gummow J refers to *Sale I* with approval stating that the 'provisions of the Convention assume a situation in which refugees, possibly by irregular means, have somehow managed to arrive at or in the territory of the contracting State'. In *Minister for Immigration v Khawar* (2002) 210 CLR 1, [42] McHugh and Gummow JJ do not refer to *Sale I* directly but state that 'the protection obligations imposed by the Convention upon Contracting States concern the status and civil rights to be afforded to refugees who are within Contracting States'.

Judge Pinto De Albuquerque, this 'is not decisive'.[73] The view that Article 33(1) of the Refugee Convention does not have territorial limits is the much stronger position given the context, object and purpose of the Convention and in light of the United States' own prior practice. This view is shared by the Inter-American Commission on Human Rights, which found in the case of *Haitian Centre for Human Rights et al. v US*[74] that 'Article 33 had no geographical limitations'.[75] This view is also shared by a number of eminent scholars.[76]

It therefore follows that the United States is bound by its obligations under Article 33(1) of the Refugee Convention in its exercise of jurisdiction under the MIP, including in its interdiction of vessels in waters outside the U.S. territorial sea.

4.3 Convention Against Torture and Other Cruel, Inhuman or Degrading Treatment or Punishment and Its Scope of Application

As with its *non-refoulement* obligation under the Refugee Convention, the United States has an extraterritorial *non-refoulement* obligation under Article 3 of the CAT. The United States signed the CAT on 18 April 1988 and ratified it on 21 October 1994.[77] In 2006, under the administration

[73] See n 62 in this chapter. Considerations of the Italian government's obligations under the Refugee Convention were not determinative of the Court's decision in the case.

[74] Case No 10.675, Report No 51/96, Inter-AmCHR Doc. OEA/Ser.L/V/II.95 Doc. 7.

[75] *Haitian Center for Human rights et al. v United States*, Case No 10.675, Report No 51/96, Inter-AmCHR Doc. OEA/Ser.L/V/II.95 Doc. 7, [157]. The finding of the Inter-American Commission for Human Rights was cited in the UK Court of Appeal's finding that 'the Sale case as wrongly decided; it certainly offends one's sense of fairness': *R (European Roma Rights Centre and Others) v Immigration Officer at Prague Airport* [2004] QB 811, 824.

[76] See, for example, Guy Goodwin-Gill, 'The Right to Seek Asylum: Interception at Sea and the Principle of *Non-Refoulement*' (2011) 23 *International Journal of Refugee Law* 443; Hathaway, n 56 in this chapter, 335–42; Stephen Legomsky, 'The USA and the Caribbean Interdiction Program' (2006) 18 *International Journal of Refugee Law* 677, 1361–63; Elihu Lauterpacht and Daniel Bethlehem 'The Scope and Content of the Principle of Non-Refoulement: Opinion' in Erika Feller, Volker Türk, Frances Nicholson and UNHCR (eds) *Refugee Protection in International Law: UNHCR's Global Consultations on International Protection* (Cambridge University Press, 2003); Gammeltoft-Hansen, n 57 ion this chapter, 98; Frelick, n 38 in this chapter, 252–53; Joan Fitzpatrick, 'Revitalizing the 1951 Refugee Convention' (1996) 9 *Harvard Human Rights Journal* 229.

[77] The CAT came into force for the United States on 20 November 1994.

of George W. Bush, the United States informed the Committee Against Torture (CAT Committee) that

> Regarding the Committee's question concerning implementation of Article 3 to persons outside of U.S. territory, the United States, while recognizing that some members of the Committee may disagree, believes that Article 3 of the CAT does not impose obligations on the United States with respect to an individual who is outside the territory of the United States ... Neither the text of the Convention, its negotiating history, nor the U.S. record of ratification supports a view that Article 3 of the CAT applies to persons outside the territory of the United States.[78]

The United States' interpretation of Article 3 of the CAT under the George W. Bush administration turned on its understanding of the terms 'expel, return ('*refouler*') or extradite'. It argued that such terms refer to 'conduct taken against individuals within a State party's territory'.[79] The U.S. executive used the Supreme Court's interpretation of '*refouler*' with regard to Article 33(1) of the Refugee Convention in *Sale I* to justify its position that Article 3 of the CAT does not apply extraterritorially. Yoo further elaborated on this view by arguing:[80]

> Although the U.S. Supreme Court has never interpreted the scope of Article 3, under which the United States cannot "expel," "return," or "extradite" individuals to countries in which it is more likely than not that they will be tortured, it has interpreted identical language elsewhere. In [*Sale I*] the Supreme Court held that the Refugee Convention's use of the words "return" and "expel" means that the treaty's requirements apply only to individuals being held within the territory of the United States.... Because the interdiction and detention of Haitian refugees occurred outside the territorial United States,

78 U.S. Department of State, *United States Written Response to Questions Asked by the Committee Against Torture* (2006) <www.state.gov/documents/organization/68662.pdf>.

79 Ibid.

80 John Yoo served as a Deputy Assistant Attorney General in the Office of Legal Counsel of the United States Department of Justice under the George W. Bush administration between 2001 and 2003. A series of legal memos authored by Yoo, which authorised harsh interrogation tactics, including sleep deprivation, stress positions, isolation, and extremes of temperature, light and darkness, have been labelled the 'Torture Memos'. See Warren Richey, 'Bush-Era Lawyer Could Stand Trial For Penning "Torture Memos"' *The Christian Science Monitor*, 16 June 2009 <www.csmonitor.com/2009/0617/p02s13-usju.html>.

> the Court held, the Refugee Convention did not apply to the operation. Thus, in the context of international treaties such as the Torture Convention, the word "return" refers to the involuntary removal of individuals who have not been legally admitted into the territory of the host country, but rather have been turned back or detained at the border.[81]

However, as with its denial of the extraterritorial application of other human rights and refugee law treaty obligations, the United States was incorrect in holding that the *non-refoulement* obligation under the CAT does not apply extraterritorially. A reading of Article 3 of the CAT that supports its extraterritorial application is consistent with the ordinary words of the treaty in their context and in the light of the treaty's object and purpose, as required under Article 31 of the VCLT. As Satterthwaite argues

> Given the wording of [CAT] Article 3's directive – "[n]o State Party shall" – the most ordinary meaning would be that a State party may not, regardless of where it is acting, "expel, return (*refouler*), or extradite a person" who is in its custody or control ... In light of the object and purpose of the treaty, this reading is not only the best one, it is also in line with the rules that have developed concerning extraterritorial application of human rights treaties generally.[82]

With regard to the reliance on *Sale I* to support the inapplicability of the CAT extraterritorially, as stated earlier, it is widely believed – and it is the opinion of this author – that the case was decided wrongly. Yet even if *Sale I* was correctly decided, the denial of the extraterritorial application of Article 33(1) was in part based on the Supreme Court's reading of the interplay between Article 33(1) and Article 33(2) of the Refugee Convention. Article 3 of the CAT is not followed by a provision similar to Article 33(2)

[81] John Yoo, 'Transferring Terrorists' (2004) 79 *Notre Dame Law Review* 1183, 1229. This position should be contrasted with that of Harold Hongju Koh, legal advisor to the Obama administration's Department of State in the 2009–2013 period. Koh argued for the extraterritorial application of the *non-refoulement* obligation under Article 3 of the CAT: Harold Hongju Koh, 'Memorandum Opinion on the Geographic Scope of the Convention Against Torture and Its Application in Situations of Armed Conflict', 21 January 2013 <www.documentcloud.org/documents/1053901-state-department-cat-memo.html>.

[82] Margaret Satterthwaite, 'Rendered Meaningless: Extraordinary Rendition and The Rule of Law' (2007) 75 *George Washington Law Review* 1333, 1368.

of the Refugee Convention, so it is unsound to rely on the decision in *Sale I* as a basis for denying the extraterritorial application of the CAT.[83]

As with its views on the Refugee Convention, the United States also believed that the negotiating history of the CAT supported its view that Article 3 of the CAT applies only to the territory of a State party. The United States made references to the fact that the original Swedish proposal of Article 3 in the *travaux préparatoires* of the CAT referred only to 'expulsion' and 'extradition' but not 'return' or '*refouler*'.[84] The introduction of the words 'return' or '*refouler*' into the draft of the treaty was followed by discussion about the term '*refoulement*', but there was no agreement that the *non-refoulement* provision should apply extraterritorially to a State party.[85] The drafters of the CAT are unlikely to have contemplated the extraterritorial *refoulement* of individuals who may be in danger of torture.[86] However, this failure of foresight should not be construed as approval for the *refoulement* of individuals to torture from outside the territorial boundaries of a State[87]

Importantly, the CAT Committee holds the view that the CAT does apply extraterritorially.[88] In its General Comment No 2, the CAT Committee stated

> The Committee also understands that the concept of "any territory under its jurisdiction," linked as it is with the principle of non-derogability, includes any territory or facilities and must be applied to protect any person, citizen or non-citizen without discrimination subject to the dejure or *de facto* control of a State party.[89]

83 Michael Garcia, 'Renditions: Constraints Imposed by Laws on Torture' *Congressional Research Service*, 12 October 2007 <http://assets.opencrs.com/rpts/RL32890_20071012.pdf>.

84 Yoo, n 81 in this chapter, 1229.

85 See U.S. Department of State, n 78 in this chapter.

86 Satterthwaite, n 82 in this chapter, 1368.

87 Ibid.

88 Committee Against Torture, *Concluding Observations: United States of America*: UN Doc CAT/C/USA/CO/2 (25 July 2006), [20].

89 Committee Against Torture, *General Comment No 2: Implementation of Article 2 by State Parties*, 39th sess, UN Doc CAT/C/GC/2 (24 January 2008), [7]. These comments were made with respect to the implementation of Article 2 of CAT. However, in *J.H.A v Spain*, UN Doc CAT/C/41/D/323/2007 (21 November 2008), [8.2], the CAT Committee clarified that '[t]his interpretation of the concept of jurisdiction is applicable in respect not only of article 2, but of all provisions of the Convention'.

In *J.H.A v Spain*,[90] the CAT Committee had the opportunity to decide on a matter involving interception of a distressed vessel in international waters. The author of the complaint was a member of a Spanish non-governmental organisation (NGO) acting on behalf of a number of individuals intercepted by the Spanish Coast Guard and detained in Mauritania at the time of the complaint. The CAT Committee found that the complainant did not have *locus standi*, and thus that the communication was inadmissible. The CAT Committee did not go on to consider the substantive allegations in the claim. However, the Committee did recall its General Comment No 2,

> in which it states that the jurisdiction of a State party refers to any territory in which it exercises, directly or indirectly, in whole or in part, *de jure* or *de facto* effective control, in accordance with international law … In the present case, the Committee observes that the State party maintained control over the persons onboard the [distressed vessel] from the time the vessel was rescued and throughout the identification and repatriation process that took place.… Consequently, the Committee considers that the alleged victims are subject to Spanish jurisdiction in so far as the complaint that forms the subject of the present communication is concerned.[91]

The interdiction operations of the United States are relevantly similar in fact to the activities of the Spanish Coast Guard considered in *J.H.A v Spain*. In fact, the United States exercises more control in its interdiction operations than was exercised by the Spanish Coast Guard, because the Spanish Coast Guard detained the persons on board their own distressed vessels. In contrast, the United States brings interdictees on board U.S. vessels. The control exercised by the United States on board its own vessels is greater than the control exercised by Spain on a foreign vessel.[92]

More specifically, in response to U.S. allegations that its *non-refoulement* obligations under Article 3 of the CAT do not extend to persons detained in Guantánamo Bay and the rendition of suspects by the United States

[90] UN Doc CAT/C/41/D/323/2007 (21 November 2008).

[91] Ibid [8.2]. Emphasis added.

[92] *United Nations Convention on the Law of the Sea*, opened for signature 10 December 1982, 1833 UNTS 3 (entered into force 14 November 1994), art 92 provides that vessels are subject to the exclusive jurisdiction of the State to which they are flagged.

to a State where they may face a real risk of torture, the CAT Committee found in 2006 that the United States

> should apply the *non-refoulement* guarantee to all detainees in its custody [and] cease the rendition of suspects, in particular by its intelligence agencies, to States where they face a real risk of torture, in order to comply with its obligations under article 3 of the Convention. The State party should always ensure that suspects have the possibility to challenge decisions of *refoulement*.[93]

It should also be noted that the extraterritorial obligation to refrain from the *refoulement* to torture of individuals interdicted by a State was also considered by the European Court of Human Rights in *Hirsi Jamaa*. The European Court did not decide on the extraterritorial application of Article 3 of the CAT but was concerned with a provision under Article 3 of the ECHR which states that '[n]o one shall be subjected to torture or to inhuman or degrading treatment or punishment'. The Court unanimously found a breach of Article 3 of the ECHR by Italy despite the fact that the interdiction took place outside the territorial boundaries of Italy. The Court's jurisdiction was determined on the basis that Italy exercised continuous de jure and de facto control over the interdictee applicants from the time the interdictees boarded the Italian vessels until they were handed over to Libyan authorities.[94] Of course, this decision of the European Court of Human Rights concerning the ECHR is not conclusive on the applicability of Article 3 of the CAT on the United States during interdiction operations. However, the decision, which concerns a similar situation to that of interdiction operations by the United States extraterritorially, and considers a similar provision to Article 3 of the CAT in an analogous treaty, adds further weight to the argument that Article 3 of the CAT is applicable to interdiction operations extraterritorially.

Under the Obama administration, the United States initially sent mixed messages regarding its position on the extraterritorial application of Article 3

[93] Committee Against Torture, *Consideration of Reports Submitted by State Parties under Article 19 of the Convention Conclusions and Recommendations of the CAT Committee: United States of America*, 36th sess, UN DOC CAT/C/USA/CO/2 (25 July 2006) [20].

[94] *Hirsi Jamaa and Others v Italy* (European Court of Human Rights, Grand Chamber, Application No 27765/09, 23 February 2012), [81]. See discussion of jurisdiction in the context of rescue at sea in subsection 3.3.4.1.

of the CAT.[95] For example, the Obama administration maintained that 'extraordinary rendition' (transferring suspects to third countries where they may be subjected to torture) was not inherently unlawful.[96] However, the Obama administration nevertheless applied the extraterritorial application of the CAT as a matter of policy (with some notable exceptions in the case of 'extraordinary rendition').[97]

In its 2013 periodic report to the CAT Committee, the United States confirmed that 'United States policy is not to transfer any person to a country where it is more likely than not that the person will be tortured'.[98] However, the United States also clarified that its report to the Committee 'does not address the geographic scope of the Convention as a legal matter, although it does respond to related questions from the Committee in factual terms.'[99] In other words, the United States left the door open to argue that it is not *legally* bound by Article 3 of the CAT extraterritorially.

In its 2014 appearance before the CAT Committee, however, the United States was much more willing to accept its extraterritorial obligations. In what appears to be a considerable departure from the previously held position, the CAT committee reported in its 2014 *Concluding Observations on the Third to Fifth Periodic Report of the United States of America* that the United States now accepts that the CAT

95 The Obama administration received legal advice supporting the extraterritorial application of Article 3 of the CAT from the Legal Advisor to the Department of State. See Harold Hongju Koh, 'Memorandum Opinion on the Geographic Scope of the Convention Against Torture and Its Application in Situations of Armed Conflict', 21 January 2013 <www.documentcloud.org/documents/1053901-state-department-cat-memo.html>. See, however, Charlie Savage, 'U.S. Seems Unlikely to Accept that Rights Treaty Applies to Its Actions Abroad', *New York Times*, 6 March 2014 <www.nytimes.com/2014/03/07/world/us-seems-unlikely-to-accept-that-rights-treaty-applies-to-its-actions-abroad.html>.

96 Greg Miller, 'Obama Preserves Rendition as Counter-Terrorism Tool', *L.A. Times*, Feb. 1, 2009, A1. For a discussion of the United States' attitude towards the CAT under the Obama administration, see Manfred Nowak, Moritz Birk and Tiphanie Crittin, 'The Obama Administration and Obligations Under The Convention Against Torture' (2011) 20 *Transnational Law & Contemporary Problems* 33.

97 U.S. Department of Justice Press Release No 09-835, *Special Task Force on Interrogations and Transfer Policies Issues Its Recommendations to the President* (24 August 2009) <www.justice.gov/opa/pr/2009/August/09-ag-835.html>. See also John Bellinger III and Vijay Padmanabhan, 'Detention Operations in Contemporary Conflicts: Four Challenges for the Geneva Conventions and Other Existing Law' (2011) *American Journal of International Law* 105.

98 Committee Against Torture, *Periodic Report of the United States of America*, www.state.gov/documents/organization/213267.pdf (12 August 2013), [66].

99 Ibid [6].

> applies to "certain areas beyond" [U.S.] sovereign territory, and more specifically to "all places that the State party controls as a governmental authority", noting that it currently exercises such control at "the U.S. Naval Station at Guantanamo Bay, Cuba, and over all proceedings conducted there, and with respect to U.S.-registered ships and aircraft".[100]

As Cleveland points out, this is a significant change in the United States' understanding of its extraterritorial obligations under the CAT.[101]

Despite the concession of the U.S. executive that the United States may be bound by the CAT in Guantánamo Bay and on board U.S. vessels, individuals interdicted by the United States continue to have limited rights under municipal law outside the municipally defined territory of the United States. That is, as explained in subsection 4.6.2, the recognition by the Obama administration of rights under the CAT in Guantánamo Bay and on board Coast Guard vessels in international waters is yet to change the lived experience of individuals interdicted under the MIP.

4.4 International Convention on the Elimination of All Forms of Racial Discrimination and Its Scope of Application

The final human rights treaty considered here is the CERD, which prohibits discrimination between interdictees on the grounds of their race or nationality.[102] The CERD was signed by the United States on 28 September 1966 and was ratified on 21 October 1994.[103] The United States has not expressly articulated a position on the extraterritorial application of the CERD; however, the CERD applies extraterritorially irrespective of any U.S position.[104] The ICJ found in *Georgia v Russian Federation*[105] that

[100] Committee Against Torture, *Concluding Observations on the Third to Fifth Periodic Report of the United States of America*, 53rd sess, UN DOC CAT/C/USA/CO/3–5 (20 November 2014), [3].

[101] Sarah Cleveland, 'The United States and the Torture Convention, Part I: Extraterritoriality' *Just Security* (14 November 2014). <http://justsecurity.org/17435/united-states-torture-convention-part-i-extraterritoriality/>.

[102] See discussion of Article 5 of the CERD in Section 5.4.

[103] The CERD entered into force for the United States on 20 November 1994.

[104] Ralph Wilde, 'Complementing Occupation Law? Selective Judicial Treatment of the Suitability of Human Rights Norms' (2009) 42 *Israel Law Review* 80, 30.

[105] *Case Concerning the Application of the International Convention on the Elimination of All Forms of Racial Discrimination (Georgia v Russian Federation) (Provisional Measure)* [2008] ICJ Rep 353.

> *[T]here is no restriction of a general nature in CERD relating to its territorial application*; … in particular, neither Article 2 nor *Article 5 of CERD* … contain a specific territorial limitation … whereas the Court consequently finds that these provisions of CERD generally appear to apply, like other provisions of instruments of that nature, to the actions of a State party when it acts beyond its territory.[106]

4.5 Lack of Effective Enforcement Mechanisms in International Law

Despite the applicability of the United States' treaty obligations extraterritorially, there are no effective means of enforcing such obligations in the international arena. The United States does not recognise the competence of the HR Committee, CAT Committee or the Committee on the Elimination of Racial Discrimination (CERD Committee) to consider complaints from individuals or groups, such as interdictees, who claim their rights under international human rights law have been violated.[107] There are no individual complaint mechanisms available through the Refugee Protocol or the Refugee Convention. As such, no interdictee has the option of using individual complaint mechanisms to challenge the MIP.

The United States has made declarations recognising the competence of the CAT Committee and the HR Committee to receive and consider communications from other State parties to the effect that the United States is not fulfilling its obligations under the CAT and the ICCPR, respectively.[108] The CERD Committee is also empowered to receive and consider communications from other States parties that claim that the United States is not fulfilling its obligations under the CERD.[109] Inter-State complaints are

[106] Ibid 386. Emphasis added.

[107] The United States is not a party to the *Optional Protocol to the International Covenant on Civil and Political Rights*, opened for signature 19 December 1966, 999 UNTS 171 (entered into force 23 March 1976), which would give the HR Committee competence to examine individual complaints with regard to alleged violations of the ICCPR by States parties. The United States has also refrained from making the necessary declaration under Article 22 of the CAT and Article 14 of the CERD, which would empower the CAT Committee and the CERD Committee, respectively, to consider individual communications from individuals claiming that their rights under the CAT and CERD have been violated.

[108] The declarations are made pursuant to Article 21(1) of the CAT and Article 41 of the ICCPR.

[109] Articles 11–13 of the CERD.

not available under the Refugee Protocol, but disputes between States parties relating to the interpretation of the Refugee Convention may be brought before the ICJ under Article 38 of the Refugee Convention.

No State has ever used the procedures available for complaints against other States parties[110] or brought a complaint before the ICJ under Article 38 of the Refugee Convention.[111] It should be noted that even if the United States was found to be in violation of its international obligations by either the HR, CAT or CERD Committees as a result of an inter-State complaint, the United States would not be legally bound to implement the views of the HR, CAT or CERD Committees.

The United States would, however, be legally obliged to implement any remedies ordered against it by the ICJ. In practice this is of little significance. Despite being legally bound by the decisions of the ICJ, there are no effective enforcement mechanisms under the ICJ that could be used to implement any finding against the United States by the ICJ. Article 94(2) of the *Charter of the United Nations*[112] provides

> If any party to a case fails to perform the obligations incumbent upon it under a judgement rendered by the [ICJ], the other party may have recourse to the Security Council, which may, if it deems necessary make recommendations or decide upon measures to be taken to give effect to the judgement.

However, the United States has veto power over decisions of the Security Council.[113] As such, the United States can decide to refrain from honouring an ICJ decision by vetoing any resolution placed before the Security Council to implement an ICJ decision.[114]

110 Ilias Bantekas and Lutz Oette, *International Human Rights Law and Practice* (Cambridge University Press, 2013) 201.

111 For a discussion of the reluctance of States to make formal complaints against other States, see Scott Leckie, 'The Inter-State Complaint Procedures in International Human Rights Law: Hopeful Prospects or Wishful Thinking?' (1988) 10 *Human Rights Quarterly* 253 and Jack Donnelly, 'Virtues of Legalisation' in Saladin Meckled-García and Basak Çali (eds) *The Legalization of Human Rights: Multidisciplinary Perspectives on Human Rights and Human Rights Law* (Routledge, 2006).

112 Opened for signature 26 June 1945, 1 UNTS XVI (entered into force on 24 October 1945).

113 Ibid art 27.

114 An example of this was the ICJ's decision in the *Case Concerning the Military and Paramilitary Activities in and Against Nicaragua (Nicaragua v United States Of America) (Judgement)* [1986] ICJ Rep 14. For commentary on this case and enforcement of ICJ decisions more decisions,

Furthermore, the United States must submit periodic reports demonstrating its compliance with obligations under the CAT, ICCPR and the CERD.[115] The CAT Committee, HR Committee and the CERD Committee can make recommendations in light of submissions from States. However, as with inter-country reports, other than highlighting the breaches of their treaty obligations, treaty bodies have no means of compelling the United States to cease the abuses of human rights in international waters and in Guantánamo Bay. Monitoring bodies can chastise States, draw attention to abuses of human rights and ask States to explain their actions, but they cannot enforce international obligations.

4.6 The Interplay of International and Municipal Law

The lack of effective law enforcement mechanisms at an international level creates a vacuum in effective enforcement that could be filled by municipal law if treaty obligations were directly incorporated into the municipal law of the United States. Unfortunately, however, the problem of ineffective enforcement mechanisms at an international level is compounded by the fact that the Refugee Protocol, CAT, ICCPR and the CERD are not enforceable in the U.S. courts without further implementing legislation.

Article VI, cl 2 of the U.S. Constitution (the Supremacy Clause) states

> This Constitution, and the Laws of the United States which shall be made in pursuance thereof; and all treaties made, or which shall be made, under the authority of the United States, shall be the supreme law of the land; and the judges in every State shall be bound thereby, anything in the Constitution or laws of any State to the contrary notwithstanding.

It might appear that the Supremacy Clause provides a blanket authorisation for the incorporation of all of the United States' treaty obligations as enforceable obligations under U.S. municipal law, without the need for further legislative action. In the seminal case of *Foster v Neilson*,[116] the Supreme Court found that the U.S. Constitution

see Attila Tanzi, 'Problems of Enforcement of Decisions of the International Court of Justice and the Law of the United Nations' (1995) 6 *European Journal of International Law* 539.

[115] The UNHCR does not receive periodic reports.

[116] 27 US 253 (1829).

> declares a treaty to be the law of the land. It is, consequently, to be regarded in courts of justice as equivalent to an act of the legislature, whenever it operates of itself, without the aid of any legislative provision.[117]

However, the Court went on to state

> But when the terms of the stipulation import a contract – when either of the parties engages to perform a particular act, the treaty addresses itself to the political, not the judicial department; and the legislature must execute the contract, before it can become a rule for the Court.[118]

That is, the Court found that treaties that require further action from the legislature are not directly enforceable by the courts without legislative implementation.[119] Thus, obligations on the United States that derive from the executive's submission to a treaty agreement are not 'immediately applicable in private lawsuits or otherwise' if the courts find that the treaties do not 'operate of themselves'.[120] This qualification is at the heart of the distinction between self-executing and non-self-executing treaties.[121]

Whether or not a treaty needs further legislative action or is in fact self-executing is a matter of intent.[122] It is not always clear who is required to have the intent. In *Foster v Neilson*, the relevant intent was that of the parties to the treaty.[123] However, the intent necessary in determining the self-executing nature of a treaty has also been found to be the intent of the United States when signing the treaty.[124] Such intention is sometimes expressed through a declaration.[125] Under Section 2, Article II of the U.S.

117 Ibid 270.

118 Ibid. It is interesting to note that the very same treaty under consideration in *Foster v Neilson* was found to be self-executing when the Court was given the Spanish text of the treaty in *United States v Percheman*, 32 US (7 Pet.) 51 (1833).

119 Non-self-executing treaties can assist in statutory interpretation even if they cannot be enforced directly in the courts of the US. *Murray v Schooner Charming Betsy*, 6 US 64,118 (1804).

120 Lori Damrosch, 'The Role of the United States Senate Concerning "Self-Executing" and "Non-Self-Executing" Treaties' (1991) *Chicago-Kent Law Review* 515, 516.

121 Carlos Vazquez, 'The Four Doctrines of Self-Executing Treaties' (1995) 89 *American Journal of International Law* 695, 701.

122 *Medellin v Texas*, 552 US 491 (2008).

123 Vazquez, n 121 in this chapter, 704.

124 See *Islamic Republic of Iran v Boeing Co.*, 771 F 2d 1279, 1284 (9th Cir, 1985) cert. dismissed, 479 US 957 (1986); *United States v Postal*, 589 F 2d 862, 881–883 (5th Cir, 1979) cert. denied, 444 US 832 (1979).

125 American Law Institute, *Restatement (Third) of the Foreign Relations Law of the United States* (1987), §111.

Constitution, the U.S. Senate is required to provide 'advice and consent' for the ratification of a treaty. When consenting to the CAT, the U.S. Senate declared that Articles 1 through 16 of the CAT are not self-executing in the United States.[126] A similar declaration was made during the 'advice and consent' to the ratification of the ICCPR where the U.S. Senate qualified its consent with a declaration that Articles 1–27 of the ICCPR are not self-executing in the United States.[127] The U.S. Senate also advised that the provisions of the CERD are not self-executing.[128] Although non-self-executing declarations do not lessen the requirement that the United States comply with its obligations as a matter of international law,[129] such declarations render a treaty non-self-executing and thus unable to be applied directly to resolve human rights abuses in the U.S. courts.[130] The courts of the United States have confirmed the non-self-executing nature of the CAT,[131] ICCPR[132] and the CERD.[133]

Unlike the CAT, ICCPR and the CERD, the ratification of the Refugee Protocol was not accompanied by a declaration by the U.S. Senate that it should be considered to be non-self-executing, but the courts of the United States have nevertheless found that the Refugee Protocol is not self-executing. In 1980, the U.S. Congress passed the *Refugee Act 1980* (*Refugee Act*).[134] In the words of the U.S. Supreme Court, 'one of Congress' primary purposes in passing the Refugee Act was to implement

[126] GA Res 39/46, 10 Dec 1984. See also 136 Cong. Rec. S17492 (daily ed. 27 Oct. 1990). See also Michael Garcia, 'The U.N. Convention Against Torture: Overview of US Implementation Policy Concerning the Removal of Aliens' *Congressional Research Service*, 21 January 2009 <www.au.af.mil/au/awc/awcgate/crs/rl32276.pdf>.

[127] Senate Committee on Foreign Relations, 'Report on the International Covenant on Civil and Political Rights', S. Rep. No 23, 102d Cong., 2d sess. 25 (1992), reprinted in (1992) *International Legal Materials* 645, 651.

[128] Committee on the Elimination of Racial Discrimination, *Reports Submitted by State Parties under Article 9 of the Convention, Third Periodic Reports of State Parties due in 1999, Addendum, United States of America*, UN Doc CERD/C/351/Add.1 (10 October 2000).

[129] See Matthew Jowanna, '42 USC § 1983: A Legal Vehicle With No International Human Rights Treaty Passengers' (2010) 9 *University of New Hampshire Law Review* 31.

[130] See Damrosch, n 120 in this chapter; Louis Henkin, 'US Ratification of Human Rights Conventions: The Ghost of Senator Bricker' (1995) 89 *American Journal of International Law* 341; Stefan Riesenfeld and Frederick Abbott, 'The Scope of US Senate Control Over the Conclusion and Operation of Treaties' (1991) 67 *Chicago-Kent Law Review* 571.

[131] *Akhtar v Reno*, 123 F 2d Supp 191 (SDNY 2000).

[132] *United States v Duarte–Acero*, 208 F 3d 1282, 1040 n. 8 (11th Cir, 2000).

[133] *Johnson v Quander*, 370 F 2d Supp 79, 101 (D. DC 2005).

[134] Refugee Act, Pub L No 96–212, 94 Stat. 102.

the principles agreed to in the [Refugee Protocol]'.[135] In *Bertrand v Sava* (*Bertrand*),[136] the U.S. Court of Appeals for the Second Circuit used the very fact that congress had designed the *Refugee Act* 'at least in part, to bring the US into compliance with the Protocol'[137] to conclude that the Refugee 'Protocol's provisions were not themselves a source of rights under [US] law unless and until Congress implemented them by appropriate legislation'.[138] In *Bertrand* the Court reasoned that if the Refugee Protocol was self-executing, the United States would have been compliant with its international obligations between the time of ratifying the treaty and the implementation of the *Refugee Act*. As this was not the case, the Refugee Protocol was not self-executing and afforded the petitioners in the case no rights beyond those they had under municipal law. Although the Supreme Court has not directly decided on the question of the self-executing nature of the Refugee Protocol, it has cited without objection the finding in *Bertrand* that the Refugee Protocol's provisions are not self-executing.[139] The Refugee Protocol was also found to be non-self-executing in a number of lower court decisions, which considered the application of the Refugee Protocol to the MIP.[140] Thus, the Refugee Protocol is not itself a source of judicially enforceable legal obligations towards refugees by the executive under U.S. municipal law.

Because the Refugee Protocol, CAT, ICCPR and CERD are not self-executing, the courts must turn to municipal law, including legislation that may have been written to comply with the United States' international obligations, to determine the constraints on the U.S. executive. Unfortunately, as the following discussion shows, the United States has not implemented into municipal law many of the obligations discussed in this book, and the attempts that have been made to implement its international obligations do not apply or are unlikely to apply to interdictees in international waters or in Guantánamo Bay.

135 *INS v Aguirre-Aguirre*, 119 S. Ct. 1439, 1446 (1999).
136 684 F 2d 204 (2nd Cir, 1982).
137 Ibid 218.
138 Ibid.
139 See n 53 in this chapter.
140 *Haitian Refugee Center v Gracey*, 600 F Supp 1396 (1985); *Haitian Refugee Center, Inc. v Baker*, 949 F 2d 1109, 1110 (11th Cir, 1991); *Cuban American Bar Association v Christopher*, 43 F 3d 1412, 1417 (11th Cir, 1995).

4.6.1 Implementation of the Refugee Protocol

The first implementation of a treaty obligation under consideration here is the United States' implementation of the Refugee Protocol under the *Refugee Act* which amended the INA,[141] the fundamental body of U.S. immigration law. As Legomsky points out, the United States' attempts to implement its *non-refoulement* obligation under Article 33(1) of the Refugee Convention 'represent almost the entirety of Congress' effort to implement United States Obligations under the Refugee Convention. Other provisions of the Convention for the most part have not yet been implemented'.[142] That is, Articles 3, 26, 32 and 34 of the Refugee Convention, also discussed in this book, have not been implemented into the municipal law of the United States through legislation.[143]

The *Refugee Act*, which, as mentioned earlier, was passed in 1980 to implement the United States' obligations under the Refugee Protocol and which amended the INA, inserted a specific definition of 'refugee' into § 101(a)(42) of the INA.[144] This definition is used in refugee status determinations under the MIP and in the U.S. mainland. This is important to note because it signifies the United States' recognition that the refugees recognised under the MIP fall into the same category as refugees who receive recognition of their status in the U.S. mainland. Thus, the disadvantages suffered by refugees in international waters and at Guantánamo Bay, discussed in Chapters 5 and 6 of this book, do not result from the United States' view that refugees under the MIP are categorically different from refugees in the U.S. mainland. Rather, the fact that they are processed outside the municipally defined territory of the United States means that the United States does not consider itself to have the same legal obligations towards them.

141 Pub L No 82–414, 66 Stat. 163. The INA is codified in Title 8 USC and its implementing regulations are found in Title 8 CFR.

142 See Stephen Legomsky, 'Refugees, Asylum and the Rule of Law in the USA' in Susan Kneebone (ed) *Refugees, Asylum Seekers and the Rule of Law* (Cambridge University Press, 2009) 127.

143 Article 3 of the Refugee Convention is discussed in greater detail in 5.4; Article 26 of the Refugee Convention is discussed in greater detail in subsection 6.4.1, Article 32 of the Refugee Convention is discussed in greater detail in subsection 6.4.2; Article 34 of the Refugee Convention is discussed in greater detail in subsection 6.4.3.

144 8 USC § 1101(A)(42)(A).

Importantly for our understanding of refugee status determination procedures, the grant of asylum to refugees under the municipal law of the United States is discretionary. INA § 208(b)(1)(A)[145] provides that

> The Secretary of Homeland Security or the Attorney General *may* grant asylum to an alien who has applied for asylum in accordance with the requirements and procedures established by the Secretary of Homeland Security or the Attorney General under this section if the Secretary of Homeland Security or the Attorney General determines that such alien is a refugee within the meaning of section 101(a)(42)(A).[146]

U.S. law does contain a compulsory *non-refoulement* obligation. This *non-refoulement* obligation was formerly found under INA § 243(h).[147] The statutory *non-refoulement* obligation can now be found under INA § 241(b)(3).[148] However, the renumbering and slight rewording of the section is not significant enough to affect the discussion in this book.

Under U.S. municipal law, refugee status is not automatically linked to a *non-refoulement* obligation. A refugee may have his or her refugee status recognised by the United States but not necessarily fall within the class of non-citizens who enjoy mandated protection from *refoulement*. In *INS v Stevic* (*Stevic*),[149] the Supreme Court interpreted the mandatory obligation of *non-refoulement*[150] and found that claimants had to demonstrate 'a clear probability of persecution'[151] before the Attorney General was mandated to withhold *refoulement*. In *INS v Cardoza-Fonseca* (*Cardoza-Fonseca*),[152] the Supreme Court found, however, that under INA § 208(b)(1)(A), refugees may apply for a discretionary grant of asylum, which may be granted if they have a 'well founded fear' of persecution,[153] the standard required under international law to satisfy refugee status under Article 1(A) of the

145 8 USC § 1158 (b)(1)(A).

146 Emphasis added.

147 8 USC § 1253 (h).

148 8 USC § 1231(b)(3).

149 467 US 407 (1984).

150 Then under INA § 243(h); 8 USC § 1253(h).

151 'A clear probability of persecution' was defined under *INS v Stevic*, 480 US 421 (1987) as 'more likely than not that the alien would be subject to persecution'.

152 480 US 421 (1987).

153 Ibid 440. The Court found that the test for whether a refugee has a 'well-founded fear' of persecution is whether persecution is a 'reasonable possibility'.

Refugee Convention. Thus refugees with a 'well founded fear' of persecution must demonstrate that they have a 'clear probability of persecution' before they are *guaranteed* protection from *refoulement* under the municipal law of the United States.

A number of scholars have argued that the separation of refugee status from *non-refoulement* protections, and the higher burden of proof applied to the mandatory provision of *non-refoulement* as compared to the discretionary grant of asylee status, places U.S. jurisprudence at odds with international refugee law.[154] As Goodwin-Gill and McAdam argue, 'the legal, and to some extent logical relationship between article 33(1) and article 1 of the 1951 Convention/1967 Protocol is evident in the correlation established in State Practice'.[155] According to Goodwin-Gill and McAdam, '[a]t the international level, no distinction is recognised between refugee status and entitlement to *non-refoulement*',[156] and the United States is the only country to require that refugees (who have a well-founded fear of persecution) show that there is 'a clear probability of persecution' should they be *refouled* before they are guaranteed *non-refoulement* protection.

In practice, the United States offers two forms of protection against *refoulement* to refugees in the U.S. mainland: asylee status[157] and withholding of removal.[158] The grant of asylee status to a refugee who has a 'well founded fear' of persecution under INA § 208 (b)(1)(A)[159] is discretionary.[160] That is, there is no mandated statutory obligation on the Secretary of Homeland Security or the Attorney General to grant asylee status to any refugee who has a well-founded fear of persecution. The United States offers mandatory protection against *refoulement*, in the form of withholding of

[154] See, for example, Joan Fitzpatrick, 'The International Dimension of US Refugee Law' (1997) 15 *Berkeley Journal of International Law* 1; Bassina Farbenblum, 'Executive Deference in US Refugee Law: Internationalist Paths Through and Beyond Chevron' (2011) 60 *Duke Law Journal* 1059; Jennifer Moore, 'Restoring the Humanitarian Character of US Refugee Law: Lessons From the International Community' (1997) 15 *Berkeley Journal of International Law* 51; James Hathaway and Anne Cusick, 'Refugee Rights Are Not Negotiable' (2000) 14 *Georgetown Immigration Law Journal* 481.

[155] Goodwin-Gill and McAdam, n 58 in this chapter, 233.

[156] Ibid 234.

[157] INA § 208(b)(1)(A); 8 USC § 1158(b)(1)(A).

[158] INA § 241(b)(3); 8 USC § 1231(b)(3).

[159] 8 USC § 1158(b)(1)(A).

[160] *INS v Cardoza-Fonseca*, 480 US 421 (1987).

removal, under INA § 241(b)(3).[161] Withholding of removal applies to refugees who have not been granted asylee status because they do not meet certain criteria,[162] but for whom there exists 'a clear probability of persecution'.[163] Individuals granted asylee status may apply for permanent residency after one year and are thus on a path to U.S. citizenship. Individuals granted a withholding of removal, however, do not enjoy permanent residency and cannot qualify for citizenship.

The failure to link recognition of refugee status with mandated legal protection from *refoulement* has also had a profound effect on refugees processed under the MIP. Refugees whose status is recognised under the MIP fall into the category of refugees who do not enjoy mandated protection from *refoulement* under the municipal law of the United States. That is, whilst the United States applies the same definition of 'refugee' in the U.S. mainland as under the MIP, refugees under the MIP are not offered the same *non-refoulement* protection as their counterparts in the U.S. mainland. This is because the mandatory protection against *refoulement* of aliens under INA § 241(b)(3) does not apply in international waters and in Guantánamo Bay. As such, the separation of refugee status from *non-refoulement* protection means that refugees whose status is recognised under the MIP are not legally protected from *refoulement* under U.S. municipal law.

In *Sale I*, the Supreme Court provided three reasons as to why INA § 243(h)(I), which implemented the United States' *non-refoulement* obligation under the Refugee Convention, did not apply to the MIP. First, the Supreme Court reasoned that since Article 33(1) of the Refugee Convention does not apply outside the municipally defined territory of the United States, the implementing legislation also does not apply outside that territory. Second, the Supreme Court reasoned that the presumption that Acts of Congress do not apply outside the municipally defined

[161] 8 USC § 1231(b)(3); see *INS v Stevic*, 467 US 407 (1984). Individuals at risk of *refoulement* to torture who are not refugees can also be offered *non-refoulement* protection in the form of a withholding of removal.

[162] For example, refugees who did not lodge an application for asylum within one year of arriving in the U.S. mainland: INA § 208(a)(2)(B); 8 USC § 1158 (a)(2)(B); refugees who previously applied for asylum and were denied protection: INA § 208(a)(2)(C); 8 USC § 1158(a)(2)(C); or for refugees who have engaged in a range of terrorist related activities: INA § 212(a)(3)(B); 8 USC 1182(a)(3)(B) and INA § 237(a)(4)(B); 8 USC 1227(a)(4)(B).

[163] INA 241(b)(3); 8 USC § 1231(b)(3), *INS v Stevic*, 467 US 407 (1984).

territory of the United States meant that INA § 243(h)(I) did not apply to the exercise of jurisdiction by the U.S. executive under the MIP. Third, the Supreme Court reasoned that since INA § 243(h)(I) was found in a provision governing deportation and adjustment of status,[164] it was meant to apply only to acts of the Attorney General in the municipally defined territory of the United States. This is because the other provisions in the part did not have an extraterritorial reach.[165]

All three reasons relied on by the Supreme Court for the rejection of the application of the United States' *non-refoulement* obligations to the MIP under statute are erroneous. First, the finding by the Supreme Court that the United States' statutory *non-refoulement* obligations under its municipal law do not apply to the MIP, because the United States' international obligations under Article 33(1) of the Refugee Convention do not apply outside the municipally defined territory of the United States, is inaccurate. This is because the United States is bound by its *non-refoulement* obligation under Article 33(1) of the Refugee Convention wherever it exercises jurisdiction.[166] Thus, as the *non-refoulement* obligation under municipal law was intended to implement the United States' international obligations, it too must be found to apply wherever the United States exercises jurisdiction, including outside U.S. territory.

The second reason given as to why the United States' statutory *non-refoulement* obligation under its municipal law does not apply to the MIP is also invalid. The presumption against the extraterritorial application of statute does not apply when 'a contrary intent [on the part of Congress] appears'.[167] Given that under international law the United States is bound by its *non-refoulement* obligation wherever it exercises jurisdiction, and the courts accept that Congress intended to abide by the United States' international obligations through domestic legislation, the intention of Congress should be interpreted as being in compliance with its

[164] Part V (SubChapter II) of the INA.

[165] The application of the then *non-refoulement* obligation under INA § 243(h) extraterritorially has also been rejected in a number of decisions in lower courts, including in *Haitian Refugee Center v Gracey*, 600 F Supp 1396, 1404 (1985); *Haitian Refugee Center Inc., v Baker*, 953 F 2d 1498 (11th Cir, 1992) (*Baker III*), and *Cuban American Bar Association v Christopher*, 43 F 3d 1412, 1425–26 (11th Cir, 1995).

[166] See subsection 4.2.1.1.

[167] See *EEOC v Arabian American Oil Co*, 499 US 244, 248 (1991) (quoting *Floy Bros v Filardo*, 336 US 281, 285 (1949).

international obligations. In other words, we can conclude that Congress intended the statute to apply wherever the United States exercised jurisdiction at the time of drafting the provisions in question. Furthermore, the reading that Congress intended for the provision to apply wherever the United States exercises jurisdiction is supported by changes to the language of INA § 243(h) following the passage of the *Refugee Act* of 1980.[168] Before the section was amended by the *Refugee Act*, INA § 243 (h) read

> The Attorney General is authorized to withhold deportation of any alien *within the United States* to any country in which in his opinion the alien would be subject to persecution on account of race, religion, or political opinion and for such period of time as he deems to be necessary for such reason.[169]

After the 1980 amendment, the words 'within the United States' were removed. The section thus read

> The Attorney General shall not deport or return any alien (other than an alien described in section 1251(a)(4)(D) of this title) to a country if the Attorney General determines that such alien's life or freedom would be threatened in such country on account of race, religion, nationality, membership in a particular social group, or political opinion.

The removal of the words 'within the United States' was intentional. That is, Congress must have intended for the section to apply beyond the municipally defined borders of the United States.[170]

Finally, the third reason given as to why the United States' statutory *non-refoulement* obligation under its municipal law does not apply to the MIP is also invalid. The courts have given undue emphasis to the fact that the statutory *non-refoulement* obligation under the INA is in a part of the INA that deals with deportation and adjustment. Although the placing of a provision within a particular part can assist in the interpretation of legislation, more weight should be given in the process of interpretation to the purpose and the clear intention of Congress in implementing

[168] Pub L No 96–212, 94 Stat. 107. The *Refugee Act* of 1980 was signed into law by President Carter on 17 March 1980 and went into effect on 1 April 1980.

[169] Emphasis added.

[170] This argument was made by Refugees in *Baker III* but was rejected by the Court.

the provision. As Congress intended the section to implement the United States' international obligations at the time of drafting, and the United States' international obligations apply wherever the United States exercises jurisdiction, the United States' statutory *non-refoulement* obligation should be interpreted to apply in international waters and in Guantánamo Bay. However, INA § 241(b)(3), which is a re-codification of INA § 243(h),[171] will not apply to the MIP until the courts have remedied the above errors of interpretation.[172]

4.6.2 Implementation of the CAT, the ICCPR and the CERD

As with the Refugee Protocol, the implementation of the CAT into municipal law is also unlikely to assist interdictees. Congress implemented Article 3 of the CAT in legislative form in the United States in 1998 under the *Foreign Affairs Reform and Restructuring Act* 1998 (FARRA).[173] § 2242(a) of FARRA states

> It *shall be the policy of the United States* not to expel, extradite, or otherwise effect the involuntary return of any person to a country in which there are substantial grounds for believing the person would be in danger of being subjected to torture, regardless of whether the person is physically present in the United States.[174]

[171] The statutory *non-refoulement* obligation can now be found under INA § 241(b)(3). However, the renumbering and slight rewording of the section are not significant enough to affect the discussion in this book. As such, INA § 241(b)(3), which is a re-codification of INA § 243(h), will not apply extraterritorially under U.S. municipal law until the courts have remedied the above errors of interpretation.

[172] INA § 241(b)(3) (8 USC § 1231(b)(3)) is in Part IV (Sub Chapter II) of the INA. Part IV deals with 'Inspection, Apprehension, Examination, Exclusion, and Removal'. Thus, the Supreme Court's reasoning in *Sale I* (and the lower courts' reasoning in *Gracey* and *Baker III*) that INA § 243(h) does not apply extraterritorially because of its placement in Part V of the INA would also apply in the context of the new *non-refoulement* obligation under Part IV of the INA. As Part IV of the INA deals with matters within the municipally defined territory of the United States, the courts are likely to find that INA § 241(b)(3) is also limited to the municipally defined territory of the United States.

[173] *Foreign Affairs Reform and Restructuring Act* of 1998, Pub L No 105–277 (1998), § 2242(a). For commentary, see David Weissbrodt and Amy Bergquist, 'Extraordinary Rendition and The Torture Convention' (2006) 46 *Virginia Journal of International Law* 586, 604; Robert Chesney, 'Leaving *Guantánamo*: The Law of International Detainee Transfers' (2006) 40 *University of Richmond Law Review* 657, 680.

[174] Emphasis added.

Because § 2242(a) of the FARRA mandates only that the United States, as a matter of policy, refrain from *refoulement*, interdictees cannot use the FARRA to compel the United States to refrain from returning them to a place where they may be in danger of being tortured. The United States has a policy of refraining from *refoulement* under Article 3 of the CAT and is therefore compliant with § 2242(a) of the FARRA.[175]

The U.S. Supreme Court confirmed that it would not question the executive's compliance with its *non-refoulement* policy in *Munaf v Geren* (*Munaf*).[176] The petitioners, who were two American citizens, argued that their transfer to Iraqi custody would result in torture. The Supreme Court found that 'in the present context that concern is to be addressed by the political branches, not the judiciary'.[177] A decision of the Court of Appeals for the District of Columbia further confirms that the courts will not question the executive's compliance with its *non-refoulement* policy. In *Kiyemba v Obama* (*Kiyemba II*),[178] which concerned Chinese nationals of Uighur ethnicity who feared *refoulement* to persecution and torture,[179] the Court of Appeals relied on the decision in *Munaf*. The Court stated

> The Supreme Court's ruling in Munaf precludes the District Court from barring the transfer of a Guantánamo detainee on the ground that he is likely to be tortured or subject to further prosecution or detention in the recipient country. The Government has declared its policy not to transfer a detainee to a country that likely will torture him, and the District Court may not second-guess the Government's assessment of that likelihood.[180]

Although *Kiyemba II* concerned individuals held by the United States in the 'war on terror', there is nothing to suggest that the decision would be any different in the case of the courts attempting to second-guess the U.S. executive's return of interdictees to their home country because they may be tortured there. The similarity in the factual position of both groups wishing not to be returned to their home country makes it even more

175 See Bellinger III and Padmanabhan, n 97 in this chapter.
176 553 US 674 (2008).
177 *Munaf v Geren*, 553 US 674, 700 (2008).
178 561 F 3d 509 (DC Cir, 2009).
179 For a discussion of other litigation involving the Uighur men, see subsection 6.2.6.
180 *Munaf v Geren*, 561 F 3d 509,516 (DC Cir, 2009).

likely that the courts would treat interdictees under the MIP in the same way as the Uighurs.

Section 2242(b) of FARRA also has a regulatory mandate that states:

> Not later than 120 days after the date of enactment of this Act [21 October 1998], the heads of the appropriate agencies shall prescribe regulations to implement the obligations of the United States under Article 3 of the United Nations Convention Against Torture and Other Forms of Cruel, Inhuman or Degrading Treatment or Punishment, subject to any reservations, understandings, declarations, and provisos contained in the United States Senate resolution of ratification of the Convention.

In response to § 2242(b) of FARRA, regulations were implemented under Code of Federal Regulations (CFR) §§ 208.16–208.18 (2005) and 8 CFR §§ 1208.16–1208.18 (2005) creating *non-refoulement* safeguards in the context of removal proceedings under immigration laws. Unfortunately, these regulations do not apply to interdictees, since in accordance with municipal law they are not being removed from the United States and are not in removal proceedings. As such, the FARRA does not create any binding legal obligations which can be used to compel the executive to refrain from the *refoulement* of protection seekers to torture under the MIP.

Unlike the CAT, the ICCPR has not been implemented into U.S. municipal law through a specific piece of legislation. In ratifying the Covenant, the United States declared that

> the fundamental rights and freedoms protected by the Covenant are already guaranteed as a matter of U.S. law, either by virtue of constitutional protections or enacted statutes, and can be effectively asserted and enforced by individuals in the judicial system on those bases. For this reason it was not considered necessary to adopt special implementing legislation to give effect to the Covenant's provisions in domestic law.[181]

As with the ICCPR, the CERD has not been implemented into municipal law through a specific piece of legislation in the United States, because

[181] Human Rights Committee, *Reports Submitted By State Parties Under Article 40 Of The Covenant: Initial Reports Of State Parties Due In 1993: United States of America*, CCPR/C/81/Add.4. (24 August 1994).

the United States believes that its Constitution and other municipal laws are sufficient to comply with the treaty.[182] As shown in Chapters 5 and 6, however, the U.S. Constitution is also unable to assist interdictees in international waters and in Guantánamo Bay. Thus, interdictees are left with no avenue through which to compel the United States to abide by its international obligations to them due to the absence of effective enforcement mechanisms under international law; the non-self-executing nature of the Refugee Protocol, ICCPR, CAT and CERD; and the ineffectiveness of implementing legislation.

4.7 Conclusion

It is clear from the discussion in this chapter that, despite U.S. objections, the United States is bound by certain human rights and refugee law obligations wherever it exercises jurisdiction, including outside its territorial sea and in Guantánamo Bay. Despite the applicability of certain obligations outside the municipally defined territory of the United States, however, there are no effective mechanisms in the international legal regime that can be used to compel the United States to abide by its treaty agreements when exercising jurisdiction under the MIP. Nor can many of the treaty obligations discussed in this chapter be directly enforced under U.S. municipal law as they have been deemed not to be self-executing and thus cannot be the cause of action in U.S. courts without implementing legislation. While in some instances implementing legislation does exist, it has been found (or is likely to be found) by the U.S. courts to not apply outside the municipally defined territory of the United States, or in the case of the *non-refoulement* obligation under the CAT, to not apply to interdictees under the MIP. The practical consequence of this is that litigation in the U.S. courts will not in itself be an effective means of redressing the plight of interdictees until there is law reform to ensure that the United States' international obligations are implemented within domestic law and are applicable to interdictees outside the municipally defined territory of the United States.

[182] Hadar Harris, 'Race Across Borders: The U.S. and ICERD' (2008) 24 *Harvard Blackletter Law Journal* 61.

The lack of effective mechanisms to enforce international human rights and refugee law treaties heightens the potential for States parties to violate their international obligations. As shown in Chapters 5 and 6, the United States does in fact violate numerous obligations under international human rights and refugee law in the course of MIP operations. It is to these specific violations that we now turn.

5

Status Determinations in International Waters and in Guantánamo Bay, Cuba

The previous two chapters of this book examined the municipal and international legal frameworks governing the MIP. This chapter begins the analysis of specific rights under international human rights and refugee law that are violated by the United States under the MIP. In particular, this chapter is concerned with the procedural deficiencies in status determinations by the United States – that is, the process for the identification and protection of individuals who are owed a *non-refoulement* obligation.

This chapter consists of four parts. It begins with an overview of status determination procedures at sea and in Guantánamo Bay under the MIP. The second part of this chapter will provide an analysis of the municipal laws governing status determinations under the MIP. Part three will consider the United States' *non-refoulement* obligations, including interrelated and partially overlapping elements of fair and effective status determinations: the requirements that are implied by the *non-refoulement* obligations themselves and the express obligations prohibiting discrimination. Part four of this chapter provides an assessment of the U.S. compliance with its international obligations when conducting status determinations under the MIP.

It will be argued that whilst it may be theoretically possible to provide fair and effective status determinations that are compliant with the United States' *non-refoulement* and non-discrimination obligations at sea and in Guantánamo Bay, the complicated logistics associated with such procedures may be prohibitive. A much easier and more certain way of ensuring the United States' compliance with its international obligations is for the United States to conduct status determinations in the U.S. mainland. In addition, the United States must refrain from discriminating between protection seekers on the basis of their nationality and must recognise and protect all individuals at risk of *refoulement* to death or to cruel, inhuman or degrading treatment or punishment, even if they are not refugees or at risk of being returned to torture.

5.1 Status Determinations and the Migrant Interdiction Program

As discussed in the previous chapter, the United States does not believe itself to be bound by international legal obligations to people interdicted in international waters. Nevertheless, the United States provides status determination, as a matter of policy, in international waters and in Guantánamo Bay. As the Coast Guard website provides

> Protection from *political persecution and torture* are important concerns for the U.S. During the course of migrant interdictions, Coast Guard crews may encounter migrants requesting protection. The Department of State (Bureau of Population, Refugees, and Migration) and the Bureau of Citizenship and Immigration Services establish the policies in this area and handle all potential asylum cases on our cutters.[1]

The United States differentiates between Cuban and non-Cuban nationals during interdiction operations and provides Cuban nationals with privileges that are not afforded to protection seekers of other nationalities. For this reason, we turn first to status determination procedures for Cuban protection seekers before examining the procedures for non-Cubans.

Cuban protection seekers undergo two steps in their status determination during the MIP. The first step for Cuban nationals is a 'credible fear' determination. This is referred to as a 'pre-screening' by the Coast Guard who describe it as 'a limited scope interview'.[2] The task of interviewing any protection seekers in a pre-screening interview is not undertaken by the Coast Guard themselves but by a Protection Screening Officer (PSO), a representative of the Refugee Affairs Division of the U.S. Citizenship and Immigration Services (USCIS) who is trained in asylum law and policy.[3]

1 U.S. Coast Guard, *Alien Migrant Interdiction* <www.uscg.mil/hq/cg5/cg531/AMIO/amio.asp>. Emphasis added.

2 U.S. Coast Guard, *Maritime Law Enforcement Manual* <www.uscg.mil/hq/cg5/cg531/AMIO/FOIA_Docs.pdf>, D.4.

3 Ibid.

A PSO is called every time the Coast Guard interdicts a vessel carrying a Cuban national. All interdicted Cubans are read a statement in Spanish by a PSO that provides

> You are being taken back to Cuba. You will not be taken to the United States. US Government officials in Havana will meet the ship and will provide information to you if you wish to apply to go to the United States through established migration programs. The government of Cuba has provided a commitment to the United States that you will suffer no adverse consequence of reprisals of any sort for illegal departure or for making applications for legal migration to the United States at the US Interests Section. Only those people who are approved by the US Interests Section in Havana can be assured of entry to the United States. I or a US Government official will be available to speak with you if you have any concerns about returning to Cuba. This will be done in a completely confidential setting and no information regarding your concern will be given to the Cuban authorities. If you would like to speak with me or this officer please let me or this officer know.[4]

If a PSO is satisfied that a Cuban national has a 'credible fear' of persecution or torture, the protection seeker is transferred to Guantánamo Bay where he or she will undergo further status determination. Cuban nationals unsuccessful in establishing that they have a credible fear of persecution or torture during interdiction operations are repatriated.

Figure 2 provides a visual guide to status determinations for Cubans under the MIP.

Status determinations on board Coast Guard vessels are different for protection seekers who are not Cuban nationals. A PSO is not automatically alerted after the interdiction of non-Cubans. Instead, non-Cubans must first alert the Coast Guard to their fears of *refoulement* (which will be referred to in this book as a 'pre-pre-screening') before they are given the opportunity to raise their protection needs with a PSO in a pre-screening interview. It is very difficult for non-Cuban protection seekers to communicate their protection needs to Coast Guard personnel. The 'pre-pre-screening' is sometimes referred to as the 'shout test' because 'only those who wave their hands, jump up and down, and shout the

[4] INS Memorandum, *Shipboard Processing of Cubans* (9 August 1995).

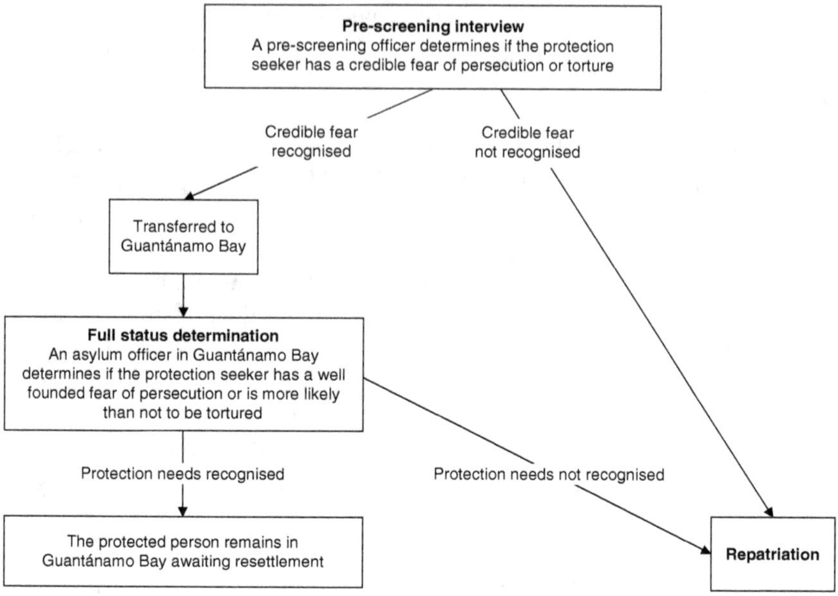

Figure 2. Status determination procedures for interdicted Cubans.

loudest – and are recognized as having done such – are even afforded, in theory, a shipboard refugee pre-screening interview'.[5] Furthermore, Coast Guard personnel are ordered to 'NOT elicit statements from [protection seekers] unless and until directed to do so'[6] and are told to limit communication to things 'necessary to accomplish embarkation, initial briefing, security, safety, medical care, food distribution and disembarkation'.[7]

In deciding if a PSO should be alerted for a pre-screening interview, the Coast Guard is also advised to look for verbal or physical manifestations of fear such as 'evidence of an injury (eg. burn, bruise etc.) … [or] non-verbal actions such as self-inflicted harm or other gestures'.[8] That is, non-Cuban protection seekers who do not speak up about their fears (and thus self-identify) may nevertheless be referred to a PSO if a member of

5 Bill Frelick, '"Abundantly Clear": *Refoulement*' (2004) 19 *Georgetown Immigration Law Journal* 245, 245.

6 U.S. Coast Guard, n 2 in this chapter', D.4.b. The original text refers to migrants rather than protection seekers. Emphasis in the original.

7 Ibid D.4.c.

8 Ibid D.4.b.

the Coast Guard suspects that they may have been persecuted or tortured in the past.

Only after successfully alerting the Coast Guard to their protection needs in a 'pre-pre-screening' do non-Cuban protection seekers have access to a pre-screening in the form of a 'credible fear' determination on board Coast Guard vessels before a PSO. It therefore follows that non-Cuban protection seekers who are unsuccessful in alerting the Coast Guard to their protection needs and have not been identified as having been subjected to persecution or torture in the past, may be repatriated before they are given a pre-screening interview with a person qualified and tasked with the specific job of hearing their protection claims.

Unlike Cuban nationals, non-Cubans are not read a statement at any point during their status determination at sea, alerting them to the opportunity to speak up about their fears.[9] As with Cuban protection seekers, non-Cubans determined to have a 'credible fear' of persecution or torture during a pre-screening interview with a PSO are transferred to Guantánamo Bay.

Figure 3 provides a visual guide to status determinations for non-Cubans under the MIP.

Under a policy introduced in 2010, PSOs now also collect biographical information about all protection seekers interviewed, regardless of their nationality, as part of the Migrant Information Tracking System (MITS). The information collected may be used by the United States in any further status determination procedures. Protection seekers may decline to provide information for the purposes of the MITS; however, this is not a real choice since refusal to provide information to the MITS disqualifies protection seekers from participating in a pre-screening interview.[10]

9 This is an issue for all non-Cubans except for Chinese nationals. The Coast Guard Manual provides that

> All PRC migrants receive a questionnaire to elicit the reason(s) for their departure from China … which the Coast Guard transmits to USCIS Headquarters. After reviewing the response to the questionnaires, USCIS determines whether any migrants' response requires further inquiry or a pre-screening interview.

Ibid D.4.a.

10 Department of Homeland Security, 'Privacy Impact Statement: US Citizenship and Immigration Services, Migrant Information Tracking System' (3 February) <www.dhs.gov/xlibrary/assets/privacy/privacy_pia_uscis_mits.pdf>.

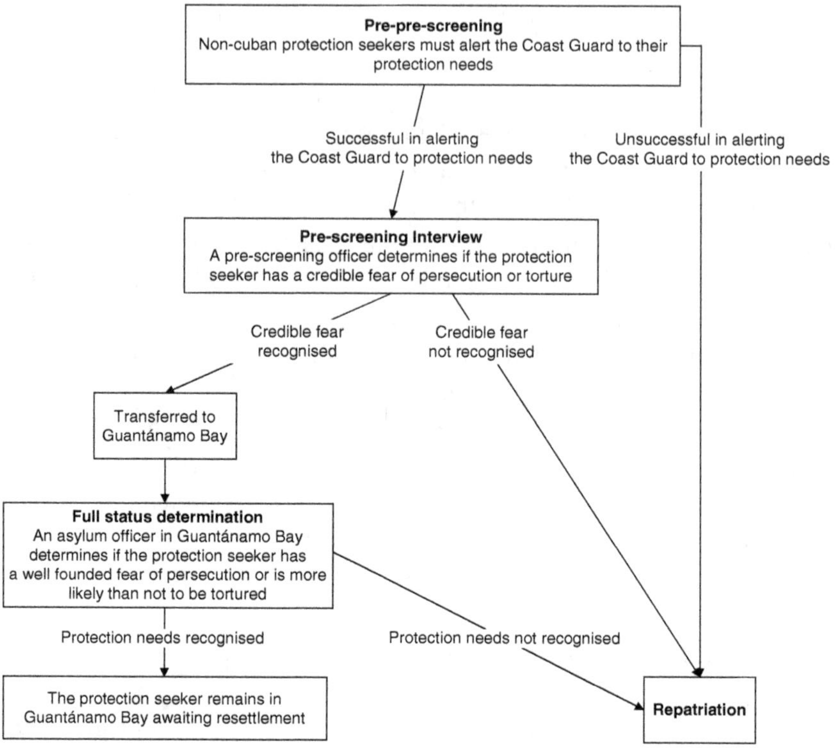

Figure 3. Status determination procedures for interdicted Non-Cubans.

The final step for all protection seekers (including non-Cubans), who have been identified as having a credible fear of persecution or torture at sea is a face-to-face interview with an USCIS Asylum Officer, trained in asylum law and policy, to assess if they are a refugee and have a 'well founded fear' of persecution.[11] The Asylum Officer also determines if the protection seeker transferred to Guantánamo Bay is more likely than not to be tortured if repatriated.

The status determination interviews in Guantánamo Bay are non-adversarial. The Asylum Officer asks each protection seeker about his or her experiences in his or her country of origin, including any fears they

[11] The Asylum Officer will be guided by the definition of a 'refugee' under INA § 101(a)(42); 8 USC § 1101(A)(42)(A) but is not bound by the provision extraterritorially. See discussion in subsection 4.6.1.

may have about returning. The interviews may take several days.[12] Since 2009, the UNHCR has also assisted the United States in conducting status determinations in Guantánamo Bay by interviewing protection seekers and referring individuals for resettlement to third countries.[13] UNHCR does not have a permanent presence in Guantánamo Bay.[14]

Protection seekers processed at sea and in Guantánamo Bay are not provided access to legal assistance or the opportunity to review a status determination before an independent body, at any stage of the status determination process under the MIP.

5.2 Municipal Law Governing Status Determinations under the MIP

Status determinations in international waters, outlined earlier, are governed by Executive Order 12807 (Kennebunkport Order)[15] as amended by Executive Order 13286.[16] This states that 'the [Secretary of Homeland Security] in his *unreviewable discretion*, may decide that a person who is a refugee will not be returned without his consent.'[17] Therefore, status determinations for protection seekers interdicted by the United States under the MIP are part of a policy pursuant to an unreviewable discretion. As such, status determinations on board Coast Guard vessels do not grant any entitlements under domestic law. The same is true for protection seekers in Guantánamo Bay. Current status determinations in Guantánamo Bay are governed by Executive Order 13276,[18] as amended by Executive Order 13286,[19] which under 1(a) (ii) provides

> The [Secretary of Homeland Security] may conduct any screening of such aliens that he deems appropriate, including screening to

[12] Interview with member of the Refugee and Asylum Law Division, U.S. Citizenship and Immigration Services, U.S. Department of Homeland Security (Fairfax, Virginia, 24 October 2008).

[13] E-mail to author from PRM Press, Bureau of Population, Refugees, and Migration, U.S. Department of State, 12 March 2013 (on file with author).

[14] Ibid.

[15] 57 *Federal Register* 23, 133 (1992).

[16] 68 *Federal Register* 10619 (2003). See Section 3.1.

[17] Emphasis added.

[18] 67 *Federal Register* 69 (2002).

[19] 68 *Federal Register* 10619 (2003).

> determine whether such aliens should be returned to their country of origin or transit, or whether they are persons in need of protection who should not be returned without their consent.

The power to screen in Guantánamo Bay does not equate to a mandated duty to conduct status determinations under domestic law. Executive Order 13276 also states: 'This order shall not be construed to require any procedure to determine whether a person is a refugee or otherwise in need of protection'.[20] Therefore, protection seekers do not have any legal rights that can be enforced in the U.S. courts under Executive Order 13276 and the Kennebunkport Order (as amended by Executive Order 13286) with regards to the determination of their status.

Nevertheless, the U.S. executive must act in the framework of law established by the common law and the U.S. Constitution when engaging in status determinations under the MIP. Unfortunately, the two constitutional provisions that are likely to be of most value to protection seekers undergoing status determination procedures under the MIP – the First and Fifth Amendments of the U.S. Constitution – do not apply to status determinations under the MIP.

The First Amendment of the U.S. Constitution is relevant to the plight of protection seekers in the MIP because it guarantees freedom of speech and association. If protection seekers were found to have rights under the First Amendment of the U.S. Constitution, they would have a right, under U.S. municipal law, to speak with legal counsel to seek assistance and advice during status determinations. The relevant provision in the Fifth Amendment of the U.S. Constitution provides that no person shall be 'deprived of life, liberty, or property, without due process of law'. Thus if the Fifth Amendment of the U.S. Constitution was to apply under the MIP, the United States would have to provide procedural safeguards to protection seekers during their status determination (which also includes access to counsel).

The leading case for the denial of protections under the First and Fifth Amendment of the U.S. Constitution for protection seekers interdicted by the United States as part of the MIP is *Cuban American Bar Association v Christopher* (*Christopher*).[21] This case concerned the right of protection

[20] Executive Order 13276, 67 *Federal Register* 69 (2002), § 3(e).

[21] 43 F. 3d 1412, 1417 (11th Cir, 1995). For a discussion of the historical and political events leading up to the case, see subsection 2.2.2.

seekers in Guantánamo Bay to lawyers and procedural safeguards. The protection seekers sought an order that 'lawyers and clients may talk to one another before defendants coerce the clients to waive their rights and return to a repressive regime from which they have fled at great risk'.[22] They argued that the denial of legal assistance raised issues under the First Amendment of the U.S. Constitution.[23] The protection seekers also argued in *Christopher* that they had a right to obtain counsel under the Fifth Amendment's Due Process Clause.[24] The 11th Circuit rejected the arguments put forward by the protection seekers and found that non-citizens in Guantánamo Bay did not enjoy rights under the First and Fifth Amendments of the U.S. Constitution as the U.S. Constitution did not apply to aliens in Guantánamo Bay.

To understand the rejection of the application of the U.S. Constitution to Guantánamo Bay in *Christopher*, it is necessary to understand its history. In the 1950 case of *Johnson v Eisentrager* (*Eisentrager*),[25] the extraterritorial application of the U.S. Constitution was tested for German nationals who were prisoners of war in occupied Germany. The prisoners of war had been prosecuted and convicted by a U.S. military commission in China under the charge of engaging in military activity against the United States and had been convicted of war crimes. It had been argued before the Supreme Court that the convictions for war crimes had violated the Fifth Amendment of the prisoners. The Supreme Court found that the extent of constitutional protections enjoyed by an alien depends on the alien's relationship with the United States. The Court asserted that '[t]he alien, to whom the US has been traditionally hospitable, has been accorded a generous and ascending scale of rights as he increases his identity with our society'.[26] In that case, the prisoners of war did not demonstrate the requisite attachment to the United States.

The extraterritorial application of the Fourth Amendment of the U.S. Constitution as it applies to aliens was tested in *US v Verdugo-Urquidez*

[22] Brief of Plaintiffs-Appellees, Christopher v Cuban-American Bar Association, No 94–5138(7 December 1994), 14.

[23] Ibid 14.

[24] Ibid 11.

[25] 339 US 763 (1950).

[26] Ibid 770–71.

(*Verdugo-Urquidez*).[27] Importantly for the purposes of this book, in *Verdugo-Urquidez* the Supreme Court restated the precedential effect of its earlier decision in *Eisentrager*, arguing that in *Eisentrager* it had 'rejected the claim that aliens are entitled to Fifth Amendment rights outside the sovereign territory of the US'.[28]

Protection seekers in Guantánamo Bay had put to the Court in *Christopher* that *Eisentrager* was not binding precedent because it addressed the incarceration of an enemy alien in a German prison on German soil, a situation very different to people interdicted by the United States and 'detained on territory subject to exclusive jurisdiction of the US'.[29] Nevertheless, the Court relied heavily in its decision on *Eisentrager* and the interpretation of that earlier decision in *Verdugo-Urquidez*. The Court of Appeals for the 11th Circuit found in *Christopher* that the protection seekers have no First or Fifth Amendment rights and that this 'is supported by the Supreme Court's decisions declining to apply extraterritorially either the Fourth Amendment, [*Verdugo-Urquidez*] … or the Fifth Amendment [*Eisentrager*]'.[30]

Whilst no constitutional protections have been found to apply to protection seekers in Guantánamo Bay, prisoners in the 'war on terror' have had more success in establishing the constitutional guarantee of *habeas corpus* in Guantánamo Bay. In *Boumediene v Bush* (*Boumediene*),[31] handed down on 12 June 2008, the Supreme Court found that Article 1, Section 9, Paragraph 2 (suspension clause) of the U.S. Constitution prohibited the suspension of the writ of *habeas corpus* in Guantánamo Bay for non-citizens. The writ of *habeas corpus*, and its lack of effectiveness for protection seekers in the MIP, is discussed further in subsections 6.2.5 and 6.2.6. For present purposes, it suffices to note that the Supreme Court found in *Boumediene* that '[n]othing in *Eisentrager* says that *de jure* sovereignty is or has ever been the only relevant consideration in determining the geographic reach of the Constitution or of *habeas corpus*'.[32]

27 494 US 259 (1990). For a more in-depth discussion of *United States v Verdugo-Urquidez*, 494 US 259, 269 (1990), see subsection 3.2.1.
28 *United States v Verdugo-Urquidez*, 494 US 259, 269 (1990).
29 Brief of Plaintiffs-Appellees, Christopher v Cuban-American Bar Association, No 94–5138 (12 December 1994), n12.
30 *Cuban American Bar Association v Christopher*, 43 F 3d 1412, 1428–29 (11th Cir, 1995).
31 553 US 723 (2008).
32 Ibid 764.

Thus the Supreme Court stated in *Boumediene* that its earlier decision in *Eisentrager* did not prohibit it from examining the constitutional claims of the non-citizens in Guantánamo Bay as they related to *habeas corpus* rights of detainees.

Boumediene did not decide on the full range of grounds for *habeas corpus* in Guantánamo Bay. The Supreme Court in *Boumediene* emphasised that its decision did not extend beyond the specific case before the Court, stating that its 'decision today holds only that petitioners before [it] are entitled to seek the writ [of *habeas corpus*]'.[33] As Geltzer points out,

> Much of the Court's analysis [in *Boumediene*] sounded distinctly Suspension Clause-specific, emphasizing the unique importance of the availability of *habeas* relief in order to keep the judiciary present and active, rather than permitting it to be sidelined by the political branches.[34]

The fact that *Boumediene* is a decision concerning the suspension clause and not other rights under the U.S. Constitution has been confirmed by the DC Circuit which has interpreted the *Boumediene* decision as being limited to the extension of the writ of *habeas corpus*. In *Kiyemba v Obama* (*Kiyemba* I),[35] the Court explained that the Supreme Court 'had never extended any constitutional rights to aliens detained outside the United States; *Boumediene* therefore specifically limited its holding to the Suspension Clause'.[36] As such, until there is a clear guidance to the contrary from the Supreme Court, *Christopher* remains the binding precedent for the proposition that the First and Fifth Amendments of the U.S. Constitution do not apply to protection seekers in Guantánamo Bay and on board Coast Guard vessels.[37]

33 Ibid 795.

34 Joshua Geltzer, 'Of Suspension, Due Process, and Guantánamo: The Reach of the Fifth Amendment after *Boumediene* and the Relationship between Habeas Corpus and Due Process' (2012) 14 *University of Pennsylvania Journal of Constitutional Law* 719, 738.

35 555 F 3d 1022 (DC Cir, 2009). See also discussion in subsection 6.2.6.

36 *Kiyemba v Obama*, 555 F 3d 1022 (DC Cir, 2009). The procedural history and findings of the Kiyemba litigation is discussed in greater detail in subsection 6.2.5.1.

37 On the issue of the extension of other constitutional protections to Guantánamo Bay following the decision in *Boumediene*, see Marc Falkoff and Robert Knowles, 'Bagram, Boumediene, and Limited Government' (2010) 59 *DePaul Law Review* 851, 871; Gerald Neuman, 'The Extraterritorial Constitution after Boumediene v Bush' (2009) 82 *Southern California Law Review* 259, 26; and Stephen Vladeck, 'Boumediene's Quiet Theory: Access to Courts and the Separation of Powers' (2009) 84 *Notre Dame Law Review* 2107, 2143.

An additional argument that could be made in support of protection seekers interdicted by the United States is that the extension of the writ of *habeas corpus* to aliens detained in Guantánamo Bay itself carries procedural safeguards, independently of those governed by the Fifth Amendment.[38] That is, some procedural safeguards, such as access to legal assistance, are an intrinsic component of a right to the writ of *habeas corpus*. However, 'simply put, existing case law offers no clarity regarding the relationship between *habeas* and due process'.[39] That is, there is great uncertainty over this issue, which has not been clarified by the Supreme Court. Justice Kennedy, writing for the majority in *Boumediene*, stated that the Supreme Court made 'no attempt to anticipate all of the evidentiary and access-to-counsel issues that will arise during the course of the detainees' *habeas corpus* proceedings'.[40]

Even if protection seekers in Guantánamo Bay were able to bring *habeas* claims and even if, as Neuman argues, the writ of *habeas corpus* inherently offered 'certain minimum content',[41] this would not overcome the inadequacy of status determination procedures in Guantánamo Bay for protection seekers. This is because, as Justice Kennedy explained in *Boumediene*, 'the essence of *habeas corpus* is an attack by a person in custody upon the legality of that custody'.[42] The suspension clause in the U.S. Constitution 'protects the rights of the *detained* by a means consistent with the essential design of the Constitution'.[43] The issue of detention of protection seekers in Guantánamo Bay and the prospect of a *habeas corpus* claim is explored in further detail in Chapter 6. For present purposes, it suffices to note that status determinations under the MIP do not result in the release of people from detention. People who are found to have protection needs under the MIP remain detained in Guantánamo Bay until they can be resettled in a third country. As such, even were a court to order the release of protection

38 Mary Van Houten argues for example that 'at least some substantive due process protection follow on the heals of habeas corpus and that the two clauses may be inextricable in some extent': Mary Van Houten, 'The Post Boumediene Paradox: Habeas Corpus or Due Process' (2014) 67 *Stanford Law Review* 9, 11.

39 Geltzer, n 34 in this chapter, 749.

40 *Boumediene v Bush* 553 US 723, 796 (2008).

41 Gerald Neuman, 'The Habeas Corpus Suspension Clause After Boumediene v Bush' (2010) 110 *Columbia Law Review* 537, 541.

42 *Boumediene v Bush* 553 US 723, 745 (2008).

43 Ibid 745. Emphasis added.

seekers from detention, the United States would remain at liberty to conduct status determinations in accordance with Executive Orders discussed earlier in the book.

It thus follows that in the absence of the application of the First and Fifth Amendments of the U.S. Constitution to protection seekers undergoing status determinations under the MIP, no other provisions of the U.S. Constitution require the U.S. executive to offer procedural safeguards to protection seekers during status determinations under the MIP. As such, protection seekers do not have any avenues through which they can challenge status determination procedures carried out under the MIP in U.S. courts.

5.3 The United States' *Non-Refoulement* Obligations under International Law

The status determination procedures carried out by the U.S. executive under the MIP may comply with U.S. municipal law, but it is unlikely that the regime is compliant with the United States' *non-refoulement* obligations under international law.

The essential characteristic of a State's *non-refoulement* obligation is the prohibition on the return of certain people to a place where they are at risk of exposure to specific, predefined, harms.[44] The United States has *non-refoulement* obligations under the Refugee Convention (which the United States must adhere to because it is a party to the Refugee Protocol), the CAT and the ICCPR.

The United States' *non-refoulement* obligation under the Refugee Convention is found under Article 33(1).[45] The Article prohibits the return of a refugee 'to the frontiers of territories where his life or freedom would be threatened on account of his race, religion, nationality, membership of a particular social group or political opinion'. Article 33(1) of the Refugee Convention is binding on all organs of a State party to the Refugee Convention or Refugee Protocol,[46] and 'constitutes the cornerstone of

44 Guy Goodwin-Gill, 'The Right to Seek Asylum: Interception at Sea and the Principle of *Non-Refoulement*' (2011) 23 *International Journal of Refugee Law* 443, 444.

45 See discussion in subsection 4.2.1.1.

46 This includes any other person or entity acting on behalf of the State party. See UNHCR, *Advisory Opinion on the Extraterritorial Application of Non-Refoulement Obligations under*

international refugee protection'.[47] The significance of Article 33(1) of the Refugee Convention is emphasised by the fact that States parties to the Refugee Convention and the Refugee Protocol are not permitted to make reservations with respect to the Article.[48] However, Article 33(2) of the Refugee Convention does provide an exception to Article 33(1) protection for certain individuals who are convicted of a serious crime and are 'a danger to the security' of the State party.

In addition to the obligation to protect refugees from *refoulement* to persecution, the United States also has an obligation to protect individuals from *refoulement* when there are substantial grounds for believing that the individual would be in danger of being subjected to torture. The *non-refoulement* obligation under the CAT is based on Article 33(1) of the Refugee Convention.[49] This obligation of *non-refoulement* is outlined under Article 3 of the CAT, which states

> No State Party shall expel, return ('refouler') or extradite a person to another State where there are substantial grounds for believing that he would be in danger of being subjected to torture.

Status determination procedures adopted for the identification of refugees may not be sufficient to identify individuals in need of protection from *refoulement* under Article 3 of the CAT. This is because, unlike Article 33 of the Refugee Convention, Article 3 of the CAT is not limited to the *refoulement* of refugees, but protects anyone who is in danger of being

the 1951 Convention Relating to the Status of Refugees and Its 1967 Protocol (26 January 2007) <www.unhcr.org/refworld/docid/45f17a1a4.html>.

47 Ibid. See also James Hathaway and Michelle Foster, *The Law of Refugee Status* (Cambridge University Press, 2nd ed., 2014) 36.

48 Article 7(1) of the Refugee Protocol prohibits reservations to Article 33 of the Refugee Convention. Article 42(1) of the Refugee Convention also prohibits reservations to Article 33 of the Refugee Convention. However, as the United States is not party to the Refugee Convention, it is bound only by Articles 2–34 of the Refugee Convention (pursuant to Article 1(1) of the Refugee Protocol).

49 David Weissbrodt and Isabel Hortreiter, 'The Principle of *Non-Refoulement*: Article 3 of the Convention Against Torture and Other Cruel, Inhuman or Degrading Treatment or Punishment in Comparison with the *Non-Refoulement* Provisions of Other International Human Rights Treaties' (1999) 5 *Buffalo Human Rights Review* 1, 7. The interrelationship between the *non-refoulement* obligations under the CAT and the ICCPR has also been noted by the Executive Committee of the High Commissioner's Programme (UNHCR ExCom). See UNHCR ExCom, *Conclusion No 79: General Conclusion on International Protection*, 51st sess, A/51/12/Add.1 (11 October 1996), [j].

subjected to torture. Thus, the torture being feared need not be related to the victim's race, religion, nationality, membership of a particular social group or political opinion, but can be inflicted for any reason. Furthermore, unlike the Refugee Convention, the CAT does not permit exceptions from the protection of *non-refoulement* for anyone.[50] That is, even individuals who are convicted of a serious crime and are a danger to the security of a State party must be protected from *refoulement* under Article 3 of the CAT.

5.3.1 *Non-Refoulement* Obligations under the ICCPR

Additional *non-refoulement* obligations are owed by the United States under Articles 6 and 7 of the ICCPR. Article 6 of the ICCPR states

> Every human being has the inherent right to life. This right shall be protected by law. No one shall be arbitrarily deprived of his life.

Article 7 provides

> No one shall be subjected to torture or to cruel, inhuman or degrading treatment or punishment. In particular, no one shall be subjected without his free consent to medical or scientific experimentation.

The United States has made reservations with regard to Articles 6 and 7 of the ICCPR.[51] The validity of these reservations is contested.[52] However,

[50] Article 3 of the CAT does not contain an express non-derogation clause; however, as Olivier De Schutter argues, 'the absence of an express prohibition against derogation in Article 3 of the CAT together with the "without prejudice" language of Article 15 do not seem to permit derogation': Olivier De Schutter, *International Human Rights Law: Cases, Materials, Commentary* (Cambridge University Press, 2010) 276. See also Robert Chesney, 'Leaving *Guantánamo*: The Law of International Detainee Transfers' (2006) 40 *University of Richmond Law Review* 657, 701 n 204; Weissbrodt and Hortreiter, n 49 in this chapter, 50.

[51] The 'United States reserves the right, subject to its constitutional constraints, to impose capital punishment on any person (other than a pregnant woman) duly convicted under existing or future laws permitting the imposition of capital punishment, including such punishment for crimes committed by persons below eighteen years of age'. The United States has also made a reservation with regard to Article 7 so that '"cruel, inhuman or degrading treatment or punishment" means the cruel and unusual treatment or punishment prohibited by the Fifth, Eighth and/or Fourteenth Amendments to the Constitution of the United States'. See United States Reservations, Declarations, and Understandings, International Covenant on Civil and Political Rights, 138 *Congressional Record* S4781-01 <www1.umn.edu/humanrts/usdocs/civilres.html>.

[52] See Human Rights Committee, *Concluding Observations of the Human Rights Committee: United States of America*, 53rd sess, UN Doc CCPR/C/79/Add.50 (6 April 1995),

even if valid, the reservations may narrow the scope of the obligation (that is, they may affect which individuals are protected from *refoulement*), but they do not affect the *non-refoulement* obligations and the associated procedural safeguards, which are the topic of study in this chapter.

Both Articles 6 and 7 of the ICCPR prohibit *refoulement.* In General Comment No 31, the HR Committee held that parties to the ICCPR shall not remove a person to another country 'where there are substantial grounds for believing that there is a real risk of irreparable harm, such as that contemplated by articles 6 and 7'.[53] In General Comment No 20, the HR Committee stated:

> In the view of the Committee, States parties must not expose individuals to the danger of torture or cruel, inhuman or degrading treatment or punishment upon return to another country by way of their extradition, expulsion or *refoulement.*[54]

In its decision of 30 March 2012, the HR Committee reiterated

> States parties are under an obligation not to extradite, deport, expel or otherwise remove a person from their territory, where there are substantial grounds for believing that there is a real risk of irreparable harm, such as that contemplated by articles 6 and 7 of the Covenant, either in the country to which removal is to be effected or in any country to which the person may subsequently be removed.[55]

One significant gap in the United States' compliance with its international obligations when carrying out status determinations as part of the MIP is that the United States denies its *non-refoulement* obligations under Articles 6 and 7 of the ICCPR. The United States does not believe the

[279]. Eleven European States have formally objected to U.S. reservation with regard to Article 6(5) of the ICCPR believing the reservation to be invalid in as much as they are incompatible with the object and purpose of the Convention. See Human Rights Committee, *Reservations, Declarations, Notifications and Objections Relating to the International Covenant on Civil and Political Rights and the Optional Protocols Thereto,* UN Doc CCPR/C/2/Rev.4 (24 August 1994).

53 Human Rights Committee, *General Comment No 31: Nature of the General Obligation on States Parties to the Covenant,* 80th sess, 12 UN Doc CCPR/C/21/Rev1/Add.13 (26 May 2004), [12].

54 Human Rights Committee, *General Comment No 20: Replaces General Comment No 7 Concerning Prohibition of Torture and Cruel Treatment or Punishment,* 44th sess, UN Doc HRI/GEN/1/Rev6 (10 March 1992), [9].

55 *K.A.L. and A.A.M.L. v Canada,* UN Doc CCPR/C/104/D/1816/2008 (26 March 2012), [6.7].

text of Articles 6 and 7 of the ICCPR contain a prohibition on *refoulement* and has expressly stated that it does not intend to be bound by any *non-refoulement* obligations under the ICCPR.[56] Although the HR Committee has expressed concern with the United States' refusal to recognise the Committee's interpretation of Articles 6 and 7, the United States has not changed its position.[57] With regard to Article 7, the United States has explicitly stated

> [U]nlike the Convention Against Torture and Other Cruel, Inhuman, Degrading Treatment or Punishment ... the [ICCPR] does not impose a *non-refoulement* obligation upon States Parties. [The United States is] familiar with the [HR Committee's] statement in General Comment 20 regarding Article 7 of the Covenant.... However, the United States disagrees that States Parties have accepted that obligation under the Covenant.[58]

As the United States does not recognise its *non-refoulement* obligations under Articles 6 and 7 of the ICCPR, no attempts are made to ascertain the protection needs of people who are at risk of *refoulement* to death, cruel, inhuman or degrading treatment or punishment (within the meaning of Article 6 and 7 of the ICCPR) who are not refugees or at risk of *refoulement* to torture during interdiction operations.

The denial of *non-refoulement* obligations to individuals under Articles 6 and 7 of the ICCPR places the United States in potential breach of its obligations under the ICCPR because it increases the likelihood that protected persons will be returned to harm. As with Article 3 of the CAT, status determination procedures created for the identification of refugees only may not be sufficient to identify individuals in need of protection under Articles 6 and 7 of the ICCPR. This is because Articles 6 and 7 of the ICCPR are not limited to the *refoulement* of refugees, but protect anyone who is in

56 U.S. Department of State, *List of Issues to Be Taken Up in Connection with the Consideration of the Second and Third Periodic Reports of the United States of America* (17 July 2006) <http://www.state.gov/g/drl/rls/70385.htm>.

57 See Human Rights Committee, *Consideration of Reports Submitted by States Parties under Article 40 of the Covenant: Concluding Observations of the Human Rights Committee: United States of America*, 87th sess, UN Doc CCPR/C/USA/CO/3 (15 September 2006). See also Yvonne Dutton, 'Pirates and Impunity: Is the Threat of Asylum Claims a Reason to Allow Pirates to Escape Justice?'(2011) 34 *Fordham International Law Journal* 236.

58 U.S. Department of State, n 56 in this chapter.

danger of being denied their right to life or subjected to torture, cruel, inhuman or degrading treatment or punishment. Thus, whilst some protected persons who are at risk of being deprived of their life or being subjected to torture, cruel, inhuman or degrading treatment or punishment may be refugees (thus leading to an overlap between Article 33(1) of the Refugee Convention and Articles 6 and 7 of the ICCPR), not all individuals protected under Article 6 and 7 of the ICCPR are refugees.[59] Furthermore, unlike the Refugee Convention, the ICCPR does not permit exceptions from the protection of *non-refoulement* for anyone. That is, even individuals who may be a danger to the security of a State party who satisfy Articles 6 and 7 of the ICCPR must be protected from *refoulement*.[60]

In addition, status determinations for the identification of people owed protection under Article 3 of the CAT only identify individuals at risk of *refoulement* to torture and not all the harms protected within the meaning of Articles 6 and 7 of the ICCPR. As such, status determinations for individuals in need of protection under Article 3 of the CAT can only identify a subset of protected persons (those at risk of torture) under Article 7 of the ICCPR. This leaves individuals at risk of *refoulement* to cruel, inhuman or degrading treatment or punishment within the meaning of Article 7 of the ICCPR, or those in need of protection from *refoulement* to a place where they are at risk of death within the meaning of Article 6 of the ICCPR, without protection. As a consequence, people interdicted by the United States who are owed protection from *refoulement* under Articles 6 or 7 of the ICCPR (who are not refugees or at risk of *refoulement* to torture) are in grave danger of *refoulement* by the United States, in violation of the United States' international obligations.

5.3.2 What Is Required for Fair and Effective Status Determination Procedures

Compliance with a State's *non-refoulement* obligations necessitates an accurate system of status determination to ensure that no protected person

[59] This is because the feared harm that triggers Article 6 and 7 protections under the ICCPR need not be related to the victim's race, religion, nationality, membership in a particular social group or political opinion.

[60] Article 4(2) of the ICCPR prohibits derogation from Articles 6 and 7 of the ICCPR even in 'times of public emergency which threatens the life of the nation'.

is returned to harm. This is well established in refugee law scholarship.[61] The importance of status determination has also been repeatedly highlighted by the UNHCR ExCom in a number of Conclusions.[62] The same reasoning can, of course, be applied to *non-refoulement* obligations

[61] See, for example, Guy Goodwin-Gill and Jane McAdam, *The Refugee in International Law* (Oxford University Press, 3rd ed., 2007) 528; James Hathaway, *The Rights of Refugees Under International Law* (Cambridge University Press, 2005) 319, 159–60; Michelle Foster and Jason Pobjoy, 'A Failed Case of Legal Exceptionalism? Refugee Status Determination in Australia's "Excised" Territory' (2011) 23 *International Journal of Refugee Law* 583, 601; Kelley Loper, 'Human Rights, *Non-Refoulement* and the Protection of Refugees in Hong Kong' (2010) 22 *International Journal of Refugee Law* 404, 404; Geoff Gilbert, 'Editorial' (2006) 18 *International Journal of Refugee Law* 487, 488; Gerald Heckman, 'Securing Procedural Safeguards For Asylum Seekers In Canadian Law: An Expanding Role For International Human Rights Law?' (2003) 15 *International Journal of Refugee Law* 212, 301–02; Mark Pallis, 'Obligations of States Towards Asylum Seekers at Sea: Interactions and Conflicts Between Legal Regimes' (2002) 31 *International Journal of Refugee Law* 329, 342.

[62] See, for example, UNHCR ExCom, *Conclusion No 2: Function of the Subcommittee and General Conclusion on International Protection*, 27th sess, UN Doc 12A A/10012/Add.1 (14 October 1975), [c]; UNHCR ExCom, *Conclusion No 8: Note on the Extraterritorial Effect of the Determination of Refugee Status under the 1951 Convention and the 1967 Protocol Relating to the Status of Refugees*, 29th sess, UN Doc EC/SCP/9 (24 August 1978), [a], [d]; UNHCR ExCom, *Conclusion No 11: General Conclusion on International Protection*, 29th sess, UN Doc 12A A/33/12/Add.1 (17 October 1978), [i]; UNHCR ExCom, *Conclusion No 14: General Conclusion on International Protection*, 30th sess, UN Doc 12A A/34/12/Add.1 (16 October 1979), [f]; UNHCR ExCom, *Conclusion No 16: General Conclusion on International Protection*, 31st sess, UN Doc 12A A/35/12/Add.1 (16 October 1980), [h]; UNHCR ExCom, *Conclusion No 20: Protection of Asylum-Seekers at Sea*, 31st sess, UN Doc No 12A A/35/12/Add.1 (16 October 1980), [d]; UNHCR ExCom, *Conclusion No 21: General Conclusion on International Protection*, 32nd sess, UN Doc 12A A/35/12/Add.1 (21 October 1981), [d]; UNHCR ExCom, *Conclusion No 25: General Conclusion on International Protection*, 33rd sess, UN Doc 12A A/37/12/Add.1 (20 October 1982), [h]; UNHCR ExCom, *Conclusion No 28: Follow-up on Earlier Conclusions of the Sub-Committee of the Whole on International Protection on the Determination of Refugee Status, Inter Alia, with Reference to the Role of UNHCR in National Refugee Status Determination Procedures*, 33rd sess, UN Doc 12A A/36/12/Add. 12 (20 October 1982), [c]; UNHCR ExCom, *Conclusion No 29: General Conclusion on International Protection*, 34th sess, UN Doc 12A A/38/12/Add.1 (20 October 1983), [h]; UNHCR ExCom, *Conclusion No 44: Detention of Refugees and Asylum-Seekers*, 37th sess, UN Doc 12A A/41/12/Add.1, (13 October 1986), [c]; UNHCR ExCom, *Conclusion No 46: General Conclusion on International Protection*, 38th sess, UN Doc12A A/42/12/Add.1 (12 October 1987), [r]; UNHCR ExCom, *Conclusion No 55: General Conclusion on International Protection*, 40th sess, UN Doc 12A A/44/12/Add.1 (13 October 1989), [f]; UNHCR ExCom, *Conclusion No 71: General Conclusion on International Protection*, 44th sess, UN Doc 12A A/48/12/Add.1 (8 October 1993), [i]; UNHCR ExCom, *Conclusion No 74: General Conclusion on International Protection*, 45th sess, UN Doc 12A A/49/12/Add.1, (7 October 1994) [i]; UNHCR ExCom, *Conclusion No 81: General Conclusion on International Protection*, 48th sess, UN Doc 12A A/52/12/Add.1 (17 October 1997), [h]; UNHCR ExCom, *Conclusion No 82: Safeguarding* Asylum, 48th sess, UN Doc A/52/12/Add.1, (17 October 1997), [d]; UNHCR ExCom, *Conclusion No 85: Conclusion on*

under the CAT and the ICCPR. That is, unless a State party to the CAT and the ICCPR is willing to afford protection from *refoulement* to all in its jurisdiction who claim such protection, at a minimum the obligation to refrain from *refoulement* under Article 3 of the CAT and Articles 6 and 7 of the ICCPR requires that protection seekers have access to status determination procedures that can accurately identify protected persons. This was confirmed by the CAT Committee in *Agiza v Sweden*[63] where the CAT Committee found that Article 3 of the CAT carries with it an implicit right to an 'effective, independent and impartial review of a decision to expel'.[64] The HR Committee also found in *Alzery v Sweden*[65] that effective, independent review of the decision to expel prior to expulsion was necessitated by the nature of the *non-refoulement* obligation under Article 7 of the ICCPR as read with a right to effective remedies under Article 2 of the ICCPR.[66]

The Refugee Convention, Refugee Protocol, CAT and the ICCPR do not provide for specific status determination procedures for evaluating who is in need of protection from *refoulement*. Each State can create its own adjudication mechanisms as long as these procedures are in line with the obligation of *non-refoulement*.[67] Nevertheless, UNHCR ExCom has called for status determination regimes to be fair and effective.[68] The call for fair

International Protection, 49th sess, UN Doc 12A A/53/12/Add.1 (9 October 1998), [q], [r]; UNHCR ExCom, *Conclusion No 87: General Conclusion on International Protection*, 50th sess, UN Doc 12A A/54/12/Add.1 (8 October 1999), [j]; UNHCR ExCom, *Conclusion No 93: Conclusion on Reception of Asylum Seekers in the Context of Individual Asylum Systems*, 53rd sess, UN Doc 12A A/57/12/Add.1(8 October 2002), [a].

63 UN Doc CAT/C/34/D/233/2003 (20 May 2005).

64 Ibid., [13.8].

65 UN Doc CCPR/C/88/D/1416/2005 (10 November 2006).

66 For a discussion of Article 2 of the ICCPR, see Section 4.1.

67 *UNHCR, Handbook and Guidelines on Procedures and Criteria for Determining Refugee Status Under the 1951 Convention and the 1967 Protocol Relating to the Status of Refugees* (1992, reissued 2011) 37 states that the Refugee Convention 'does not indicate what type of procedures are to be adopted for the determination of refugee status'.

68 UNHCR ExCom, *Conclusion No 81: General Conclusion on International Protection'*, 48th sess, UN Doc A/52/12/Add.1, (17 October 1997), [h]; UNHCR ExCom, *Conclusion No 82: Conclusion on Safeguarding Asylum*, 48th sess, UN Doc A/52/12/Add.1 (17 October 1997), [d] (iii); UNHCR ExCom, *Conclusion No 85: Conclusion on International Protection'*, 49th sess, UN Doc A/53/12/Add.1 (9 October 1998), [q]; UNHCR ExCom, *Conclusion No 99: Conclusions Adopted by the Executive Committee on the International Protection of Refugees*, 55th sess, UN Doc A/59/12/Add.1, (8 October 1997), [l].

and effective procedures has also been reiterated by the International Law Association.[69]

Effectiveness in status determinations includes the principle of accuracy and is clearly necessary for compliance with a State's *non-refoulement* obligations, since effectiveness reduces the likelihood of a wrong determination and thus *refoulement*. The principle of fairness should not, however, be overlooked. Fairness embodies the ideas of justice and equality and can not only enhance accuracy but also ensure the legitimacy of the status determination process.[70] This in turn enhances the acceptance of the outcomes by the parties involved and thereby the stability of the protection regime. There is often much overlap between the concepts of fairness and effectiveness, for both aim to reduce mistakes in status determinations. As Legomsky has argued, 'no process can be considered fair if the probability of error is too high'.[71]

UNHCR ExCom has outlined certain basic requirements for status determinations. Each requirement ensures not only greater accuracy but also greater justice. The basic requirements outlined by UNHCR ExCom for status determinations are

(i) The competent official (e.g., immigration officer or border police officer) to whom the applicant addresses himself at the border or in the territory of a Contracting State, should have clear instructions for dealing with cases that might be within the purview of the relevant international instruments. He should be required to act in accordance with the principle of *non-refoulement* and to refer such cases to a higher authority.

69 International Law Association, 'Resolution 6/2002 on Refugee Procedures (Declaration on International Minimum Standards for Refugee Procedures)' (70th Conference of the International Law Association, New Delhi, India, 2–6 April 2002).

70 See Tom Tyler, 'Procedural Fairness and Compliance with the Law' (1997) *Swiss Journal of Economics and Statistics* 219; Robert MacCoun, 'Voice, Control, and Belonging: The Double-Edged Sword of Procedural Fairness' (2005) 1 *Annual Review of Law and Social Science* 171; Stefan Machura, 'Introduction: Procedural Justice, Law and Policy' (1998) 20 *Law & Policy* 1; Eric Tucker, 'The Political Economy of Administrative Fairness: A Preliminary Enquiry' (1987) 25 *Osgoode Hall Law Journal* 555.

71 Stephen Legomsky, 'An Asylum Seeker's Bill of Rights In a Non-Utopian World' (2000) 14 *Georgetown Immigration Law Journal* 619, 623.

(ii) The applicant should receive the necessary guidance as to the procedure to be followed.

(iii) There should be a clearly identified authority – wherever possible a single central authority – with responsibility for examining requests for refugee status and taking a decision in the first instance.

(iv) The applicant should be given the necessary facilities, including the services of a competent interpreter, for submitting his case to the authorities concerned. Applicants should also be given the opportunity, of which they should be duly informed, to contact a representative of UNHCR.

(v) If the applicant is recognised as a refugee, he should be informed accordingly and issued with documentation certifying his refugee status.

(vi) If the applicant is not recognised, he should be given a reasonable time to appeal for a formal reconsideration of the decision, either to the same or to a different authority, whether administrative or judicial, according to the prevailing system.

(vii) The applicant should be permitted to remain in the country pending a decision on his initial request by the competent authority referred to in paragraph (iii) above, unless it has been established by that authority that his request is clearly abusive. He should also be permitted to remain in the country while an appeal to a higher administrative authority or to the courts is pending.[72]

The preceding list of basic requirements that can be seen to be both 'fair' and 'effective' are equally applicable to individuals seeking protection from *refoulement* under Article 3 of the CAT and Articles 6 and 7 of the ICCPR (except for provisions that call for access to the UNHCR).

[72] UNHCR ExCom, *Conclusion No 8: Determination of Refugee Status*, 28th sess, UN Doc A/10012/Add.1 (14 October 1975). See also UNHCR, *Note on Determination of Refugee Status under International Instruments*, 28th sess, UN Doc EC/SCP/5 (24 August 1977), [16]. It should be noted that UNHCR ExCom Conclusion No 8 led the UNHCR to issue the UNHCR, *Handbook and Guidelines on Procedures and Criteria for Determining Refugee Status Under the 1951 Convention and the 1967 Protocol Relating to the Status of Refugees* (1992, reissued 2011), the reissued 2011 version of which is referred to in this book. Paragraph 192 of the Handbook sets out many of the core principles on procedure and safeguards in refugee determination and reiterates the basic requirements outlined in this list.

The United States fails to meet many of the basic requirements identified in that list during interdiction operations, in particular for non-Cuban protection seekers subject to a 'pre-pre-screening' at sea. Non-Cuban protection seekers are not advised of their right to raise protection concerns and are not, in the first instance, provided a clearly identified authority, such as a PSO, with whom they must communicate their fears of *refoulement*. The United States' failure to provide non-Cuban protection seekers with the 'necessary guidance as to the procedure to be [followed]'[73] for obtaining protection from *refoulement* and the lack of a 'clearly identified authority ... with responsibility for examining requests'[74] leads the United States to fall short of the basic procedural requirements (ii) and (iii) identified by UNHCR ExCom under Conclusion No 8.

It is true that non-Cuban protection seekers who do not speak up about their fears may nevertheless be referred to a PSO if a member of the Coast Guard suspects that they may have been persecuted or tortured in the past. However, this does not remedy the United States' failures to meet requirements (ii) and (iii) identified in Conclusion No 8. Whilst looking for evidence of past persecution and torture may increase the likelihood of a protected persons being identified, visible evidence of past persecution and torture is not a reliable indicator of future risk. First, experience of persecution or torture may not result in any visible evidence. Second, and most importantly, evidence of past persecution and torture does not in itself trigger protection from *refoulement* under international law.[75] A State's *non-refoulement* obligation is to shield protected persons from future harm. As such, non-Cuban protected persons who are unable to self-identify remain at risk of being overlooked by the Coast Guard. The repatriation of a protected person under such circumstances would constitute *refoulement* in breach of the United States' international obligations.

There is also a significant issue with the provision of Creole interpreters to Haitian protection seekers interdicted at sea that does not meet basic requirement (iv) – 'to provide necessary facilities, including the services of a competent interpreter'. Although the Coast Guard will, as a matter of

[73] UNHCR ExCom, *Conclusion No 8: Determination of Refugee Status*, 28th sess, UN Doc A/10012/Add.1 (14 October 1975), (e)(ii).

[74] Ibid (e)(iii).

[75] See James Hathaway and Michelle Foster, n 47 in this chapter, 161–69.

policy,[76] attempt to provide interpreters on board Coast Guard cutters used for interdictions, there is no requirement that an interpreter be present at every interdiction.[77] Attempts are made to provide Creole interpreters in the Windward Passage and Spanish interpreters in the Mona Passage.[78] However, this is not always possible. Spanish interpreters for interdicted Cubans are readily available in interdiction operations, but the Coast Guard has found it more difficult to provide interdicted Haitians with Creole interpreters.[79] When an interpreter is not available and it is not operationally feasible to make one available on the Coast Guard vessel, translation services are provided via the telephone.[80] Telephone interpretation requires a protection seeker to speak about their fears to a person they cannot see, do not know and may not trust. In addition, the process can become more time-consuming and frustrating. Failure to provide competent interpreters to Haitian protection seekers could lead to breakdowns in communication between protection seekers and a decision maker, which could result in their protection needs not being correctly identified by the State.[81] As Barsky has shown in his detailed analysis of asylum hearings in Canada in the late 1980s, a protection seeker's chance of having his or her protection needs recognised is affected by language problems, misunderstandings and cultural differences that can be remedied by the provision of competent interpreters.[82] There is thus a greater danger of miscommunication, which could lead to the *refoulement* of protected persons who were not able or willing to communicate their protection needs.

76 U.S. Coast Guard, n 2 in this chapter, D.4.d.

77 Jonathan Friedman et al., *Maritime Interception: History, Practice and Emerging Issue*, Yale Law School, Allard K. Lowenstein International Human Rights Clinic (Unpublished, 2002) 27.

78 U.S. Coast Guard, n 2 in this chapter, D.4.d.

79 See Frelick, n 5 in this chapter.

80 U.S. Coast Guard, n 2 in this chapter, D.4.d.

81 Walter Kälin, 'Troubled Communication: Cross-Cultural Misunderstandings in the Asylum Hearing' (1986) 20 *International Migration Review* 230.

82 See, for example, Robert Barsky, 'The Interpreter as Intercultural Agent in Convention Refugee Hearings' (1996) 2 *The Translator* 45; Robert Barsky, 'The Construction of the other and the Destruction of the Self: Efficacious Discursive Production in the Convention Refugee Hearing' in Gisela Brinker-Gable (ed) *Encountering the Other/s* (SUNY Press, 1995); Robert Barsky *Constructing a Productive Other Discourse Theory and the Convention Refugee Gearing* (John Benjamins Publishing, 1994); Robert Barsky, 'The Interpreter and the Canadian Convention Refugee Hearing: Crossing the Potentially Life-Threatening Boundaries Between "coccode-e-eh," "cluck-cluck, and "cot-cot-cot"' (1993) 6 *Traduction, Terminologie, Racdaction* 13.

Furthermore, the United States fails to meet certain basic requirements for status determinations that affect all protected persons assessed under the MIP at sea, regardless of their nationality. First, protection seekers lack privacy in their interview with a PSO on board Coast Guard vessels. This fails to meet UNHCR ExCOM's basic requirement (iv) – 'necessary facilities'. As a former member of the Immigration and Nationality Service has reported, 'shipboard [status determination] interviews are never private because privacy is too difficult to achieve in that setting'.[83] Privacy is important for status determination interviews, as the protection seeker may fear that others on the vessel could report their claims to the government of their home countries, which may result in further persecution or torture. Therefore, lack of privacy could lead certain protected persons not to come forward with their protection concerns and thus fail to be identified and protected from *refoulement*, in breach of the United States' international obligations.

Second, the right to seek review of a status determination by an independent tribunal, identified under basic requirement (vi), is critical and is denied protected persons of all nationalities during status determinations both at sea and in Guantánamo Bay. It should be noted that whilst UNHCR ExCom posited in Conclusion No 8 that 'if the applicant is not recognised, he [or she] should be given a reasonable time to appeal for a formal reconsideration of the decision, either to the same or to a different authority', the UNHCR had changed its position by 2001 and found it unacceptable to have 'the same authority' conduct the review of a status determination.[84] UNHCR ExCom has identified 'an authority different from and independent of that making the initial decision', '[a] key procedural safeguard'.[85]

Rights of review, in particular the rights of review of a negative status determination,[86] are important in ensuring effectiveness, since denying

83 Telephone interview with an anonymous former INS employee (31 March 2001): Ibid 25.

84 See UNHCR, Global Consultations on International Protection/Third Track: Asylum Processes (Fair and Efficient Asylum Procedures), UN Doc EC/GC/01/12 (31 May 2001), [43].

85 Ibid.

86 Negative status determinations in particular should be subjected to review, as mistakes in granting protection from *refoulement* to individuals who did not need it would not place a State party in breach of its international obligations. However, an incorrect negative determination that may result in the *refoulement* of a protection seeker would breach a State party's international human rights and refugee law obligations.

access to review by an independent tribunal exposes protection seekers to increased danger of *refoulement*. Mistakes are possible during status determinations. An opportunity to have a decision reviewed safeguards against such mistakes. Furthermore, a review body has an advantage over the initial decision maker in so far as it can build on the articulated reasons of the first decision maker and to respond to the perceived weaknesses and strengths of the initial decision.[87] 'Thus, the second decision reflects not only increased attention to the main disputed issues, but also the combined insights of two decision makers'.[88]

As Legomsky also points out, a right to the review of a status determination can affect the initial asylum determination. Legomsky asserts

> [The] benefit of [a right to review is] considerable. In any asylum adjudication system, it might turn out that only a small proportion of unsuccessful claimants exercise their right of review. I submit, though, that the mere prospect of review encourages decision-makers to devote more care to the decision and to its articulation than they otherwise would. If that submission is right, then a review process accomplishes more in the vast majority of cases that never get to the review stage than in the smaller number that do.[89]

A right to seek review ensures not only accuracy in decision making but also fairness of procedure because it provides protection seekers with an opportunity to remedy any mistakes made in the initial decision. Here the importance of an *independent* review of a status determination must be stressed both for ensuring fairness and effectiveness. A right to seek review before a body that is removed from political considerations insulates decision makers from the political process and provides greater accuracy and impartiality.[90] The more a review body is independent vis-á-vis the initial decision maker, the more plausible it becomes that a decision would not be unduly influenced by the initial decision maker for the sake of expediency.[91] The denial of the right to independent review of status

87 Stephen Legomsky, 'Refugees, Administrative Tribunals, and Real Independence: Dangers Ahead for Australia' (1998) 76 *Washington University Law Quarterly* 243, 246.
88 Ibid.
89 Legomsky, n 71 in this chapter, 641.
90 Legomsky, n 87 in this chapter, 246.
91 Crépeau and Nakache, writing about the refugee determination process in Canada, argue that '[I]ndependence is a key feature of any tribunal. It is the precondition of credibility'.

determinations during the MIP thus places protected persons at grave risk of being returned to harm.

A further critical feature of a fair and effective status determination procedure is access to legal assistance that is denied protection seekers of all nationalities both at sea and in Guantánamo Bay. Several studies have shown that there is a clear correlation between having legal advice and the recognition of a refugee's status. Schoenholtz and Jacobs found in 2002 that asylum seekers who had legal assistance in the U.S. mainland were four to six times more likely to have their refugee status recognised by the United States as compared to asylum seekers who did not have the assistance of legal counsel.[92] In Schoenholtz and Jacobs's study, a legal advisor improved the chance of a refugee being recognised as needing protection regardless of the refugee's country of origin and at every stage of the determination process studied.[93] A study of legal advisors in Cairo, Egypt, has also found that refugees who had legal advice had nearly double the chance of having their refugee status recognised after a UNHCR interview than other, unrepresented asylum seekers.[94] As UNHCR has concluded:

> Asylum-seekers are often unable to articulate the elements relevant to an asylum claim without the assistance of a qualified counsellor because they are not familiar with the precise grounds for the recognition of refugee status and the legal system of a foreign country. Quality legal assistance and representation is, moreover, in the interest of States, as it can help to ensure that international protection needs are properly identified.[95]

Individuals at risk of *refoulement* under Article 3 of the CAT also benefit from access to legal advice for the same reasons as refugees do. Access to legal assistance ensures greater effectiveness of status determination

Their argument is equally applicable to status determinations undertaken by the US: François Crépeau and Delphine Nakache, 'Critical Space in the Canadian Refugee Determination System: 1989–2002' (2008) 20 *International Journal of Refugee Law* 50, 53.

92 Andrew Schoenholtz and Jonathan Jacobs, 'The State of Asylum Representation: Ideas for Change' (2002) 16 *Georgetown Immigration Law Journal* 739, 740.

93 Ibid.

94 Michael Kagan, 'Frontier Justice: Legal Aid and UNHCR Refugee Status Determination in Egypt' (2006) 19 *Journal of Refugee Studies* 45, 54.

95 UNHCR, *Fair and Efficient Asylum Procedures: A Non-Exhaustive Overview of Applicable International Standards* (2 September 2005), 3 <www.unhcr.org/refworld/pdfid/432ae9204.pdf>.

because it increases the likelihood that a State will recognise the protection needs of an individual at risk of being subjected to *refoulement*; it also provides greater fairness for protection seekers as they become more aware of their rights and can better articulate their claims. Thus the denial of access to legal assistance also increases the likelihood that protected persons will not have their protection needs recognised by the United States and will be subject to *refoulement* in violation of the United States' international obligations.

The need for legal assistance is particularly acute for protection seekers assessed at sea because protection seekers whose records are stored in the MITS do not have an opportunity to review the records or contest the accuracy of the information contained therein.[96] The inability to amend or contest inaccurate information is highly problematic in itself for it may result in future decision makers relying on erroneous information and thus failing to recognise protected persons. The United States should amend its procedures to provide protection seekers with an opportunity to review and amend information as part of the MITS. The presence of lawyers would also assist protection seekers in understanding the consequences of the information they provide to a PSO.

Finally, it should be noted that protection seekers at sea are denied the opportunity 'to contact a representative of UNHCR', which is basic requirement (iv) as outlined earlier. Furthermore, individuals recognised as refugees in Guantánamo Bay are not issued with documentation certifying their status, but are instead labelled as 'protected migrants'.[97] Failure to issue processed refugees with documentation certifying their refugee status leads the United States to fall short of a basic procedural requirement (v) that requires refugees to be 'informed accordingly and issued with documentation certifying his [or her] refugee status'.

5.4 Non-Discrimination

Another important feature of fair and effective status determinations, which is an intrinsic component of a State's *non-refoulement* obligations, is freedom from discrimination. Status determination procedures that deny

96 Department of Homeland Security, n 10 in this chapter, 12.

97 See Section 4.2 and the opening section of Chapter 6.

certain procedural safeguards to a subset of protection seekers because of their country of origin or nationality are discriminatory and hence unfair. They can also be ineffective because protected persons who are denied procedural safeguards may not have their protection needs recognised.

Discrimination during a status determination is also expressly prohibited in the Refugee Convention, ICCPR and the CERD. The inferior status determination procedures provided at sea for non-Cubans as compared to Cuban nationals place the United States in breach of its non-discrimination obligations under international refugee law and human rights law. These obligations will now be discussed in turn.

Article 3 of the Refugee Convention states 'The Contracting States shall apply the provisions of this Convention to refugees without discrimination as to race, religion or country of origin'. For the obligation under Article 3 of the Refugee Convention to be triggered, discrimination must be related to a further right under the Refugee Convention.[98] That is, a State is prohibited from discrimination between refugees when honouring obligations under the Refugee Convention. Article 3 can be breached if the provision of the Convention to which it is directly related is not itself violated,[99] but a State discriminates between refugees in applying that provision. Importantly, Article 3 can be triggered if a State discriminates in applying a law or policy related to a provision in the Refugee Convention even if on its face the law or policy is not directly linked to an interest protected by the Refugee Convention. Status determination procedures are an example of laws or policies that are linked to a State's *non-refoulement* obligation but are not expressly regulated by the Refugee Convention. Nevertheless, as Hathaway argues

> To the extent that it can be shown that a heightened risk of rejection is the foreseeable consequence of [a particular status determination procedure] an issue of compliance with Art.33's duty of *non-refoulement* arises. Because the duty of *non-refoulement* is set by the Convention

[98] Erick Roxtrom and Mark Gibney, 'The Legal and Ethical Obligations of UNHCR: The Case of Temporary Protection in Western Europe' in Niklaus Steiner, Mark Gibney and Gil Loescher (eds) *Problems of Protection: The UNHCR, Refugees and Human Rights* (Routledge, London, 2003) 278–79, n 52.

[99] Felix Marx and Weiebke Staff, 'Article 3 1951 Convention' in Andreas Zimmermann (ed) *The 1951 Convention Relating to the Status of Refugees and its 1967 Protocol: A Commentary* (Oxford University Press, 2011) 650.

> itself, the discriminatory nature of the ... inferior procedures can be challenged by reference to Art. 3's duty of non-discrimination.[100]

Therefore, the United States violates its obligation under Article 3 of the Refugee Convention by providing inferior status determination procedures to non-Cuban refugees on the basis of their nationality even in cases where the inferior status determinations do not result in actual *refoulement* and Article 33(1) of the Refugee Convention is not violated.

Discrimination is also prohibited under the ICCPR. Article 26 of the ICCPR provides

> All persons are equal before the law and are entitled without any discrimination to the equal protection of the law. In this respect, the law shall prohibit any discrimination and guarantee to all persons equal and effective protection against discrimination on any ground such as race, colour, sex, language, religion, political or other opinion, national or social origin, property, birth or other status.

Article 26 of the ICCPR imposes an obligation on the United States to refrain from discriminating on the grounds of an individual's national origin. The Article refers to equality before the law as well as equal protection of the law. Therefore, it prohibits discriminatory statutes that govern status determination procedures. The HR Committee has clarified that the provision 'prohibits discrimination in law *or in fact* in any field regulated and protected by public authorities'.[101] That is, Article 26 of the ICCPR is not only concerned with discriminatory municipal law; it also addresses the enforcement of any law[102] and prohibits discriminatory application of laws by public officials, including the exercise of discretion granted public officials under law.[103] As such, the United States is in breach of its obligation under Article 26 of the ICCPR in exercising the discretion provided for status determinations under Executive Order 12807 (Kennebunkport

[100] See Hathaway, n 100 in this chapter, 253.

[101] Human Rights Committee, *General Comment No 18: Non-Discrimination*, 37th Sess (10 November 1989), [12]. Emphasis added.

[102] Manfred Nowak, *UN Covenant on Civil and Political Rights: CCPR Commentary* (N.P Engel Publisher, 2nd ed., 2005) 606.

[103] Christian Tomuschat, 'Equality and Non-Discrimination under the International Covenant on Civil and Political Rights' in Hans-Jürgen Schlochauer and Ingo von Münch (eds) *Staatsrecht – Völkerrecht – Europarecht* (Walter de Gruyter, 1981) 707.

Order)[104] and Executive Order 13276.[105] This is because despite the neutral language of the Executive orders, public officials discriminate between protection seekers on the basis of their national origin.

A significant difference between Article 3 of the Refugee Convention and Article 26 of the ICCPR is that Article 26 of the ICCPR is 'a free-standing guarantee of non-discrimination in relation to all rights',[106] not just rights under the ICCPR itself. The CERD also contains a non-discrimination obligation that applies to all rights, not just rights under the CERD. Article 5 of the CERD states

> In compliance with the fundamental obligations laid down in article 2 of this Convention, States Parties undertake to prohibit and to eliminate racial discrimination in all its forms and to guarantee the right of everyone, without distinction as to race, colour, or national or ethnic origin, to equality before the law.

The right to be free from discrimination under Article 5 of the CERD is very broad for it calls for the elimination of racial discrimination (which includes discrimination on the grounds of national origin) in *all its forms*. Discriminating between Cuban and non-Cuban protection seekers on the basis of their national origin in determining their status therefore place the United States in breach of its obligations under Article 5 of the CERD.

5.5 The Need for Status Determinations to Be Conducted in the U.S. Mainland

The United States must respect its obligations to refrain from discrimination and *refoulement* when conducting status determinations under the MIP. It is theoretically possible, if difficult in practice, for the United States to meet the international obligations outlined in this chapter to protected persons in international waters and in Guantánamo Bay. For example, the United States could refrain from discriminating on the

104 57 *Federal Register* 23, 133 (1992) as amended by Executive Order 13286, see n 16 in this chapter.
105 67 *Federal Register* 69 (2002) as amended by Executive Order 13286, see n 19 in this chapter.
106 Sarah Joseph, and Melissa Castan, *The International Covenant on Civil and Political Right: Cases, Materials, and Commentary* (Oxford University Press, 3rd ed., 2013) 768.

grounds of the nationality of protection seekers by providing all protection seekers with the same rights as it does Cuban protection seekers during status determinations at sea. To do this, the United States would need to read a statement alerting all protection seekers to their right to seek protection, provide all protection seekers with the opportunity to raise protection claims with a PSO and ensure that interpreters are present on every Coast Guard vessel for all languages spoken by protection seekers, in particular Creole.

The United States' non-discrimination obligations would also be met by removing the privileged status of Cuban nationals and subjecting all protection seekers to the inferior status determination process of non-Cubans. However, it is important to emphasise that removing the discrimination suffered by non-Cuban protection seekers in any form would not make the United States compliant with all of the breaches of its international obligations outlined earlier. The United States would still need to address the lack of fairness and effectiveness in its status determination procedures under the MIP to ensure that it is not in breach of any *non-refoulement* obligation to protected persons in the MIP. Creating inferior status determination procedures for all protection seekers by simply removing the privileges afforded to Cubans would lead status determinations for all protection seekers to become less fair and effective and thus place the United States in greater danger of violating its *non-refoulement* obligations.

Greater safeguards that would result in fair and effective procedures outside the U.S. mainland are also not impossible in theory but would be very difficult in practice. For example, privacy is an important procedural safeguard that is currently absent in status determinations on board Coast Guard vessels. To provide greater privacy, the United States would need to provide purpose-built interview facilities on board Coast Guard cutters, or to transfer all protection seekers to another vessel or State for status determinations.

The absence of access to legal assistance was also identified as a factor in fair and effective status determinations. The United States could provide all interdicted protection seekers with access to legal counsel under the MIP, but to do this some lawyers would need to travel with the Coast Guard and some lawyers would need to be stationed in Guantánamo Bay. Access to independent advice from lawyers via the telephone would be a more practical compromise to ensure that protection seekers are provided access to some assistance; however, establishing trust between protection seekers and legal counsel and ensuring effective communication would be difficult over the telephone and would diminish the effectiveness of the assistance that could be provided.

Finally, providing a right to seek independent review of status determinations was also identified in this chapter as an important feature of fair and effective status determination procedures. To provide such a right under the MIP, the United States would need to establish an independent tribunal that could fairly and effectively assess the protection needs of protection seekers. Alternatively, the United States could change existing municipal law so that review bodies operating in the U.S. mainland, such as the Board of Immigration Appeals and U.S. courts, could review determinations regarding the status of protection seekers under the MIP. The review bodies would need to make determinations very quickly to ensure that protection seekers on board Coast Guard vessels received a review of their status determination prior to their repatriation. Very short turnaround times and the difficulty of communicating with protection seekers in international waters would make the task of fair and effective review of status determinations by an independent body practically unworkable.

A much easier and more certain way of ensuring the United States' compliance with its international obligations would be for status determinations to be conducted in the U.S. mainland. The link between compliance with a State's *non-refoulement* obligation under the Refugee Convention and access to territory has been made by refugee scholars and the UNHCR but is equally applicable to people owed protection against *refoulement* under the CAT and the ICCPR. As Hathaway points out, where there is a real risk of persecution due to a Convention ground, a duty of *non-refoulement* amounts to 'a *de facto* duty to admit the refugee since admission is normally the only means of avoiding the alternative, impermissible consequence of exposure to risk'.[107] The UNHCR ExCom in its 1997 Conclusions on Safeguarding Asylum considered it timely to draw attention to the importance of the principle of *refoulement* and the need 'to *admit refugees into the territories of States*, which includes no

[107] Hathaway, n 100 in this chapter, 301.

rejection at frontiers without fair and effective procedures for determining status and protection needs'.[108]

The UNHCR ExCom in its 1998 Conclusion strongly deplored the *refoulement* of refugees and reiterated

> the need to *admit refugees to the territory of States*, which includes no rejection at frontiers without access to fair and effective procedures for determining their status and protection needs.[109]

Finally, in its Protection Policy Paper on Maritime Interception Operations the UNHCR noted in 2010 'that claims for international protection made by intercepted persons are in principle to be processed in procedures within the territory of the intercepting State'.[110] Thus admission of protection seekers in the MIP to the U.S. mainland complies with best-practice models identified by the UNHCR.

In addition, the United States must put in place procedures for the identification and protection from *refoulement* of persons at risk of death or cruel, inhuman or degrading treatment or punishment if repatriated who are not refugees or at risk of torture. The U.S.' denial of its *non-refoulement* obligations under the ICCPR places protected persons at risk of being returned to harm, in violation of the United States' obligations.

5.6 Conclusion

The urgency of the need for changes to the MIP, in particular to status determinations at sea, is evident in the alarming statistic that between 1996 and 2013, only 404 Cuban nationals,[111] of the 24,021 interdicted,[112] were found to have a credible fear of persecution or torture and were transferred

[108] UNHCR ExCom, *Conclusion No 82: Conclusion on Safeguarding Asylum*, 48th sess, UN Doc A/52/12/Add.1 (17 October 1997), [d].

[109] UNHCR ExCom, *Conclusion No 85: Conclusion on International Protection'*, 49th sess, UN Doc A/53/12/Add.1 (9 October 1998), [q]. Emphasis added.

[110] UNHCR, *Protection Policy Paper: Maritime Interception Operations and the Processing of International Protection Claims* (November 2010) <www.unhcr.org/refworld/docid/4cd12d3a2.html>.

[111] E-mail to author from PRM Press, Bureau of Population, Refugees, and Migration, U.S. Department of State, 15 July 2014 (on file with author).

[112] U.S. Coast Guard, *Statistics: Alien Migrant Interdiction* <www.uscg.mil/hq/cg5/cg531/AMIO/FlowStats/currentstats.asp>.

to Guantánamo Bay. That is, less than 1.7 per cent of all Cuban nationals interdicted were identified as having any form of protection needs under the MIP.[113] More alarmingly still, in the same time period, only 21 of the 27,685 Haitians interdicted by the United States[114] – less than 0.07 per cent of Haitians interdicted – were the only other group to be found to have a credible fear of persecution or torture and were transferred to Guantánamo Bay for further status determination.[115]

The statistics on status determinations at sea provided here do not in and of themselves prove the problematic nature of status determinations in international waters. There is, for example, the possibility that individuals who were subject to status determination at sea during the period identified were not persons in need of protection from *refoulement* under international law. However, when viewed in light of the preceding analysis, the statistics support the evidence, provided in this chapter, that protected persons in the MIP are likely to be subjected to *refoulement*, at sea in contravention of the United States' international obligations.

The denial of rights to protected persons in the MIP is not, however, limited to the process of status determinations. The next chapter builds on the discussion in this chapter by showing that individuals who gain recognition of their protection needs in Guantánamo Bay are subjected to further breaches of their rights under international human rights and refugee law.

[113] In contrast, all Cubans who reached the U.S. mainland were eligible to apply for an adjustment of status after one year under the *Cuban Adjustment Act* of 1966. See Section 2.2.

[114] E-mail to author from PRM Press, see n 111 in this chapter.

[115] Ibid.

6

Detention and Related Issues in Guantánamo Bay

In Chapter 5 this book focused on status determination procedures and the United States' failure to comply with its legal obligations during interdiction operations. Protection seekers undergoing status determinations are not, however, the only group to be denied rights under the MIP. The very few protection seekers fortunate enough to have their protection needs recognised must endure long waits at the Migrant Operations Center (MOC) in Guantánamo Bay, where they are denied many rights, prior to being resettled in a third country.

As explained in Chapter 2, the United States first introduced an offshore processing and immigration detention facility in Guantánamo Bay in 1991 as a response to the mass movement of Haitians fleeing the rule of the junta leader, Raoul Cédras.[1] The MOC began as a series of tent cities guarded by U.S. troops and surrounded by barbed wire. The centre has, however, become much more sophisticated over time. Individuals at the MOC are now housed in an apartment-style setting,[2] and the facility is used to accommodate all who are found to have a credible fear of persecution or torture during interdiction operations at sea or make their way to the U.S. naval base in search of protection.

The United States and its service providers separate individuals at the MOC into three categories: 'non-protected migrants' are individuals who have been found not to be refugees and are not considered to be at risk of torture if repatriated (members of this group are repatriated very quickly,

[1] See subsection 2.1.2.

[2] U.S. Immigration and Customs Enforcement, *Fact Sheet: Guantánamo Bay Migrant Operations* (23 July 2004) <http://web.archive.org/web/20070711063736/http://www.ice.gov/pi/news/factsheets/072304gitmo.htm>.

if possible, normally within twenty-four hours); 'undetermined migrants' are individuals seeking protection whose status has not yet been resolved; and 'protected migrants' are refugees or individuals who are more likely than not to be tortured if returned to their home countries,[3] what this book refers to as 'protected persons' or the 'protected population'.[4]

The use of the term 'migrants' to describe refugees whose status is confirmed pursuant to a status determination procedure in Guantánamo Bay highlights the United States' unwillingness, discussed earlier in Chapters 4 and 5, to accept its *non-refoulement* obligation under international refugee law outside its municipally defined territory. However, the choice of terminology adopted by the United States in no way obviates its obligation to afford refugees the rights owed to them under the Refugee Convention[5] and Refugee Protocol,[6] wherever the United States exercises jurisdiction, including in Guantánamo Bay.[7]

The vast majority of individuals transferred to Guantánamo Bay under the U.S. interdiction program are never permitted to enter the U.S. mainland, even if they are assessed as having a well-founded fear of persecution or to be at risk of *refoulement* to torture.[8] For example, of the 100 people found to have protection needs in Guantánamo Bay in the period from 1 October 2009 to 5 August 2014 only 5 were admitted or paroled into the U.S. mainland.[9] As a

3 Contract between Wackenhut Corrections Corporation, GEO Group and the United States. Requisition/Reference Number: DRO-3M-RQ0216, DRO-04-RQ0314, DRO-06-RQ0333, DRO-05-003A, FOW060019A, DDP-07-235, FDNDRO070027.1 # .2. See also Sonia Farber, 'Forgotten at Guantánamo: The Boumediene Decision and Its Implications for Refugees at the Base Under the Obama Administration' (2010) 98 *California Law Review* 989, 990.

4 This is to avoid conflating the category of 'refugee', which is a legally defined status that carries certain obligation on behalf of States parties to the Refugee Convention and Refugee Protocol, with the category of 'migrant' which is not an internationally protected status.

5 Opened for signature 28 July 1951, 189 UNTS 150 (entered into force 22 April 1954).

6 Opened for signature 31 January 1967, 606 UNTS 267 (entered into force 4 October 1967).

7 The United States became party to the Refugee Protocol on 1 November 1968 but is not party to the Refugee Convention. However, as a result of being party to the Refugee Protocol, the United States is obliged to abide by Articles 2 to 34 inclusive of the Refugee Convention.

8 Harold Hongju Koh, Sterling Professor of International Law, Yale Law School, former Legal Adviser, U.S. Department of State from 2009 to 2013, *The Globalization of High Seas Interdiction: Sale's Legacy and Beyond* (Yale Law School, 8 March 2014).

9 U.S. Immigration and Customs Enforcement, ICE FOIA Case Number 2014-ICFO-03555 (30 September 2014), copy on file with author; Interview with Deputy Assistant Secretary Bureau of Population, Refugees, and Migration, U.S. Department of State (Fairfax, Virginia, 25 October 2008). The U.S. mainland refers to the municipally defined territory of the United States under INA § 101(a)38; 8 USC § 1101(a)(38). See Section 1.2.

consequence, the vast majority of individuals in the protected category must endure lengthy and potentially indefinite waits in this isolated location prior to being resettled in a third country. The longest period between the recognition of protection needs and resettlement from Guantánamo Bay has been four years.[10] Resettlement countries for individuals found to have protection needs in Guantánamo Bay have included Australia, Canada, Slovakia, Costa Rica, the Netherlands, Spain, Honduras, Guatemala, the Czech Republic, Hungary, Uruguay, Argentina, Venezuela and Bolivia.[11] This chapter provides an analysis of the United States' compliance with its international obligations towards the protected population in Guantánamo Bay.

6.1 Arrangements in Guantánamo Bay

The MOC has the capacity to accommodate 130 individuals with additional capacity for approximately 400 individuals in the event of a surge.[12] The facility can house single men and women, families and even unaccompanied children.[13] On 8 February 2012, MVM Inc., a private security company, was awarded the contract for provision of security services at and operation of the MOC with four one-year renewal option periods.[14]

[10] E-mail to author from Deputy Assistant Secretary Bureau of Population, Refugees, and Migration, U.S. Department of State, 14 November 2008 (on file with author). In July 2014, eight people were awaiting resettlement in Guantánamo Bay under the MIP. They had been there for periods ranging from nine months to more than two years: e-mail to author from PRM Press, Bureau of Population, Refugees, and Migration, U.S. Department of State, 15 July 2014 (on file with author).

[11] U.S. Immigration and Customs Enforcement, n 9 in this chapter; interview with Deputy Assistant Secretary Bureau of Population, Refugees, and Migration, U.S. Department of State (Fairfax, Virginia, 25 October 2008); e-mail to author from Deputy Assistant Secretary Bureau of Population, Refugees, and Migration, U.S. Department of State, 14 November 2008 (on file with author).

[12] GEO Group, *Guantánamo Bay (GTMO) Migrant Operations Center* (2008) <www.thegeogroupinc.com/locations_na.asp>. The GEO Group, previously known as the Wackenhut Corrections Corporation, a company that operates private prisons in the United States and abroad, provided 'Management and Operations [as well as] unarmed custody officers' in Guantánamo Bay for the U.S. government between 2006 and 2012.

[13] Ibid.

[14] Federal Business Opportunities, *Guard Services for the Migrant Operations Center* (8 February 2012) <www.fbo.gov/index?s=opportunity&mode=form&tab=core&id=264814fc2dd263475076cde797036eec>. This is at a cost of $2,319,711.76 for the base year and $8,556,801.24 over the four one-year option periods for a total of $10,876,513.00.

Members of the protected population are provided with community liaison assistance, translation and interpreting services, education and recreation programs and employment facilitation by the International Organization for Migration (IOM).[15] The protected population is also provided with medical and dental care, may establish bank accounts and can attend religious services.[16]

The United States does not deny that individuals awaiting status determination and those found not to have protection needs are detained. However, the United States argues that the protected population is not detained in Guantánamo Bay. According to the website for the U.S. Immigration and Customs Enforcement, the protected population

> is not incarcerated or detained. They live in a relatively unrestricted environment, and have substantial freedom of movement in that they are permitted to sign themselves in and out of the facility to participate in activities on the leeward side of the base.[17]

Whilst the protected population may leave the MOC during the day, they have a curfew and must return to the MOC by 11 PM each night.[18] They are also required to account for their whereabouts at all time.[19]

Furthermore, despite enjoying the right to leave the MOC during the day, the freedom of movement of the protected population is severely limited by the geography of Guantánamo Bay. Guantánamo Bay is a relatively small military naval base. As shown on the map in Figure 4, it is divided into two distinct areas by the 4-kilometre-wide bay. The MOC is located on the lower part of the west side of the bay, which is commonly referred to as the Leeward side. Much of the rest of the lower part of the Leeward side is occupied by an airfield and hosts the Department of Defense, the Coast Guard and chartered commercial aircraft. Members of

15 E-mail from Regional Coordinator, Media and External Relations IOM to author, 27 October 2008 (on file with author).

16 U.S. Immigration and Customs Enforcement, n 2 in this chapter.

17 Ibid.

18 Carol Rosenberg, 'Cuban Migrants at Guantánamo Base "Broke Rules", Face Restrictions' *Miami Herald*, 7 February 2012 <www.miamiherald.com/2012/02/07/2629897/cuban-migrants-at-Guantánamo-base.html>.

19 Harold Hongju Koh, Sterling Professor of International Law, Yale Law School, former Legal Adviser, U.S. Department of State from 2009 to 2013, *The Globalization of High Seas Interdiction: Sale's Legacy and Beyond* (Yale Law School, 8 March 2014).

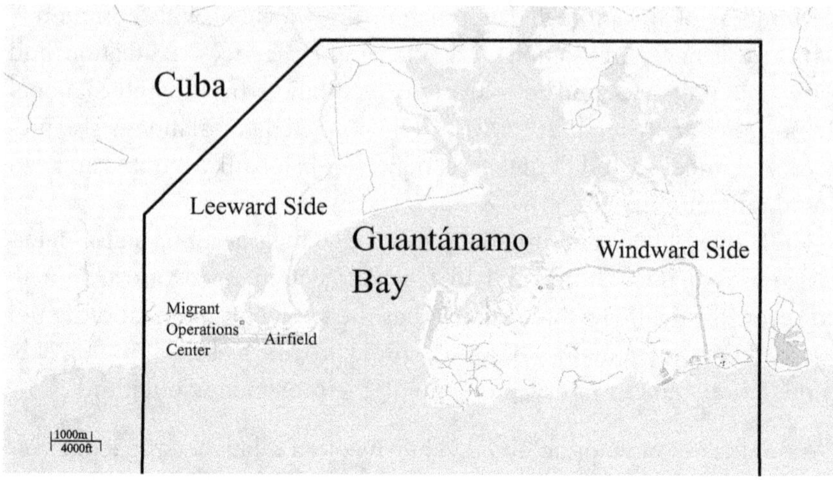

Figure 4. Map of Guantánamo Bay. Open Street Maps <www.openstreetmap.org/>. Modifications by author.

the protected population are subjected to significant restrictions on their movement in the airfield and surrounding areas 'due to security concerns surrounding other [U.S. naval base] missions'.[20] Furthermore, much of the Leeward side of Guantánamo Bay is strictly forbidden and reserved for military exercises.[21] The rest of the Leeward side is desolate and undeveloped, and there is therefore very little for the protected population to do.

The eastern side of the base is commonly referred to as the Windward side, and is where the detention facilities in the 'war on terror' are located. The Windward side of Guantánamo Bay is considerably more developed than the Leeward side is. Several commercial enterprises, including McDonald's and Subway restaurants, a Wal-Mart shopping mall and even a gift shop currently operate on the Windward side of Guantánamo Bay. The Windward side also contains a school, a hospital, a sports arena, an outdoor cinema, a nine-hole golf course and a large church. In contrast with the Windward side, 'little of the business of [Guantánamo] is done on the Leeward side of the Bay.'[22]

[20] U.S. Immigration and Customs Enforcement, n 2 in this chapter.

[21] Precise information regarding the exact areas in Guantánamo Bay in which military exercises are undertaken have not been made publically available by the United States.

[22] Defense System Journal, *Inside GTMO* <www.dsjournal.com/insidegtmo.html>.

A ferry is available between the Leeward side and the Windward side, although individuals in the protected category are only permitted to participate in activities on the Windward side of the base with an escort.[23] This is in part to ensure that the protected population do not disturb activities on the Windward side of Guantánamo Bay and do not engage in disorderly behaviour.

Given the severe restrictions on the movement of the protected population within the narrow space of the Leeward side of Guantánamo Bay, the question arises as to whether or not the protected population is in fact detained.

6.2 Detention in Guantánamo Bay

Detention is governed under the ICCPR by Article 9(1), which provides:

> Everyone has the right to liberty and security of person. No one shall be subjected to arbitrary arrest or detention. No one shall be deprived of his liberty except on such grounds and in accordance with such procedure as are established by law.

A determination as to whether or not the United States complies with its obligations under Article 9 of the ICCPR with regard to the protected population in Guantánamo Bay raises three separate questions: (1) Are individuals awaiting resettlement in Guantánamo Bay detained for the purposes of Article 9 of the ICCPR? (2) If so, is this detention 'arbitrary'? (3) Do detainees have a right to challenge their detention in a court of law?

6.2.1 Is the Protected Population Detained in Guantánamo Bay?

Turning first to the issue of detention under Article 9 of the ICCPR, the HR Committee has stated that 'deprivation of liberty involves more severe restrictions of motion within a narrower space than mere interference with liberty of movement under article 12',[24] which governs freedom of

[23] E-mail from Bureau of Population, Refugees, and Migration, U.S. Department of State, 20 May 2013 (on file with author).

[24] Human Rights Committee, *General Comment No 35 – Article 9: Liberty and Security of Person*, 112th sess, UN Doc CCPR/C/GC/35 (28 Oct 2014), [5]. This General Comment replaced Human Rights Committee, *General Comment No 8: Right to Liberty and Security of Persons (Art. 9)*, 16th sess, UN Doc 30/06/82 (30 June 1982).

movement.[25] However, the HR Committee has not clarified at what point restrictions of motion will be of such severity as to constitute deprivation of liberty, nor what size space will lead to the characterisation of an area as a place of detention. In other words, it is not clear from this statement from the Committee whether the limitations placed on the movement of protected persons (including curfews) due to military exercises and other activities on the U.S. naval base, in the relatively narrow space of the Leeward side of Guantánamo Bay, constitutes detention.

In *Celepli v Sweden*,[26] the HR Committee expressed the view that confinement of the author to his home municipality of Västerhaninge, a town of approximately 9.32 square kilometres which at that time had a population of 10,000 inhabitants, did not constitute 'deprivation of liberty within the meaning of Article 9 of the Covenant.'[27] Mr Celepli was required to report to the police three times per week and to seek permission before changing his employment or residence.

In *Karker v France*,[28] limitation of movement under a compulsory residence order to 15.6 square kilometres and later 117.07 square kilometres was also found not to constitute 'deprivation of liberty' for the purposes of Article 9(1) of the ICCPR.[29] The HR Committee observed that the residency order

> allowed [the author] to reside in a comparatively wide area. Moreover, the restrictions on Mr Karker's freedom of movement were examined by the domestic courts which, after reviewing all the evidence, held them to be necessary for reasons of national security.[30]

The restrictions placed on members of the protected population in Guantánamo Bay are considerably more severe than those that had been placed on Mr Celepli or Mr Karker. Members of the protected population are subjected to a curfew, a restriction that was not placed on either Mr Celepli or Mr Karker. Unlike Mr Celepli, who was required to report his whereabouts three times per week, and Mr Karker, who was required to

[25] Freedom of movement under Article 12 of the ICCPR is considered in Section 6.3.
[26] UN Doc CCPR/C/51/D/456/1991 (18 July 1994).
[27] Ibid [5.2].
[28] UN Doc CCPR/C/70/D/833/1998 (26 October 2000).
[29] Ibid [8.5].
[30] Ibid [9.3].

report once per day, members of the protected population must account for their whereabouts at all times.[31] Significantly, Mr Celepli and Mr Karker were not taken to a prison island; rather, their movement was restricted within an area in which they were already residing. Thus, the restrictions placed on Mr Celepli and Mr Karker were less severe than those placed on the protected population who are confined to a restricted area within a foreign military base rather than their homes. The difference in the severity of the restrictions on the protected population as compared to Mr Celepli and Mr Karker is determinative of whether or not their situation is one of 'detention'.

Unfortunately, the HR Committee did not clarify, in the communications discussed above, what circumstances would constitute a deprivation of liberty or detention. Therefore, whilst it can be argued that individuals in the situation of Mr Karker or Mr Celepli are not deprived of their liberty or detained, greater guidance is needed from the HR Committee to clarify under what circumstances an individual can be said to be detained pursuant to Article 9 of the ICCPR.

In the Concluding Observations on the United Kingdom of Great Britain and Northern Ireland, in 2008, the HR Committee did express concern about a control order regime under the *Terrorism Act 2005* 'which involved the imposition of a wide range of restrictions including curfews'.[32] By citing Article 9 of the ICCPR (which regulates detention) rather than Article 12(1) of the ICCPR (which regulates freedom of movement) as a provision of the ICCPR implicated by the control orders, the HR Committee suggested that the control orders could constitute detention. That is, the Committee suggested that curfews of the kind under the *Terrorism Act* 2005, in combination with other restrictions, could constitute detention.

The curfews considered by the HR Committee were for sixteen hours. Although members of the protected population have a curfew of 11 PM, it is

[31] It should be noted, however, that Mr Karker complained of being subject to additional around-the-clock surveillance by the police. See ibid [5.2].

[32] Human Rights Committee, *Concluding Observations of the Human Rights Committee: United Kingdom of Great Britain and Northern Ireland*, UN Doc CCPR/C/GBR/CO/6 (30 July 2008), [17]. This Concluding Observation was cited with approval by the Committee in Human Rights Committee, *General Comment No 35 – Article 9: Liberty and Security of Person*, 112th sess, UN Doc CCPR/C/GC/35 (28 Oct 2014), [5], n 4.

not known what time in the morning they are permitted to leave the MOC. Therefore, a direct comparison with the curfews under the *Terrorism Act* 2005 is not possible. Furthermore, the HR Committee was unclear as to which other elements in the 'wide range of restrictions' under the *Terrorism Act* 2005 contributed to the characterisation of the restrictions under the *Terrorism Act* 2005 as detention. What the HR Committee's statement does suggest, however, is that certain restrictions, including curfews, can be an element of detention under certain circumstances. Greater guidance is needed from the HR Committee to confirm this and to resolve the current state of uncertainty in this area.

Some additional guidance regarding the definition of 'deprivation of liberty' is provided by the European Court of Human Rights with regard to Article 5(1) of the *Convention for the Protection of Human Rights and Fundamental Freedoms* (ECHR).[33] Article 5(1) of the ECHR states

> Everyone has the right to liberty and security of person. No one shall be deprived of his liberty save in [a number of limited] cases and in accordance with a procedure prescribed by law.

The findings of the European Court of Human Rights regarding Article 5 of the ECHR are helpful for present purposes because the drafters of the ICCPR were guided by Article 5 of the ECHR when drafting Article 9(1) of the ICCPR.[34] That is, given the derivative nature of Article 9(1) of the ICCPR to Article 5 of the ECHR, the reasoning of the European Court of Human Rights can assist in determining whether the United States has deprived protection seekers in Guantánamo Bay of their liberty.

The jurisprudence of the European Court of Human Rights holds that the question of whether or not an individual is deprived of his or her liberty is a question of the 'degree or intensity, and not one of nature or substance' of the restrictions.[35] That is, it is the cumulative impact of the restrictions that must be considered in determining whether or not an individual is detained. The leading judgment for this proposition is *Guzzardi v Italy*,[36] which concerned a suspected member of the Italian Mafia. Mr Guzzardi

33 Opened for signature 4 November 1950, 213 UNTS 222 (entered into force 3 September 1953).

34 Manfred Nowak, *UN Covenant on Civil and Political Rights: CCPR Commentary* (N.P Engel Publisher, 2nd ed., 2005) 216.

35 *Amuur v France* (1996) 22 EHRR 533, [42].

36 [1981] 3 EHRR 333.

was arrested in 1973 for conspiracy and for being an accomplice in an abduction. He was placed in detention on remand in Milan. According to Italian domestic law at the time, the detention on remand of Mr Guzzardi could not continue for more than two years. Subsequently, in 1975, Mr Guzzardi was removed from the jail in Milan and taken to the island of Asinara (which lies off the north-west tip of Sardinia) where he was ordered to remain for three years. The island is approximately 52 square kilometres. The Italian government argued in the case that Mr Guzzardi was free to move around on the island, but Mr Guzzardi claimed that he was limited to a radius of approximately 800 meters. Mr Guzzardi could apply for authorisation to visit Sardinia or the Italian mainland if he had good reasons, such as for medical treatment, family matters or because of a court order. Any visits outside of the island were made with strict supervision of the police. Mr Guzzardi was also permitted to go to Porto Torres to shop at least once per week. Mr Guzzardi was housed in one of two buildings on the island and was not permitted to leave his accommodation between 10 PM and 7 AM except in case of necessity and after having notified the authorities in due time. Mr Guzzardi was also permitted to work if he wished to do so and could find employment.

The European Court of Human Rights accepted the Italian government's reasoning that Mr Guzzardi's treatment was very different from 'classic detention in prison or strict arrest imposed on a serviceman'.[37] However, the Court found

> Deprivation of liberty may, however, take numerous other forms. Their variety is being increased by developments in legal standards and in attitudes.... Whilst the area around which the applicant could move far exceeded the dimensions of a cell and was not bounded by any physical barrier, it covered no more than a tiny fraction of an island to which access was difficult.[38]

After considering the number of restrictions placed upon Mr Guzzardi, the Court concluded

> It is admittedly not possible to speak of "deprivation of liberty" on the strength of any one of [the restrictions placed on Mr Guzzardi] taken

[37] Ibid [95].
[38] Ibid.

> individually, *but cumulatively and in combination* they certainly raise an issue of categorization from the viewpoint of Article 5 [of the ECHR]. In certain respects the treatment complained of resembles detention in an "open prison" or committal to a disciplinary unit.[39]

Therefore, in combination, the restrictions set out above led the European Court of Human Rights to find that Mr Guzzardi had been subjected to a deprivation of liberty.

The European Court of Human Rights was also asked to consider whether restricting the movement of asylum seekers in a French airport transit zone and a hotel constituted detention in *Amuur v France*.[40] The Court relied on its earlier decision of *Guzzardi v. Italy*, stating

> In order to determine whether someone has been "deprived of his liberty" within the meaning of Article 5 (art. 5) [of the ECHR] the starting-point must be his concrete situation, and account must be taken of a whole range of criteria such as the *type, duration, effects and manner of implementation of the measure* in question. *The difference between deprivation of and restriction upon liberty is merely one of degree or intensity, and not one of nature or substance.*[41]

The European Court of Human Rights found in *Amuur v France* that confinement of asylum seekers at an airport's transit zone and the Hotel Arcade for twenty days constituted a 'deprivation of liberty' under Article 5 of the ECHR.

Applying the reasoning of the European Court of Human Rights in the cases of *Guzzardi v Italy* and *Amuur v France* to the analogous situation of the protected population in Guantánamo Bay, it is clear that in combination, the restrictions placed on the protected population lead to a deprivation of their liberty and, like Mr Guzzardi, their treatment resembles detention in an 'open prison'.[42] Like Mr Guzzardi, members of the protected population in Guantánamo Bay are permitted to work and walk around a restricted area, although they have the additional requirement of signing in and out of the MOC. Like Mr Guzzardi, their motion on the island is limited. Like Mr Guzzardi, members of the protected population

39 Ibid. Emphasis added.
40 (1996) 22 *EHRR* 533.
41 Ibid [42]. Emphasis added.
42 *Guzzardi v Italy* [1981] 3 EHRR 333, [95].

have a curfew. Unlike Mr Guzzardi, however, whose detention was fixed to end after the completion of his compulsory residence order, members of the protected population awaiting resettlement in a third country have no fixed end date to their detention (since finding resettlement places in third countries does not follow a predictable timeframe). The detention of the protected population is also longer than that considered by the European Court of Human Rights in *Amuur v France*.

A factor contributing to the characterisation of the restrictions on Mr Guzzardi as detention was the fact that there 'were few opportunities for social contacts available to the applicant other than with his near family, his fellow "residents" and the supervisory staff'.[43] The social isolation of members of the protected population in Guantánamo Bay is more severe than that of Mr Guzzardi. For example, whereas Mr Guzzardi could be joined by his family, members of the protected population are isolated from members of their family who are not in Guantánamo Bay. Furthermore, whereas Mr Guzzardi could visit Sardinia or the Italian mainland if he had good reasons, members of the protected population are prevented from entering the U.S. mainland. Cumulatively and in combination, therefore, the restrictions placed on the protected population in Guantánamo Bay can be seen to constitute deprivation of liberty or detention.

The UNHCR also supports the idea that it is the cumulative impact of restrictions on detainees rather than where they are detained that constitutes detention. The UNHCR has defined detention as

> deprivation of liberty or confinement in a closed place which an asylum-seeker is *not permitted to leave at will* ... Distinctions between deprivation of liberty (detention) and lesser restrictions on movement is one of "degree or intensity and not one of nature or substance".[44]

As such, given the degree and intensity of the restrictions on the protected population in Guantánamo Bay, and the fact that members of the

[43] Ibid.

[44] UNHCR, *Guidelines on the Applicable Criteria and Standards Relating to the Detention of Asylum-Seekers and Alternatives to Detention* (2012) <www.unhcr.org/refworld/docid/503489533b8.html>, 9. These guidelines replace the UNHCR, *Revised Guidelines on Applicable Criteria and Standards relating to the Detention of Asylum-Seekers* (1999) <www.unhcr.org/refworld/docid/3c2b3f844.html>.

protected population are not permitted to leave at will, it is highly likely that the UNHCR would also view their situation as one of detention.

6.2.2 Prohibition of Arbitrary Detention

Having established that the protected population in Guantánamo Bay is liable to be viewed as 'detained', the question arises as to whether this detention is *arbitrary* within the meaning of the second sentence of Article 9(1) of the ICCPR. To avoid the characterisation of detention as 'arbitrary', it is not enough that detention be justified by law; the law itself must not be arbitrary. The HR Committee has stated

> The notion of "arbitrariness" is not to be equated with "against the law", but must be interpreted more broadly to include elements of inappropriateness, injustice, lack of predictability, and due process of law, as well as elements of reasonableness, necessity, and proportionality.[45]

The term 'arbitrary' is not defined under the ICCPR, and there are some uncertainties as to its meaning. In drafting Article 9(1) of the ICCPR, there was an initial attempt to prohibit detention except in cases provided by an exhaustive list 'corresponding to those set down in Article 5(1) of the ECHR in 1950'.[46] However, it soon became clear during the drafting process that no agreement could be reached on a list of permissible reasons for detention. Thus, a proposal by Australia to prohibit 'arbitrary detention' rather than provide a catalogue of reasons to justify detention akin to Article 5(1) of the ECHR was adopted.[47] In light of the desire during the drafting process to capture the categories of detention explicitly listed under Article 5(1) of the ECHR, it can be inferred that the listed categories of detention under Article 5(1) of the ECHR are not inherently 'arbitrary' under the ICCPR.[48] This includes Article 5(1)(f) of the ECHR, which provides an exception to the prohibition against the deprivation of liberty in

45 Human Rights Committee, *General Comment No 35 – Article 9: Liberty and Security of Person*, 112th sess, UN Doc CCPR/C/GC/35 (28 Oct 2014), [12]. See also *Van Alphen v The Netherlands*, UN Doc CCPR/C/39/D/305/1988 (15 August 1990), [5.8].

46 Nowak, n 34 in this chapter, 216.

47 Ibid 218.

48 Ibid 225.

the case of 'the lawful arrest or detention of a person to prevent his effecting an unauthorized entry into the country or of a person against whom action is being taken with a view to deportation or extradition'.

Thus, detention for the purposes of preventing entry into a State party would not *ipso facto* constitute arbitrary detention.[49] This was confirmed by the HR Committee in A *v Australia*,[50] which concerned a complaint by a Cambodian asylum seeker that Australia had violated his rights under the ICCPR by detaining him in immigration detention for more than four years. The HR Committee stated that there is no basis to argue that

> it is *per se* arbitrary to detain individuals requesting asylum. Nor [did the HR Committee] find any support for the contention that there is a rule of customary international law which would render all [immigration] detention arbitrary.[51]

However, the HR Committee expressed the view that 'detention should not continue beyond the period for which the State can provide appropriate justification'.[52] In A *v Australia*, the HR Committee also stated

> [R]emand in custody could be considered arbitrary if it is not necessary in all the circumstances of the case, for example to prevent flight or interference with evidence. The element of proportionality becomes relevant in this context.[53]

Australia argued that the detention was justified on the grounds that the asylum seeker in question 'entered Australia unlawfully' and also by the perceived incentive for the asylum seeker to 'abscond if left in liberty'.[54] The HR Committee did not accept this justification and found the asylum seeker's detention to be arbitrary. In *Shafiq v Australia*,[55] which also considered the mandatory detention of an asylum seeker in Australia, the HR Committee succinctly reiterated the view first expressed in A *v*

[49] The HR Committee hold the view that detention 'in the course of proceedings for the control of immigration is not *per se* arbitrary'; Human Rights Committee, *General Comment No 35 – Article 9: Liberty and Security of Person*, 112th sess, UN Doc CCPR/C/GC/35 (28 Oct 2014), [18].

[50] A *v Australia*, UN Doc CCPR/C/59/D/560/1993 (30 April 1997).

[51] Ibid [9.3].

[52] Ibid [9.2].

[53] Ibid.

[54] Ibid.

[55] UN Doc CCPR/C/88/D/1324/2004 (13 November 2006).

Australia that 'remand in custody could be considered arbitrary if it is not necessary in all the circumstances of the case and proportionate to the ends sought'.[56]

Finally, in A *v Australia*, the HR Committee also stated that the factors necessitating detention must be 'particular to the individual'.[57] The State party was found not to have provided any particular grounds for justifying the detention of the asylum seeker in question for four years, and the detention was therefore found to have been arbitrary. That is, unlawful entry and fears of the asylum seeker absconding if left at liberty were not particular to the author of the complaint.

The requirement for the detention to be particular to the individual has been reiterated in a number of communications concerning Australia's policy of mandatory immigration detention. For example, in *Kwok v Australia*,[58] Ms Kwok also alleged that her detention in an immigration detention facility was arbitrary. Australia attempted to justify her detention by arguing that

> [m]andatory immigration detention is a measure for, among others, people who arrive in the State party without a valid visa. The detention of such persons is necessary to ensure that they are available for processing of any protection claims, to enable essential identity, security, character and health checks to be carried out, and to ensure that they are available for removal if found not to have a basis to lawfully remain in the State party.[59]

The HR Committee expressed the view that despite Australia providing 'general reasons to justify the author's detention,'[60] Ms Kwok was arbitrarily detained in contravention of Article 9(1) of the ICCPR, because the 'State party has not demonstrated that, in the light of the author's particular circumstances, there were no less invasive means of achieving the same ends'.[61]

56 Ibid [7.2].

57 *A v Australia*, UN Doc CCPR/C/59/D/560/1993 (30 April 1997), [9.4]. See also Human Rights Committee, *General Comment No 35 – Article 9: Liberty and Security of Person*, 112th sess, UN Doc CCPR/C/GC/35 (28 Oct 2014), [18].

58 UN Doc CCPR/C/97/D/1442/2005 (23 October 2009).

59 Ibid [9.3].

60 Ibid [4.7].

61 Ibid [9.3].

Arbitrary detention has also been linked to the denial of a right to the review of detention.[62] In A v *Australia*, the HR Committee stated that 'every decision to keep a person in detention should be open to review periodically so that the grounds justifying the detention can be assessed'.[63] That is, since detention must be justified and particular to the circumstances of each detainee, periodic review of detention is necessary to ensure that the detention continues to be justified. Detention that continues beyond the period for which a State can provide appropriate justification is arbitrary and places a State in breach of its obligations under Article 9(1) of the ICCPR.[64]

6.2.3 Right to Review

Closely related to Article 9(1) of the ICCPR is Article 9(4) of the ICCPR which provides

> Anyone who is deprived of his liberty by arrest or detention shall be entitled to take proceedings before a court, in order that that court may decide without delay on the lawfulness of his detention and order his release if the detention is not lawful.

The HR Committee has interpreted Article 9(4) to mean that a detainee must have a right to appeal his or her detention in a court to determine the legality of the detention, and the court must be empowered to order the release of the detainee if there is a violation of Article 9(1) of the ICCPR.[65] In the case of A v *Australia*, the HR Committee found that '[c]ourt review available to A was, in fact, limited to a formal assessment of the self-evident fact that he was indeed a "designated person" within the meaning of municipal law'.[66] The Committee found that review of detention which was 'limited to mere compliance of the detention with domestic law'[67] did

[62] Human Rights Committee, *General Comment No 35 – Article 9: Liberty and Security of Person*, 112th sess, UN Doc CCPR/C/GC/35 (28 Oct 2014), [15]. It is interesting to note that the HR Committee has also called for 'access to independent legal advice, preferably selected by the detainee'.

[63] A v *Australia*, UN Doc CCPR/C/59/D/560/1993 (30 April 1997), [9.4].

[64] Ibid.

[65] Human Rights Committee, *General Comment No 35 – Article 9: Liberty and Security of Person*, 112th sess, UN Doc CCPR/C/GC/35 (28 Oct 2014), [39].

[66] Ibid [9.5].

[67] Ibid.

not comply with the requirements under Article 9(4) of the ICCPR. The HR Committee expressed the following view

> While domestic legal systems may institute differing methods for ensuring court review of administrative detention, what is decisive for the purposes of article 9, paragraph 4, is that such review is, in its effects, real and not merely formal. By stipulating that the court must have the power to order release "if the detention is not lawful", article 9, paragraph 4, requires that the court be empowered to order release, if the detention is incompatible with the requirements in article 9, paragraph 1, or in other provisions of the Covenant.[68]

As such, Australia was found to be in violation of Article 9(4) of the ICCPR because the right to question the legality of detention under municipal law was merely formal and not real in its effect, and the courts were not empowered to release A from immigration detention.[69]

6.2.4 Is the Protected Population Arbitrarily Detained?

Like Australia's policy of mandatory detention, which has been found by the HR Committee to be in violation of Article 9(1) of the ICCPR,[70] the United States mandatorily detains all individuals it transfers to Guantánamo Bay under the MIP. This is because the current confinement arrangements for the protected population in Guantánamo Bay constitute detention.[71] Thus, all individuals transferred there under the interdiction program are currently detained. No assessment is made of the individual

68 Ibid.

69 Australia's immigration detention regime has also been found to be in violation of Article 9(4) of the ICCPR in a number of other decisions. See, for example, *C v Australia*, UN Doc. CCPR/C/76/D/ 900/1999 (28 October 2002); *Baban v Australia*, UN Doc CCPR/C/78/D/1014/2001 (6 August 2003), [7.2]; *Bakhtiyari v Australia*, UN Doc CCPR/C/79/D/1069/2002 (29 October 2003) [9.4]-[9.5]; *Shams v Australia*, UN Doc CCPR/C/90/D/1255, 1256, 1259, 1260, 1266, 1268, 1270, 1288/2004 (11 September 2007), [7.3]; *Shafiq v Australia*, UN Doc CCPR/C/88/D/1324/2004 (13 November 2006), [7.4].

70 *C v Australia*, UN Doc. CCPR/C/76/D/ 900/1999 (28 October 2002); *Baban v Australia*, UN Doc CCPR/C/78/D/1014/2001 (12 August 2003); *Bakhtiyari v Australia*, UN Doc CCPR/C/79/D/1069/2002 (29 October 2003); *D & E v Australia*, UN Doc CCPR/C/87/D/1050/2002 (11 July 2006); *Shafiq v Australia*, UN Doc CCPR/C/88/D/1324/2004 (13 November 2006); *Shams v Australia*, UN Doc CCPR/C/90/D/1255 (11 September 2007), *Kwok v Australia*, UN Doc CCPR/C/97/D/1442/2005 (23 November 2009).

71 See discussion in subsection 6.2.1.

circumstances of any detainee and no alternatives are considered. This detention is indefinite because it only comes to an end if the detainees are repatriated or resettled. The detention of members of the protected population in Guantánamo Bay thus lasts longer than 'absolutely necessary'[72] because all members of the protected population could be brought to the U.S. mainland rather than kept on the U.S. naval base. It therefore follows that the protected population is arbitrarily detained, and the United States acts in violation of its obligations under Article 9(1) of the ICCPR.

6.2.4.1 Deterrence as Arbitrariness

A further issue relevant to arbitrariness is the use of detention as a deterrent. The United States has stated that its interdiction program (which includes as an element the use of Guantánamo Bay) acts as a deterrent to others who may attempt to enter the United States by sea without valid authority. In 2005, for example, the George W. Bush administration maintained that admitting Haitians interdicted by the United States into the country might 'encourage other Haitians to embark on the risky sea travel and potentially trigger a mass asylum from Haiti to the US'.[73]

In A *v Australia*, the author of the complaint contended that Australia's

> policy of detaining boat people is inappropriate, unjustified and arbitrary, as its principal purpose is to deter other boat people from coming to Australia, and to deter those already in the country from continuing with applications for refugee status.[74]

Unfortunately, the HR Committee did not express a view as to the appropriateness of deterrence as a justification for detention, finding for the author of the complaint on other grounds. However, despite the HR Committee's lack of comment on the issue, detention for the purpose of deterrence is clearly arbitrary as it is not 'particular to the individual'.[75] That is, as UNHCR points out, 'detention policies aimed at deterrence are generally unlawful under international human rights law as they are

[72] See n 65 in this chapter.

[73] Ruth Wasem, Congressional Research Service, 'US Immigration Policy on Haitian Migrants' (2 February 2009) <www.fas.org/sgp/crs/row/RS21349.pdf>.

[74] A *v Australia*, UN Doc CCPR/C/59/D/560/1993 (30 April 1997), [9.2].

[75] Ibid [9.4].

not based on an individual assessment as to the necessity to detain'.[76] The United States does not consider the special circumstance of each member of the protected population in Guantánamo Bay before subjecting them to detention. As such, the detention is arbitrary.

6.2.5 Right of Review and *Habeas Corpus* for Detainees in Guantánamo Bay

In addition, members of the protected population in Guantánamo Bay have no right to have their detention reviewed, in violation of Article 9(4) of the ICCPR. One means of ensuring that detainees in Guantánamo Bay are able to have their detention reviewed would be to give them access to *habeas corpus* in U.S. courts.[77]

The discussion of *habeas corpus* here is separated into two parts. The first part deals with the right of *habeas corpus*, which should now be available to all non-citizens in Guantánamo Bay, including the protected population. The second part will show that the operation of an Executive Order and the continuing operation of the doctrine of plenary power means that *habeas corpus* rights available to detainees cannot be used for their release from detention. This results in the United States' continuing violation of Article 9(4).

6.2.5.1 Extension of Habeas Corpus *to Guantánamo Bay*

In the 2004 case of *Rasul v Bush* (*Rasul*),[78] the U.S. Supreme Court found that the U.S. District Court had jurisdiction to hear *habeas corpus* challenges to the legality of the detention of aliens in the Guantánamo Bay Naval Base, basing its decision on statute.[79] That is, rather than deciding on the constitutional rights of aliens in Guantánamo Bay, the Court found a power to grant a writ under 28 USC § 2241. Whilst not deciding on the issue of the constitutional rights of the detainees, the Court did suggest

[76] UNHCR, *Guidelines on the Applicable Criteria and Standards Relating to the Detention of Asylum-Seekers and Alternatives to Detention* (2012) <www.unhcr.org/refworld/docid/503489533b8.html>, 7.

[77] The link between Article 9(4) of the ICCPR and the right to *habeas Corpus* was made by the Human Rights Committee in Human Rights Committee, *General Comment No 35 – Article 9: Liberty and Security of Person*, 112th sess, UN Doc CCPR/C/GC/35 (28 Oct 2014), [39].

[78] 542 US 466, 484 (2004).

[79] Ibid.

in a footnote to the decision that the detainees in Guantánamo Bay were held in 'custody in violation of the Constitution or laws or treaties of the US'.[80] Therefore the Court in *Rasul* implied that in light of the particular circumstances surrounding their imprisonment, the Guantánamo detainees were entitled to fundamental constitutional rights. Following the decision in *Rasul*, the U.S. Congress passed the *Detainees Treatment Act of 2005* (DTA)[81] which amended 26 USC § 2241 on which the *Rasul* decision had been based.[82] Thus Congress removed any statutory right for a court to consider a *habeas corpus* claim on behalf of detainees in Guantánamo Bay.

In *Boumediene v Bush* (*Boumediene*),[83] the Supreme Court was once again asked to decide on the right of aliens in Guantánamo Bay to *habeas corpus*. Given the change to the statutory provision on which the Court had decided *Rasul*, the Court was forced to decide the matter on constitutional grounds and found that Article 1, Section 9, Paragraph 2 of the U.S. Constitution prohibited the suspension of the writ of *habeas corpus* in Guantánamo Bay. *Boumediene* concerned individuals detained under criminal law. In writing for the majority, however, Justice Kennedy emphasised the importance of *habeas corpus* in cases of non-criminal detention. According to the Court in *Boumediene*:

> It appears the common-law habeas court's role was most extensive in cases of pretrial and noncriminal detention, where there had been little or no previous judicial review of the cause of detention.[84]

It follows that the reasoning of the Court in *Boumediene* can be applied to provide the protected population in Guantánamo Bay with the right to *habeas corpus*. *Boumediene* stated that, as a minimum, the writ of *habeas corpus*

> entitles the prisoner to a meaningful opportunity to demonstrate that he is being held pursuant to "the erroneous application or

80 Ibid 484 n15.

81 Pub L No 109–148, § 1005(e), 119 Stat. 2680, 2742–44.

82 28 USC § 2241(e)(1) now provides that 'no court, justice, or judge shall have jurisdiction to … consider … an application for … habeas corpus filed by or on behalf of an alien detained … at Guantánamo'.

83 *Boumediene v Bush*, 553 US 723 (2008).

84 Ibid 780.

> interpretation" of relevant law … and the habeas court must have the power to order the conditional release of an individual unlawfully detained – though release need not be the exclusive remedy and is not the appropriate one in every case in which the writ is granted.[85]

6.2.6 The Continuing Operation of the Plenary Power Doctrine and Indefinite Detention

At a minimum, therefore, the protected population in Guantánamo Bay should have a right to a 'meaningful opportunity to demonstrate that [they are] being held pursuant to [an] erroneous application or interpretation'[86] of the law. However, it is unlikely that the U.S. courts will release the protected population from their detention by ordering their entry to the U.S. mainland under any *habeas* petition. This is because of the continuing operation of the plenary power doctrine.

Plenary power, as used in this book, refers to what Spiro calls 'immigration exceptionalism'[87] – that is, the deference of the U.S. courts to the political branches in immigration cases. Under the plenary power doctrine, only the political branches have the authority to choose who enters the U.S. mainland. Jurisprudence from the U.S. courts provides that it is the 'exclusive power of the political branches to decide which aliens may, and which aliens may not, enter the US [mainland] and on what terms'.[88] The U.S. courts have considered the plight of non-citizens in a similar situation to the protected population and have construed restraints on the freedom of movement of non-citizens resulting from their denial of entry to the U.S. mainland (or any other country) not as unlawful detention, but as a permissible exercise of the executive's plenary power to deny the entry of non-citizens.

85 Ibid 779.

86 Ibid.

87 Peter Spiro, 'Explaining the End of Plenary Power' (2002) 16 *Georgetown Immigration Law Journal* 339, 339.

88 *Kiyemba v Obama*, 555 F 3d 1022, 1025–26 (DC Cir, 2009). A similar language was used by the then prime minister of Australia, John Howard, when he too asserted the executive's right to determine the entry of non-citizens into Australia territory when he stated that 'we will decide who comes to this country and the circumstances in which they come': John Howard, Speech delivered at the Federal Liberal Party Campaign Launch, Sydney, 28 October 2001.

The first of these cases is *United States ex rel. Knauff v Shaughnessy* (*Knauff*).[89] In that case Ellen Knauff, a German national married to an American citizen, sought to enter the U.S. mainland. Upon arrival, however, Knauff was detained at Ellis Island on security grounds. The Attorney General permanently excluded her without a hearing pursuant to regulation promulgated by the Secretary of State and the Attorney General as authorised under Presidential Proclamation 2523.[90] Among other things, Proclamation 2523 stated: 'No alien shall be permitted to enter the US if it appears … that such entry would be prejudicial to the interests of the US'.

Knauff instituted *habeas corpus* proceedings. On *certiorari*, the U.S. Supreme Court found that it 'is not within the province of any court, unless expressly authorized by law, to review the determination of the political branch of the Government to exclude a given alien'.[91] That is, the Court found that it could not order Ms Knauff's entry to the U.S. mainland because decisions relating to the admission of non-citizens rested with the political rather than legislative branches of government. The Court did not consider whether Ms Knauff's exclusion from the U.S. mainland amounted to unlawful detention.

On the question of whether or not the delegation of power to the Attorney General and the Secretary of State to deny Ms Knauff entry to the U.S. mainland without hearing was lawful, the Supreme Court stated

> [T]here is no question of inappropriate delegation of legislative power involved here. The exclusion of aliens is a fundamental act of sovereignty. The right to do so stems not alone from legislative power, but is inherent in the executive power to control the foreign affairs of the nation.… Thus, the decision to admit or to exclude an alien may be lawfully placed with the President, who may, in turn, delegate the carrying out of this function to a responsible executive officer of the sovereign, such as the Attorney General. The action of the executive officer under such authority is final and conclusive.[92]

89 338 US 543, 537 (1950).

90 3 CFR 270, 271. The proclamation also authorised the promulgation of regulations jointly by the Secretary of State and the Attorney General, which 'imposed certain restrictions and prohibitions, in addition to those otherwise provided by law, upon the departure of persons from and their entry into the United States.' Revoked by Proclamation 3004, 18 *Federal Register* 489 (1953).

91 *United States ex rel. Knauff v Shaughnessy*, 338 US 543 (1950).

92 Ibid 542–43.

As was the situation in *Knauff*, members of the protected population in Guantánamo Bay seek freedom from their detention by being admitted to the U.S. mainland. As was also the case in *Knauff*, the municipal law relied on for the detention of the protected population in Guantánamo Bay is delegated authority from the president (to the Secretary of Homeland Security) for restrictions on the admission of non-citizens into the United States (in the case of Guantánamo immigration detainees, in the form of the maintenance of custody).[93] In particular, the current detention regime is authorised under municipal law under Executive Order 13276[94] as amended by Executive Order 13286,[95] which provides

> The [Secretary of Homeland Security] *may maintain custody*, at any location he deems appropriate, of any undocumented aliens he has reason to believe are seeking to enter the US and who are interdicted or intercepted in the Caribbean region. In this regard, the [Secretary of Homeland Security] shall provide and operate a facility, or facilities, to house and provide for the needs of any such aliens. *Such a facility may be located at Guantánamo Bay Naval Base* or any other appropriate location.[96]

Thus, immigration detention in Guantánamo Bay as part of the interdiction program is an exercise of executive discretion. As with *Knauff* therefore, the Executive Order and the delegation of authority is likely to be lawful.

The detention of a non-citizen as a consequence of the denial of entry to the U.S. mainland was also an issue in the Supreme Court's decision in *Shaughnessy v United States ex rel. Mezei* (*Mezei*).[97] The case considered the plight of Ignatz Mezei, a non-citizen resident who lived in the United States for more than twenty-five years before leaving to visit his dying mother overseas. Mezei was denied re-entry to the U.S. mainland on national security grounds. Attempts to resettle Mezei in countries other than the United States failed and he was kept on Ellis Island. In response, Mezei instituted *habeas corpus* proceedings arguing that his continued

93 See discussion of the municipal legal authority relied on by the U.S. executive for the operation of the interdiction program in Section 3.1.

94 Executive Order 13276, 67 *Federal Register* 69 (2002).

95 68 *Federal Register* 10619 (2003).

96 Emphasis added.

97 345 US 206 (1953).

exclusion from the country without a hearing amounted to unlawful detention. The Court, relying on the precedent in *Knauff*, found that 'neither [the] respondent's harborage on Ellis Island nor his prior residence [in the United States] transform[ed his situation] into something other than an exclusion proceeding'.[98] That is, the Court did not entertain the idea that Mr Mezei's denial of entry to the U.S. mainland constituted unlawful detention, for the Court construed his situation as a lawful exercise of the executive's power to exclude aliens.[99]

The characterisation of a denial of entry that results in detention as incidental to the executive authority to exclude (rather than as unlawful detention) was further confirmed by the U.S. courts in recent decisions concerning litigation involving men of Uighur ethnicity, detained in Guantánamo Bay as part of the 'war on terror'. In *Parhat v Gates*,[100] it was determined that the United States could not hold Parhat (one of the Uighur men) in detention pursuant to the DTA, as he had not engaged in hostilities against the United States or its coalition partners and could therefore not be held as an enemy combatant. The U.S. executive conceded that the other men of Uighur ethnicity were in the same position.[101] However the men, who are Chinese nationals, cannot be returned to China because they fear persecution, torture and execution in their home country or any country that may subsequently return them to China. At the time of initiating the litigation, the United States had been unable to find the men a suitable country to which they could be safely repatriated. In *Kiyemba v Obama* (*Kiyemba I*),[102] the U.S. Court of Appeals for the District of Columbia found that the Uighur men could not be released to the U.S. mainland because of the immigration plenary power doctrine. The Court applied *Mezei* because the Uighurs, like Mr Mezei, were found to be non-citizens at the border seeking entry into the U.S. mainland in circumstances in which no third country had been found (at the time) to resettle them.[103] Like *Mezei*, the Court found that the

98 Ibid 213.

99 In *Shaughnessy v US ex rel. Mezei*, 345 US 206, 213 (1953), the Supreme Court majority also 'sought various means to show that [Mezei's detention] was not incarceration in the normal sense': Daniel Wilsher, *Immigration Detention: Law, History, Politics* (Cambridge University Press, 2011) 60.

100 532 F 3d 834 (DC Circ, 2008).

101 *Kiyemba v Obama*, 555 F 3d 1022, 1024 (DC Cir, 2009).

102 Ibid.

103 Ibid 1027.

detainees did not have a basis to enter the U.S. mainland. The Court also stated that the 'decision whether to allow an alien to enter the country [is] for the political departments, not the Judiciary'.[104]

In March 2010, the Supreme Court granted *certiorari* to the Uighur men[105] but noted that by the time the case had come to it, each of the detainees at issue had received at least one offer of resettlement in another country and all but five of the detainees had accepted an offer of resettlement. The Supreme Court found that the change in facts may have affected the legal issues presented, and as they were a court of review and not of first instance, they declined to be the first to rule on the case in light of the new developments. As such, the Supreme Court vacated the judgment of *Kiyemba I* and remanded the case to the U.S. Court of Appeals for the District of Columbia Circuit, which decided on the issue again in *Kiyemba v Obama* (*Kiyemba III*).[106] In *Kiyemba III*, the Court found that 'the posture of the case [was] not materially different than in *Kiyemba I*'.[107] The Court of Appeals thus reinstated its opinion in *Kiyemba I* that it is 'the exclusive power of the political branches to decide which aliens may, and which aliens may not, enter the US [mainland], and on what terms'.[108] The Supreme Court denied a further petition for a writ of *certiorari*.[109]

It should also be noted that in *Kiyemba I*, the court also rejected the application of protections against indefinite detention available to detainees in the U.S. mainland.[110] In *Zadvydas v Davis* (*Zadvydas*),[111] the Supreme Court found that non-citizens in the United States could only be detained following an order of removal so long as it is 'reasonably necessary to bring about that alien's removal from the US'.[112] *Zadvydas* was only concerned with the indefinite detention of those who cannot be removed by the United States. However, the limitations on indefinite detention under INA § 241(a)(6) found in *Zadvydas* were later found to extend to 'inadmissible aliens' in *Clark v Martinez* (*Martinez*).[113] Importantly, the Supreme

104 Ibid 1028.
105 *Kiyemba v Obama*, 130 S Ct 1235 (2010).
106 *Kiyemba v Obama*, 605 F 3d 1046 (DC Cir, 2010).
107 Ibid 1047 (DC Cir, 2010).
108 *Kiyemba v Obama*, 555 F 3d 1022, 1048 (DC Cir, 2009).
109 *Kiyemba v Obama* 131 S Ct 1631 (2011).
110 *Kiyemba v Obama*, 555 F 3d 1022, 1027–28 (DC Cir, 2009).
111 533 US 678 (2001).
112 Ibid 689.
113 543 US 371 (2005).

Court relied on statutory interpretation rather than constitutional interpretation to determine that INA § 241(a)(6) implicitly includes a presumptive limit on indefinite detention in both *Zadvydas* and *Martinez*.[114] This is significant for the purposes of detainees in Guantánamo Bay because it limits the finding to the particular provisions in question. As such, the protections offered to indefinite detainees in the U.S. mainland, under the two Supreme Court decisions, do not extend to detainees in Guantánamo Bay. As the court stated in *Kiyemba I*:

> It would therefore be wrong to assert that, by ordering aliens paroled into the country in Zadvydas and Clark, the [Supreme] Court somehow undermined the plenary authority of the political branches over the entry and admission of aliens.[115]

In the Kiyemba litigation the Court of Appeals accepted the executive's argument that 'the Government retains the sovereign authority, independent of the authority to detain enemy combatants, to hold petitioners incident to barring them from the US [mainland], and pending efforts to resettle them elsewhere'.[116] It should be noted that the restrictions on the movement of the Uighur men in Guantánamo Bay was more severe than is currently experienced by members of the protected population. Unlike members of the protected population who have some level of freedom to move around the Leeward side of Guantánamo Bay, the Uighur men were held in Camp Iguana, a compound within Guantánamo Bay, surrounded by barbed wire, which they could not leave. Thus, if such severe restrictions on the Uighur men are permissible under municipal law as incidental to the executive's plenary power, then it follows that the lesser restrictions on the members of the protected population are also permitted under municipal law. Therefore, the decisions in *Knauff*, *Mezei* and *Kiyemba* stand for the proposition that detention that arises as a consequence of the denial of entry of an alien to the U.S. mainland is a lawful exercise of the executive's authority to exclude aliens under municipal law.

Interestingly, the U.S. Court of Appeals for the District of Columbia only considered three options for freeing the men from their detention

[114] *Zadvydas v Davis*, 533 US 678, 701 (2001); *Clark v Martinez*, 543 US 371, 380–81 (2005).

[115] *Kiyemba v Obama*, 555 F 3d 1022, 1028 n 12 (DC Cir, 2009).

[116] *Reply Brief for Appellants, Kiyemba v Obama*, 555 F 3d 1022, (Nos. 08-5424, 08-5425, 08-5426, 08-5427, 08-5428, 08-5429) 2009 WL 6058812, 13.

in the *Kiyemba* litigation: release to the U.S. mainland (which was not permissible under the plenary power doctrine); release into their home country of China (which would go against U.S. policy of refraining from the transfer of individuals to countries where they would be subjected to mistreatment); or released into third countries (for which diplomatic efforts were continuing).[117] The Court therefore did not consider whether the Uighur men could be released from Camp Iguana into Guantánamo Bay more generally.

There is, therefore, no precedent for the proposition that a *habeas* petition could be used to free detainees from confinement in a restricted section of Guantánamo Bay to Guantánamo Bay more generally. That is, no precedent exists to assist in determining if the protected population, currently detained in a limited area within the Leeward side of Guantánamo Bay and subjected to restrictions such as curfews, could use a *habeas* petition to grant them access to all of Guantánamo Bay currently under U.S. jurisdiction and control (including the Windward side), free from additional restrictions such as curfews or an escort. Such a challenge would not face the obstacle of the plenary power doctrine, since the protected population would not be seeking entry to the U.S. mainland.

If such a *habeas* challenge was successful and members of the protected population were no longer detained in the Leeward side (and were not subjected to additional restrictions such as curfews or an escort), it may be arguable that the constraints on them would no longer constitute detention, and thus the United States would no longer be in violation of Article 9 of the ICCPR. However, it is not possible to speculate what form such a release might take and whether it would in fact continue to constitute detention within the meaning of Article 9 of the ICCPR. Furthermore, whilst such a victory may make life marginally better for members of the protected population, it would not resolve the bigger issue of their indeterminate state in Guantánamo Bay while they await resettlement. Furthermore, as discussed later in the chapter, even if it did not amount to detention, access to the whole of Guantánamo Bay would continue to

[117] The Court stated that until their resettlement the Uighur men were 'held under the least restrictive conditions possible' in Guantánamo Bay: *Kiyemba v Obama*, 555 F 3d 1022, 1024 (DC Cir, 2009). This was not in fact true because, as discussed in the text, the men could have been released from Camp Iguana and could have been permitted to live in Guantánamo Bay more generally.

place the United States in breach of other international obligations such as freedom of movement (which requires freedom to move in all of a State party's territory, including, in this case, the U.S. mainland).

6.3 Further Rights under International Human Rights Law: Articles 12 and 13 of the ICCPR

The preceding discussion has focused on the detention of the protected population in Guantánamo Bay on the basis that the protected population can be characterised as detained. However, even if members of the protected population were found not to be in detention, the fact that their movements are restricted, by virtue of their 'harborage'[118] in Guantánamo Bay, and they are resettled in a third country without procedural safeguards, places the United States in violation of its obligations under Articles 12 and 13 of the ICCPR.

6.3.1 Application of Articles 12 and 13 of the ICCPR in Guantánamo Bay

Article 12(1) states that '[e]veryone *lawfully within the territory* of a State shall, *within that territory*, have the right to liberty of movement and freedom to choose his residence'.[119] Article 13 of the ICCPR begins with the words: 'an alien *lawfully in the territory of a State party* to the present Covenant may be expelled therefrom only in pursuance of a decision reached in accordance with law'.[120] Articles 12 and 13 of the ICCPR, therefore, specifically refer to the concept of 'territory' as a limiting principle in the scope of their application and, in contrast with Article 2(1) of the ICCPR, do not contain any reference to jurisdiction.[121] It therefore follows that the exercises of jurisdiction in Guantánamo Bay is not sufficient to trigger the United States' obligations to the protected population in Guantánamo Bay under the two Articles. The question thus arises as to

[118] As stated earlier, this was the term used by the U.S. Supreme Court to refer to the limits placed on the freedom of movement of Mezei in *Shaughnessy v United States ex rel. Mezei*, 345 US 206, 214 (1953).

[119] Emphasis added.

[120] Emphasis added.

[121] See discussion of the scope of application of Article 2 of the ICCPR in Section 4.1.

whether or not Guantánamo Bay constitutes U.S. 'territory' for the purposes of Article 12 and 13 of the ICCPR.

Article III of the agreement for the lease of Guantánamo Bay by the United States from Cuba[122] states in part that

> While on the one hand the United States recognizes the *continuance of the ultimate sovereignty of the Republic of Cuba* over the above described areas of land and water, on the other hand the Republic of Cuba consents that during the period of the occupation by the United States of said areas under the terms of this agreement the *United States shall exercise complete jurisdiction and control* over and within said areas ...[123]

As the U.S. Supreme Court has pointed out, '[w]hile obligated to abide by the terms of the lease, the US is, for all practical purposes, answerable to no other sovereign for its acts on the base'.[124] Cuba has no jurisdiction over individuals in Guantánamo Bay.[125] Furthermore, the U.S. courts have confirmed that the criminal and civil law of the United States apply in Guantánamo Bay.[126]

This is not to claim that Guantánamo Bay is U.S. territory under the municipal law of the United States, for it clearly is not.[127] However, U.S. municipal law rather than Cuban law is the governing legal regime in Guantánamo Bay. When U.S. municipal law is found not to apply in Guantánamo Bay in the courts of the United States, it is because of constraints within the municipal law itself (e.g., geographical limitations within statutes such as the INA) rather than because of a conflict between Cuban and American domestic legal regimes.[128] The United States may

[122] *Agreement between the United States and Cuba for the Lease of Lands for Coaling and Naval Stations; Lease to the United States of Lands in Cuba for Coaling and Naval Stations*, Feb. 16–23, 1903, US-Cuba, T.S. No 418.

[123] Emphasis added.

[124] *Boumediene v Bush*, 553 US 723, 770 (2008).

[125] *In Re Guzman & Latamble*, Annual Digest, 1933–34, Case No 43 p 112.

[126] For the application of criminal law in Guantánamo Bay, see *United States v Rogers*, 388 F Supp 298, 301 (ED Va, 1975). U.S. criminal law was also said to apply in Guantánamo Bay in *United States v Lee*, 906 F 2d 117, 117 n1 (4th Cir, 1990). The application of civil law in Guantánamo Bay was tested and confirmed in *Huerta v United States*, 548 F 2d 343 (Fed Cir, 1977).

[127] The definition of the 'United States' under INA § 101(a)38; 8 USC § 1101(a)(38) does not include Guantánamo Bay.

[128] See, for example, *Bird v United States* 923 F Supp 338 (D Conn, 1996).

choose not to extend certain laws to Guantánamo Bay; however, this is at the discretion of the United States rather than because of an inability by the United States to extend its laws to an area over which it exercises full jurisdiction and control.

In determining the scope of application of Article 12(1) of the ICCPR in Guantánamo Bay, U.S. jurisdiction and control of Guantánamo Bay can be compared to Israeli jurisdiction and control over Occupied Palestinian Territory. Israel's obligations to Palestinians in the Occupied Palestinian Territory under Article 12(1) were considered by the ICJ in *Legal Consequences of the Construction of a Wall in the Occupied Palestinian Territory* (*Israeli Wall*).[129] In that case the ICJ found

> that the construction of the wall and its associated régime impede the liberty of movement of the inhabitants of the Occupied Palestinian Territory (with the exception of Israeli citizens and those assimilated thereto) as guaranteed under Article 12, paragraph 1, of the International Covenant on Civil and Political Rights.[130]

The ICJ observed that the Palestinian territories had been occupied by Israel for more than thirty-seven years, were under Israeli 'effective control' and were subject to its 'territorial jurisdiction as the occupying power'.[131] It thus found that Israel was bound by Article 12(1) of the ICCPR with respect to the Occupied Palestinian Territories. That is, Palestinian territory over which Israel exercised jurisdiction and effective control constituted Israeli 'territory' for the purpose of the application of Article 12(1) of the ICCPR.

The HR Committee also considered the application of Article 12(1) in the Palestinian territories by Israel in its Concluding Observations on Israel in 2010. The Committee noted with concern Israel's

> military blockade of the Gaza Strip, in force since June 2007. While recognizing the State party's recent easing of the blockade with regard to the entry of civilian goods by land, the Committee is nevertheless concerned at the effects of the blockade on the civilian population in the

[129] *Legal Consequences of the Construction of a Wall in the Occupied Palestinian Territory* (Advisory Opinion) [2004] ICJ Rep 136.
[130] Ibid [134].
[131] Ibid [112].

> Gaza Strip, including restrictions to their freedom of movement (arts. 1, 6 and 12).[132]

The HR Committee also expressed

> concern at the restrictions to freedom of movement imposed on Palestinians, in particular persons residing in the "Seam Zone" between the wall and Israel, the frequent refusal to grant agricultural permits to access the land on the other side of the wall or to visit relatives, and the irregular opening hours of the agricultural gates (arts. 1, 12 and 23).[133]

That is, the HR Committee is also of the view that Article 12(1) of the ICCPR applies to Israel in the Occupied Palestinian Territories and for the purposes of Article 12(1), Occupied Palestinian Territories constitute the 'territory' of Israel.

Therefore, by analogy with the ICJ decision in *Israeli Wall* and the HR Committee's concluding observations on Israel, the United States exercises effective control and 'territorial jurisdiction' in the leased area of Guantánamo Bay. There is no legal impediment (such as lack of authority or a conflict of laws) in the United States' ability to grant individuals in Guantánamo freedom of movement. In fact, the degree of jurisdiction and control exercised by the United States in Guantánamo Bay is more than that exercised by Israel in the Occupied Palestinian Territories. Unlike Palestinians who continue to live in the occupied territories, the Cuban nationals (except those who are brought into Guantánamo Bay by the United States, seek authorisation to come into Guantánamo Bay or enter Guantánamo Bay through clandestine means) are in large part denied access to the area of Guantánamo Bay. Their entry into Guantánamo Bay is physically obstructed by fences and minefields.[134] Furthermore, U.S. law is the only governing law in Guantánamo Bay in contrast with the Occupied Palestinian Territories, which are governed by a mixture of Israeli law and Palestinian law.[135]

[132] Human Rights Committee, *Concluding Observations of the Human Rights Committee: Israel*, 99th sess, UN Doc CCPR/C/ISR/CO/3 (3 September 2010), [8].

[133] Ibid [16].

[134] U.S. President Bill Clinton ordered the de-mining of the U.S. side of the fence in 1997, but the mines on the Cuban side of the naval base remain.

[135] On the operation of Palestinian and Israeli law in the occupied territories, see Feras Milhem and Jamil Salem 'Building the Rule of Law in Palestine: Rule of Law Without Freedom' in

The interpretation of Article 12(1) is also relevant to the interpretation of the phrase 'territory of a State party' under Article 13 of the ICCPR. The reach of Article 13 has received little scholarly attention to date. However, in light of the ICJ's decision in *Israeli Wall* and the HR Committee's acceptance of the application of Article 12(1) to the Palestinian territories, the words 'territory of a State party' in Article 13 should be read to apply to Guantánamo Bay, which is territory in which the United States exercises jurisdiction and control.

6.3.2 Are Members of the Protected Population 'Lawfully' within the Territory of the United States for the Purposes of Articles 12 and 13 of the ICCPR?

In addition to containing a territorial limitation in their scope of application, Articles 12 and 13 of the ICCPR are also limited to individuals who are *lawfully* in the territory of a State party. As Nowak has noted, the requirement of lawful presence in Article 13 'corresponds literally to that in Art. 12(1)'.[136] As such, the analysis of the requirement of 'lawful presence' that follows applies to both Article 12(1) and Article 13 of the ICCPR.

In General Comment No 15 the HR Committee stated

> The Covenant does not recognise the right of aliens to enter or reside in the territory of a State party. *It is in principle a matter for the State to decide who it will admit to its territory.* However, in certain circumstances, an alien may enjoy the protection of the Covenant even in relation to entry or residence, for example when consideration of non-discrimination, prohibition of inhuman treatment and respect of family life arises.[137]

The requirement of lawful entry and presence in the U.S. territory (which for present purposes includes Guantánamo Bay) is thus clearly satisfied if an alien has been admitted into Guantánamo Bay by the United States itself and remains there in compliance with U.S. municipal law. It

Susan Akram, Michael Dumper, Michael Lynk and Iain Scobbie (eds) *International Law and the Israeli-Palestinian Conflict: A Rights-Based Approach to Middle East Peace* (Routledge, 2011) 253.

136 Nowak, n 34 in this chapter, 292.

137 Human Rights Committee, *General Comment No 15: The Position of Aliens under the Covenant*, 27th sess, UN Doc HRI/GEN/1/Rev.6 (11 April 1986), [5]. Emphasis added.

follows that members of the protected population are lawfully present in Guantánamo Bay for the purposes of Articles 12 and 13 of the ICCPR.

Members of the protected population are not in Guantánamo Bay of their own volition. Their vessels were interdicted outside the U.S. territorial sea (often against their will).[138] Whereas the vast majority of individuals interdicted are repatriated, members of the protected population are transferred to Guantánamo Bay by the U.S. Coast Guard because they have been found to have a credible fear of persecution or torture. That is, they have satisfied a procedure carried out by the United States and have been transferred to Guantánamo Bay by a deliberate act of the State. As such, members of the protected population have not entered Guantánamo Bay in contravention of U.S. municipal law. Furthermore, Executive Order 13276,[139] provides the Secretary of Homeland Security with an unreviewable discretion to hold protection seekers in the custody of the United States in Guantánamo Bay under municipal law and to provide them with status determinations.[140] Whilst Executive Order 13276[141] does not address the issue of resettlement (in third countries or in the United States itself), resettlement is intrinsically linked to status determination. That is, status determinations would be futile if no consequence flowed from the determination of the protection seeker's status. This means that the protected population in Guantánamo Bay continues to be present in Guantánamo Bay lawfully while they await status determination, in compliance with Executive Order 13276.[142]

6.3.3 Violations of Article 12 of the ICCPR in Guantánamo Bay

Having established the applicability of Articles 12 and 13 of the ICCPR to the protected population in Guantánamo Bay, the question arises as to the rights triggered under the two Articles. Articles 12(1) and 12(3) of the ICCPR provide

138 For a detailed account of U.S. interdiction practices at sea, see Chapter 3.

139 67 *Federal Register* 69 (2002). As amended by Executive Order 13286, 68 *Federal Register* 10619 (2003).

140 See Section 5.2 and subsection 6.2.6.

141 As amended by Executive Order 13286.

142 As amended by Executive Order 13286.

1. Everyone lawfully within the territory of a State shall, within that territory, have the right to liberty of movement and freedom to choose his residence …
3. The above-mentioned rights shall not be subject to any restrictions except those which are provided by law, are necessary to protect national security, public order (*ordre public*), public health or morals or the rights and freedoms of others, and are consistent with the other rights recognized in the present Covenant.

Article 12(1) applies equally to aliens lawfully in the territory of a State party and the citizens of a State party. According to the HR Committee, once an alien is lawfully in the territory of a State,

> any restrictions on his or her rights guaranteed under article 12, paragraphs 1 and 2, *as well as any treatment different from that accorded to nationals*, have to be justified under the rules provided for by article 12, paragraph 3 … The right to move freely relates to the whole territory of a State, including all parts of federal States … [P]ersons are entitled to move from one place to another and to establish themselves in a place of their choice.[143]

That is, the State party to the ICCPR is prohibited from preventing the entry or stay of persons to any particular part of its territory.[144] For example, in *Ackla v Togo*,[145] the prohibition on the author of entering a particular district of Togo was viewed as a violation of Article 12(1). Despite being lawfully present in the U.S. territory of Guantánamo Bay, members of the protected population are denied the right to move freely within the whole territory of the United States, which includes the U.S. mainland. As such, members of the protected population are treated differently from U.S. citizens in Guantánamo Bay whose movement to and from the U.S. mainland is not prohibited.

143 Human Rights Committee, *General Comment No 27: Freedom of Movement (Art.12)*, 67th sess, UN Doc CCPR/C/21/Rev1/Add.9 (2 November 1999), [4]-[5]. See also Human Rights Committee, *General Comment No 15: The Position of Aliens Under the Covenant*, 27th sess, UN Doc HRI/GEN/1/Rev.1 (4 November 1986), [8]. Emphasis added.

144 Sarah Joseph and Melissa Castan, *The International Covenant on Civil and Political Right: Cases, Materials, and Commentary* (Oxford University Press, 3rd ed., 2013) 393.

145 UN Doc CCPR/C/51/D/505/1992 (25 March 1996).

Turning now to Article 12(3), the United States' refusal to permit the protected population to move freely within its whole territory is not justified on the grounds of 'national security, public order (*ordre public*), public health or morals or the rights and freedoms of others'. That is, the United States' violation of Article 12(1) does not fit into any of the exceptions provided by Article 12(3). As such, regardless of whether or not the current confinement of the protected population in Guantánamo Bay constitutes detention, the United States clearly acts in violation of Article 12(1) of the ICCPR in restricting the movement of the protected population. This violation can only be remedied by providing the protected population with the right to freedom of movement in all of its territory, including the U.S. mainland.

6.3.4 Violations of Article 13 of the ICCPR in Guantánamo Bay

Article 13 of the ICCPR states

> An alien lawfully in the territory of a State Party to the present Covenant may be expelled therefrom only in pursuance of a decision reached in accordance with law and shall, except where compelling reasons of national security otherwise require, be allowed to submit the reasons against his expulsion and to have his case reviewed by, and be represented for the purpose before, the competent authority or a person or persons especially designated by the competent authority.

It should be noted that Article 13 does not prohibit expulsion of non-citizens but provides minimum procedural safeguards to non-citizens who are facing expulsion from a State party. That is, aliens protected by Article 13 of the ICCPR must only be expelled pursuant to a 'decision reached in accordance with law'.[146] In addition to a right to a hearing, Article 13 also guarantees a right to seek review of a decision to expel an alien.[147] This right to review is satisfied by access to administrative review and need not

146 The law authorising expulsion must be compatible with the provisions of the ICCPR; however, the HR Committee takes the view that 'the interpretation of domestic law is essentially a matter for the courts and authorities of the State party concerned': *Maroufidou v Sweden*, UN Doc CCPR/C/OP/1 (8 April 1981), [10.1].

147 This aspect was demonstrated in *Hammel v Madagascar*, UN Doc CCPR/C/OP/2 (3 April 1987) [19.2].

be exercised before a court.[148] Article 13 of the ICCPR also provides for a right of representation. This includes access to legal advice.[149]

As Guantánamo Bay is U.S. territory for the purposes of Article 13 of the ICCPR, the removal of members of the protected population for resettlement in third countries constitutes expulsion from U.S. territory. The United States must therefore provide members of the protected population, who will be resettled in a third country, with the procedural safeguards outlined in Article 13 of the ICCPR prior to their expulsion.

The United States is currently in violation of its obligations under Article 13 of the ICCPR because the decision to resettle members of the protected population from Guantánamo Bay in third countries is made by the U.S. executive without providing members of the protected population the right to submit reasons against their expulsion, to have their cases reviewed or to obtain legal assistance. The United States could remedy this breach of its obligations by providing individuals who will be resettled in a third country with the right to present evidence against any resettlement, to access legal representation and to request a review of any decision to expel. Alternatively, the United States could ensure its compliance with Article 13 of the ICCPR by refraining from expulsion altogether and resettling all members of the protected population in the U.S. mainland.

6.4 Rights under the Refugee Convention

In addition to the aforementioned rights under the ICCPR, refugees who are members of the protected population have further rights to freedom of movement under Article 26 of the Refugee Convention and further constraints on their expulsion under Article 32 of the Refugee Convention. As discussed earlier,[150] refugees acquire rights under the Refugee Convention in accordance with their attachment to the State party. Articles 26 and 32 of the Refugee Convention are triggered only when a refugee is lawfully present within U.S. territory.

148 *Maroufidou v Sweden* UN Doc CCPR/C/OP/1 (8 April 1981).

149 Human Rights Committee, *Concluding Observations of the Human Rights Committee: Denmark*, 70th sess, UN Doc CCPR/CO/70/DNK (31 October 2000), [17].

150 See Section 4.2.

The term 'territory' in Articles 26 and 32 of the Refugee Convention should be interpreted consistently with developing understandings of international human rights law, including developing understanding and interpretations of the term 'territory' under the ICCPR.[151] The Refugee Convention's reference to the *Universal Declaration of Human Rights* (UDHR)[152] in its Preamble places the Refugee Convention within the context of human rights law.[153] It therefore follows that the ICJ's decision in *Israeli Wall*, namely that territory for the purposes of Article 12(1) (which has an explicit territorial limit) is 'territory' over which a State exercises jurisdiction and control, is relevant in the interpretation of the term 'territory' in Articles 26 and 32 of the Refugee Convention. Just as Guantánamo Bay constitutes 'territory' for the purposes of Article 12(1) of the ICCPR, so too Guantánamo Bay constitutes 'territory' for the purposes of the Refugee Convention. To draw a distinction between the application of international human rights law and international refugee law in Guantánamo Bay would be 'to overlook the place of refugee law within the wider human rights framework'.[154]

As with the concept of territory, the concept of lawful presence, under Articles 26 and 32 of the Refugee Convention, 'should [also] be interpreted in a way that takes account of, and is consistent with, developing international human rights standards'.[155] As noted earlier, the protected population are lawfully in the territory of the United States for the purposes of Articles 12 and 13 of the ICCPR. It therefore follows that refugees among

[151] On the interrelationship of human rights law and refugee law, see Jane McAdam, *Complementary Protection in International Refugee Law* (Oxford university Press, 2007) 29–30; James Hathaway, *The Rights of Refugees Under International Law* (Cambridge University Press, 2005) 4–6; Karen Musalo, Jennifer Moore and Richard Boswell, *Refugee Law and Policy: Cases and Materials* (Carolina Academic Press, 1997) 233; and Tom Clark and François Crépeau, 'Mainstreaming Refugee Rights: The 1951 Refugee Convention and International Human Rights law' (1999) 17 *Netherlands Quarterly of Human Rights* 389, 389.

[152] GA Res 217A(III), UN GAOR, 3rd sess, 183rd plen mtg, UN Doc A/810 (10 December 1948).

[153] Michelle Foster, *International Refugee Law and Socio-Economic Rights: Refuge from Deprivation* (Cambridge University Press, 2007) 49. See also UNHCR ExCom, *Note on International Protection*, 52nd sess, UN Doc A/AC.96/951 (13 September 2001), [4]; UNHCR ExCom, *Note on International Protection*, 52nd sess, UN Doc A/AC.96/951 (13 September 2001), [4]; UNHCR, *Briefing Note: Human Rights and Refugee Protection* (1 July 1997) <www.unhcr.org/refworld/docid/3ae6b32310.html>.

[154] Jane McAdam, 'Status Anxiety: The New Zealand Immigration Bill and the Rights of Non-Convention Refugees' [2009] *New Zealand Law Review* 239, 246.

[155] Foster, n 153 in this chapter, 51.

the protected population are also in Guantánamo Bay lawfully for the purposes of Articles 26 and 32 of the Refugee Convention.

6.4.1 Freedom of Movement for Refugees

In addition to Article 12 of the ICCPR, Article 26 of the Refugee Convention further prohibits restrictions on the freedom of movement of refugees. It provides

> Each Contracting State shall accord to refugees lawfully in its territory the right to choose their place of residence and to move freely within its territory *subject to any regulations applicable to aliens generally in the same circumstances*.[156]

Non-citizens whose status has been regularised by the United States and who are lawfully in the U.S. mainland have a right to choose their place of residence and to move freely within the U.S. mainland, other than in exceptional cases (such as aliens detained because they are especially dangerous or have a highly contagious disease that is a threat to public safety; and/or due to security or terrorism concerns or the possibility of serious adverse foreign policy consequences if they were to be released, discussed earlier in the book). As Hathaway has noted, once the status of a refugee is regularised, 'all refugee-specific restrictions on the right to move freely and to choose one's residence must end in accordance with Article 26'.[157] As such, if refugees in Guantánamo Bay can be said to be 'generally in the same circumstances' as aliens who are lawfully in the U.S. mainland, then they should also have the right to choose their place of residence and to move freely within the U.S. mainland, as long as they do not fall into any of the special categories listed previously. It therefore would follow that the United States' denial of their freedom of movement would be a violation of Article 26 of the Refugee Convention.

However, it could be argued that aliens lawfully in the U.S. mainland are not a reasonable comparison class, because they are not 'generally in the same circumstances' in one very important respect: they are not located in Guantánamo Bay. If this is the case, the most appropriate comparison class

[156] Emphasis added.
[157] Hathaway, n 151 in this chapter, 708.

for refugees in Guantánamo Bay are other non-citizens on the U.S. naval base. Such individuals include non-citizen spouses or dependents of U.S. Navy personnel, or other non-citizens working in Guantánamo Bay such as the staff of the IOM.

Guantánamo Bay is 'a closed military reservation'.[158] Freedom of movement of non-citizens working and living in the military base is not governed by U.S. immigration law, but rather by the Department of Defense in conjunction with the DHS and the Department of State.[159] It is therefore not known if non-citizens lawfully in Guantánamo Bay who are not under the interdiction program are permitted to enter the U.S. mainland or not. However, what is clear is that such aliens are not restricted to a limited area within the Leeward side of Guantánamo Bay and have some access to the Windward side (provided they do not compromise the naval operations or the security of the base). As such, at the very least, Article 26 of the Refugee Convention requires the United States to allow members of the protected population in Guantánamo Bay the same freedom of movement as non-citizens more generally in Guantánamo Bay. Of course, Article 26 would also clearly be satisfied by providing refugees access to the U.S. mainland.

6.4.2 Freedom from Expulsion for Refugees

Furthermore, whilst Article 13 of the ICCPR provides procedural safeguards for members of the protected population before they can be resettled in a third country, Article 32(1) of the Refugee Convention prohibits the expulsion of any refugee (and thus their resettlement in third countries), except in cases of national security. Article 32 of the Refugee Convention states

1. The Contracting States shall not expel a refugee lawfully in their territory save on grounds of national security or public order.
2. The expulsion of such a refugee shall be only in pursuance of a decision reached in accordance with due process of law. Except where compelling reasons of national security otherwise require, the refugee shall be allowed to submit evidence to clear himself, and

[158] CNIS, *GTMO Entry Clearance Information* <www.cnic.navy.mil/guantanamo/InstallationGuide/GTMOEntryClearanceInformation/ index.htm>.

[159] Ibid.

to appeal to and be represented for the purpose before competent authority or a person or persons specially designated by the competent authority.

3. The Contracting States shall allow such a refugee a reasonable period within which to seek legal admission into another country. The Contracting States reserve the right to apply during that period such internal measures as they may deem necessary.

Because Guantánamo Bay constitutes 'territory' for the purposes of Article 32(1) of the Refugee Convention and refugees who are members of the protected population are lawfully in Guantánamo Bay, the prohibition on expulsion applies to members of the protected population who are refugees. The decision to expel a member of the protected population through their resettlement in a third country is not in pursuance of a decision reached in accordance with any due process of law. It is purely an executive decision. Furthermore, the United States does not claim that any expulsions are justified on the grounds of national security. As with other elements of the interdiction program, the only justification provided by the United States is that the program acts as a deterrent. Deterrence is not a permitted justification for expulsion under Article 32(2) of the Refugee Convention. As such, the United States must refrain from the expulsion of all refugees from Guantánamo Bay. Thus, the only means of complying with Article 32 of the Refugee Convention (in combination with the United States' other obligations) is to permanently resettle all refugees currently in Guantánamo Bay (who do not threaten the United States' national security or public order) in the U.S. mainland rather than expose them to expulsion, prolong their detention, or limit their freedom of movement in Guantánamo Bay.

6.4.3 Facilitation of Naturalisation

The resettlement of refugees from Guantánamo Bay in third countries rather than in the U.S. mainland also places the United States in breach of its obligations under Article 34 of the Refugee Convention, which states

> The Contracting States shall as far as possible facilitate the assimilation and naturalization of refugees. They shall in particular make every effort to expedite naturalization proceedings and to reduce as far as possible the charges and costs of such proceedings.

The Article is not strongly worded. The words 'shall as far as possible' mitigate the impact of the obligation. Furthermore, the Article does not require States parties to grant citizenship to refugees.[160] However, the VCLT[161] requires that treaty obligations be interpreted and performed in good faith.[162] An unwillingness to do anything about the assimilation and naturalisation of refugees when assimilation and naturalisation is a possibility places a State in breach of its obligation under Article 34.

As Field argues, the obligation to facilitate the assimilation and naturalisation of refugees is not limited by territory but by feasibility.[163] That is, the United States must do what it can, wherever it exercises jurisdiction, to ensure that refugees are facilitated in their naturalisation. The United States cannot guarantee when a refugee will be resettled in a third country and thus when they may come closer to gaining citizenship in their resettlement State. The assimilation and naturalisation of all refugees in Guantánamo Bay would be easily achieved through the parole or admission of all members of the protected population in the U.S. mainland. The denial of this resettlement option to the majority of refugees results in lengthy delays for those refugees and demonstrates unwillingness by the United States to treat Article 34 in good faith.

6.5 Conclusion

This chapter has shown that the United States contravenes the rights of refugees and individuals who have been found to be at risk of *refoulement*

[160] Paul Weis, *The Refugee Convention, 1951: The Travaux Préparatoires Analysed, With a Commentary* (Cambridge University Press, 1995) 352. This point has been accepted by UNHCR. See UNHCR, 'Outline of Submissions on Behalf of the Office of the United Nations High Commissioner for Refugees (as Amicus Curiae)' (2007) 19 *International Journal of Refugee Law* 360. As Hathaway points out, the Secretary General was emphatic that Article 34 of the Refugee Convention did not require State parties to grant citizenship to refugees. Hathaway, n 151 in this chapter, 981.

[161] Opened for signature 23 May 1969, 1155 UNTS 331 (entered into force 27 January 1980).

[162] Article 31(1) of the VCLT provides, among other things, that 'a treaty shall be interpreted in good faith'. Article 26 of the VCLT provides that '[e]very treaty in force is binding upon the parties to it and must be performed by them in good faith.'

[163] Jeannie Rose Field, 'Bridging the Gap Between Refugee Rights and Reality: a Proposal for Developing International Duties in the Refugee Context' (2010) 22 *International Journal of Refugee Law* 512.

to torture by detaining them (or in the alternative limiting their freedom of movement). Furthermore, the resettlement of the majority of the protected population in third countries rather than in the U.S. mainland results in the subjection of many members of the protected population to expulsion without procedural safeguards and denies the affected refugees the facilitation of their naturalisation. In addition to being unlawful, such actions result in great harm to at-risk individuals whose protection needs have been recognised by the United States.

It may be possible for the United States to remedy some of its present violations of international human rights and refugee law without resettling all members of the protected population permanently in the U.S. mainland – for example, by temporarily allowing members of the protected population to the U.S. mainland until arrangements are made for their resettlement in a third country. Such arrangements would ensure that members of the protected population are not arbitrarily detained (in contravention of Article 9 of the ICCPR) and are provided with freedom of movement (in accordance with Article 12 of the ICCPR and additionally under Article 26 of the Refugee Convention for refugees). However, once a resettlement option becomes available, the United States must only resettle in third countries members of the protected population who are not refugees in pursuance of a decision reached in accordance with the law. The individuals concerned must also be provided with a right to submit reasons against their resettlement and the right to have their resettlement option reviewed. Additionally, the individuals facing resettlement in a third country must also be provided the right to legal assistance during this process (in accordance with Article 13 of the ICCPR).

However, the United States cannot meet all of its obligations to members of the protected populations who are refugees without providing them all with an option for permanent resettlement in the U.S. mainland. This is because refugees are protected not only under Article 13 of the ICCPR (which provides them with certain procedural safeguards in any decision to expel) but also under Article 32 of the Refugee Convention (which protects them from expulsion once they are lawfully within the territory of a State party). Furthermore, the United States must facilitate the naturalisation of all refugees under Article 34 of the Refugee Convention, a task that is best achieved through the permanent resettlement of all refugees in Guantánamo Bay in the U.S. mainland.

At a minimum, therefore, the United States must bring all members of the protected population to the U.S. mainland prior to the availability of any settlement option. The United States is then obliged to treat refugees differently from individuals at risk of *refoulement* to torture by providing refugees with the option of settling permanently in the U.S. mainland, and the right to pursue naturalisation, whilst individuals at risk of torture can be resettled in a third country.

Given the very small numbers of individuals transferred to the MOC under the interdiction program, the operation of such a facility outside of the U.S. mainland may be deemed excessive by some. Despite this, it is unlikely that the United States will abandon the MOC in the near future. The main purpose for the facility appears to be one of contingency, to be used in case of any future influx of people attempting to enter the U.S. mainland by boat. Individuals transferred to Guantánamo Bay under the interdiction program, therefore, must pay the price for the United States' caution – a high price indeed, which leaves them in a state of limbo for many years in violation of their rights under international human rights and refugee law.

7

Conclusion

This book has provided a legal analysis of the U.S. MIP as it currently operates, examining the United States' compliance with its obligations under municipal and international law. The United States has argued that many of the international human rights and refugee law obligations discussed in this book do not apply to it when it exercises jurisdiction in international waters and in Guantánamo Bay. However, the United States' objections are unfounded. The United States is bound by relevant human rights and refugee law obligations, discussed in this book, wherever it exercises jurisdiction, including outside its municipally defined territory.

The exercise of jurisdiction by the United States over individuals interdicted under the MIP is authorised by U.S. municipal law and the international law of the sea with some important exceptions. Whilst the United States must continue to rescue vessels in grave and imminent danger, it must stop turning rescue operations into interdictions when it does not have an agreement with the vessel's flagged State authorising such interference (unless the rescued vessel is stateless or is located in the U.S. contiguous zone). The United States must also cease the practice of destroying rescued unseaworthy vessels flagged to another State with which it does not have an appropriate agreement.

Importantly, certain aspects of the MIP offend international human rights and refugee law. For example, the United States violates international law under the MIP by failing to identify and protect from *refoulement* individuals who are at risk of death or cruel, inhuman or degrading treatment or punishment, who are not refugees or at risk of torture. The United States also denies individuals owed protection against *refoulement* fair and effective status determinations (a requirement that is an intrinsic component of the United States' *non-refoulement* obligations) and discriminates against individual interdictees on the grounds of their nationality. Furthermore, the United States violates its international obligations by arbitrarily detaining members of the protected population in Guantánamo Bay or in the alternative, limiting their freedom of movement; expelling members of the protected population from Guantánamo Bay without procedural safeguards; denying refugees facilitation of their naturalisation; and resettling refugees in third countries in violation of its obligation to refrain from the expulsion of refugees lawfully in its territory.

The most effective way in which the United States can comply with all of its international human rights and refugee law obligations to interdictees is to transfer all interdictees to the U.S. mainland for status determination and, if required, resettlement. In the alternative, the United States could comply with its human rights obligations to individuals protected from *refoulement* under international human rights law, who are not refugees, by permitting them to remain in the U.S. mainland temporarily until they can be resettled in a third country. The United States must also ensure that the removal of any protected person (who is not a refugee) through resettlement in a third country complies with the requirements of Article 13 of the ICCPR.[1] However, the United States owes additional obligations to refugees. As such, in order to comply with its obligations under international refugee law, the United States must provide all refugees with the option of settling permanently in the U.S. mainland.

Unfortunately, litigation in U.S. courts is not in itself an effective means of compelling the U.S. executive to institute the aforementioned changes and thus comply with the United States' international obligations. This is because the international human rights and refugee law obligations discussed in this book are non-self-executing and are therefore not enforceable in U.S. courts without additional implementing legislation. The United States has not implemented all of its international obligations in municipal law, and the obligations that have been implemented under municipal law are unlikely to apply to the U.S. executive in international

[1] As discussed in subsection 6.3.4, the individual facing resettlement must be removed in pursuance of a decision reached in accordance with the law, must be provided with a right to submit reasons against his or her resettlement in a third country and must be provided with a right to have his or her resettlement reviewed.

waters and in Guantánamo Bay. Furthermore, the continuing operation of the plenary power doctrine means that U.S. courts will not interfere in any decision of the executive that may be construed as an exercise of its sovereign power to determine the entry of non-citizens into the U.S. mainland. Moreover, there are no effective mechanisms in the international legal regime for enforcing adherence to international human rights and refugee law obligations.

Whilst interdictees may have no means of litigating to enforce the international human rights and refugee law obligations owed them, the law remains an effective tool in procuring social change. The law can empower and legitimise the claims of advocates against States that violate the rights of at-risk groups.[2] As was shown in Chapter 2, successful advocacy and pressure on the U.S. executive led the Clinton administration to resettle HIV-positive Haitian refugees from Guantánamo Bay into the U.S. mainland rather than appeal the decision of the Second Circuit in *Haitian Centers Council v Sale* (Sale II)[3] to the Supreme Court (which was likely to rule against the refugees); to temporarily suspend the repatriation of Haitian protection seekers in March 1994; and also to resettle Cuban nationals from Guantánamo Bay into the U.S. mainland in 1995. As such, public advocacy may prove successful again in ensuring that the rights of interdictees under international law are respected by the United States.

It should be remembered, however, that policy changes can be readily altered. This was evident in the Clinton administration's short-lived policy changes that benefitted interdictees. Therefore, advocates should call for the United States to fully implement in municipal law the international obligations by which it is legally bound when it exercises jurisdiction in international waters and in Guantánamo Bay. Only changes to U.S. municipal law will ensure that any benefits to interdictees are not short-lived and that the U.S. executive can be challenged in U.S. courts should it breach its international obligations to interdictees in the future.

It should also be noted that the United States is not the only country to interdict individuals attempting to enter its territory without prior

[2] Thomas Risse and Kathryn Sikkink, 'The Socialization of International Human Rights Norms into Domestic Practices: Introduction" in Thomas Risse, Stephen Ropp and Kathryn Sikkink (eds) *The Power of Human Rights: International Norms and Domestic Change* (Cambridge University Press, 1999), 5.

[3] 823 F Supp 1028 (EDNY, 1993).

authorisation. There has been an increasing tendency by States to deny protection seekers access to their territory,[4] notably by Australia and several European States.[5] The United States is also not alone in detaining and processing protection seekers outside its municipally defined territory. Australia too detains and processes people seeking its protection outside its municipally defined territory. In contrast with the United States, however, which detains protection seekers in territory under its jurisdiction, Australia has utilised third countries such as Nauru and Papua New Guinea as sites for extraterritorial immigration detention and processing.[6] Any legal challenge to a particular extraterritorial interdiction or detention regime requires a locally grounded approach. This is because despite some overlapping legal obligations, the legal frameworks in which each regime operates differs in many respects. In particular, each regime is unique in the operation of municipal law and its interplay with international law (and even European Union Law in the context of European States). Nevertheless, extraterritorial interdiction and detention regimes share a common underlying objective: they seek to deter and prevent access to legal safeguards in the country responsible for the interception.[7] Furthermore, such regimes are attractive to States because protection seekers remain 'nameless, faceless, and voiceless' as long as they are outside the State.[8]

4 James Hathaway and Thomas Gammeltoft-Hansen, 'Non-Refoulement in a Wold of Cooperative Deterrence' (Law and Economic Working Papers, Paper 106, University of Michigan Law School, 1 August 2014); Rustvica Andrijasevic, 'From Exception to Excess; Detention & Deportation Across the Mediterranean Space' in Nicholas De Genova and Nathalie Peutz (eds) *The Deportation Regime: Sovereignty, Space, and the Freedom of Movement* (Duke University Press, 2010) 154.

5 See generally Bernard Ryan and Valsamis Mitsilegas (eds.), *Extraterritorial Immigration Control: Legal Challenges* (Martinus Nijhoff, 2010).

6 See Tania Penovic and Azadeh Dastyari, 'Boatloads of Incongruity: The Evolution of Australia's Offshore Processing Regime' (2007) 12 *Australian Journal of Human Rights* 33. For a comparative analysis of Australian and U.S. extraterritorial detention practices by the author, see also Azadeh Dastyari, 'Offshore Processing: An Australian Phenomenon?' in Marius Smith (ed) *Human Rights 2006: The Year in Review* (Castan Centre, 2007); Azadeh Dastyari, 'Refugees on Guantánamo Bay: A Blue Print for Australia's "Pacific Solution"?' (2007) 78 *Australian Quarterly* 1; Azadeh Dastyari 'Swapping Refugees: The Implications of the "Atlantic Solution" (2008) 9 *UTS Law Review* 93.

7 Angus Francis, 'Bringing Protection Home: Healing the Schism Between International Obligations and National Safeguards Created by Extraterritorial Processing' (2008) 20 *International Journal of Refugee Law* 273.

8 Janet Dench and François Crépeau, 'Introduction: Interdiction at the Expense of Human Rights: A Long-term Containment Strategy' (2003) 21 *Refuge: Canada's Journal on Refugees* 1, 5.

This book began with the plea of a Cuban mother, Arelys Valladares Prado, to not forget her and the many others detained in Guantánamo Bay after being transferred there under the MIP. The vast majority of people interdicted under the MIP remain 'nameless, faceless, and voiceless' because they are immediately repatriated, and even the very few who are lucky enough to have their protection needs recognised at sea remain largely hidden from view in Guantánamo Bay. Arelys Valladares Prado was ultimately resettled in the U.S. mainland with her family. Others have not been so lucky. With more effective advocacy, it is conceivable that the United States will cease the detention of protected persons in Guantánamo Bay and provide interdictees with rights they are owed under international law. Until then, we must endeavour to continue shining a light on the vulnerable who are denied rights and kept from view under the MIP. Only then can we ensure that the 'war on terror' prison in Guantánamo Bay is not the only detention centre set for closure on the U.S. naval base in Cuba.[9]

[9] President Obama ordered the closure of the detention centres used in the 'war on terror' on 22 January 2009 under Executive Order 13492, 74 *Federal Register* 4897 (2009). As of November 2014, the detention centres remained open.

Bibliography

U.S. Case Law and Related Documents

Abdullahi v Pfizer, Inc., 562 F.3d 163 (2nd Cir, 2009).
Akhtar v Reno, 123 F.2d Supp. 191 (SDNY, 2000).
American Bar Association v Christopher, 43 F.3d 1412 (11th Cir, 1995).
Barapind v Reno, 225 F.3d 1100 (9th Cir, 2000).
Beazley v Johnson, 242 F.3d 248 (5th Cir, 2001).
Benitez v Wallis, 337 F.3d 1289 (11th Cir, 2003).
Bertrand v Sava, 684 F.2d 204 (2nd Cir, 1982).
Bird v United States, 923 F Supp. 338 (D Conn, 1996).
Boumediene v Bush, 553 US 723 (2008).
British Caledonian Airways v Bond, 665 F.2d 1153 (DC Cir, 1981).
Calderon v Reno, 39 F.2d Supp 943 (ND Ill, 1998).
Calero-Toledo v Person Yacht Leasing Co., 416 US 663 (1974).
Cardenas v Smith, 733 F.2d 909 (DC Cir, 1984).
Clancy v Office of Foreign Assets Control of US Dept. of Treasury, 559 F.3d 595 (7th Cir, 2009).
Clark v Martinez, 543 US 371 (2005).
Cook v United States, 288 US 102 (1932).
Cuban American Bar Association v Christopher, 43 F.3d 1412 (11th Cir, 1995).
Cuban American Bar Association v Christopher, No 94–2183 (Class Action Complaints) (SD Fla, 1994).
Diggs v Richardson, 555 F.2d 848 (DC Cir, 1976).
Edwards v Carter, 580 F.2d 1055 (DC Cir, 1978).
EEOC v Arabian American Oil Co, 499 US 244 (1991).

Floy Bros v Filardo, 336 US 281 (1949).
Foster v Neilson, 27 US 253 (1829).
Frolova v Union of Soviet Socialist Republics, 761 F.2d 370 (7th Cir, 1985).
Goldstar (Panama) S.A. v United States, 967 F.2d 965 (4th Cir, 1992).
Haitian Refugee Center Inc. v Christopher, 43 F.3d 1431 (11th Cir, 1995).
Haitian Centers Council Inc. v McNary, 969 F.2d 1326 (2nd Cir, 1992).
Haitian Centers Council Inc. v McNary, 969 F.2d 1350 (2nd Cir, 1992).
Haitian Centers Council Inc. v McNary, No. 92-CV-1258 (EDNY, June 5, 1992).
Haitian Centers Council Inc. v Sale, 823 F Supp. 1028 (EDNY, 1993).
Haitian Refugee Center v Baker, 112 S Ct 1245 (1992).
Haitian Refugee Center v Baker, 789 F. Supp. 1552 (SD Fla, 1991).
Haitian Refugee Center v Baker, 949 F.2d 1109 (11th Cir, 1991).
Haitian Refugee Center v Baker, 953 F.2d 1498 (11th Cir, 1992).
Haitian Refugee Center v Gracey, 600 F Supp. 1396 (DDC, 1985).
Haitian Refugee Center v Gracey, 809 F.2d 794 (DC Cir, 1987).
Haitian Refugee Center Inc. v Christopher (District Court for the Southern District of Florida / No. 95–0022–CIV–MOORE, 5 January 1995).
Hamdan v Rumsfeld, 548 US 557 (2006).
Huerta v United States, 548 F.2d 343 (Fed Cir, 1977).
Igartua De La Rosa v United States, 32 F.3d 8 (1st Cir, 1994).
In re Extradition of Cheung, 968 F Supp. 791(D Conn, 1997).
In re Stoffregen, 6 F.2d 943 (DC Cir, 1925).
INS v Aguirre-Aguirre, 119 S.Ct. 1439 (1999).
INS v Cardoza-Fonseca, 480 US 440 (1987).
INS v Stevic, 480 US 421 (1987).
Islamic Republic of Iran v Boeing Co., 771 F.2d 1279 (9th Cir, 1985).
Jama v INS, 22 F.2d Supp. 353 (DNJ, 1 October 1998).
Johnson v Eisentrager, 339 US 763 (1950).
Johnson v Quander, 370 F.2d Supp. 79 (D DC 2005).
Kiyemba v Obama, 130 S.Ct. 1235 (2010).
Kiyemba v Obama, 555 F.3d 1022 (DC Cir, 2009).
Kiyemba v Obama, 561 F.3d 509 (DC Cir, 2009).
Kiyemba v Obama, 605 F.3d 1046 (DC Cir, 2010).
Kyler v Montezuma County, 203 F.3d 614 (9th Cir, 2000).
Lauritzen v Larsen, 345 US 571 (1953).
Leng May Ma v Barber, 357 US 185(1958).
Linder v Calero Portocarrero, 747 F Supp. 1452 (SD Fla, 1990).

United States v Marino-Garcia, 679 F.2d 1373 (11th Cir, 1982).
Martinez-Lopez v Gonzales, 454 F.3d 500 (5th Cir, 2006).
Matter of Median, 151 & N Dec. 611 (BIA, 1976).
McNary v Haitian Centers Council, Inc., 503 US 1000 (1992).
Medellin v Texas, 552 US 491 (2008).
Munaf v Geren, 128553 US 674 (2008).
Murray v Schooner Charming Betsy, 6 US 64 (1804).
Parhat v Gates, 532 F.3d 834 (DC Cir, 2008).
Pierre v Gonzales, 502 F.3d 109 (2nd Cir, 2007).
Rasul v Bush, 542 US 466 (2004).
Recinos De Leon v Gonzales, 400 F.3d 1185 (9th Cir, 2005).
Rousseau v Brown, 21 App. DC 73 (DC Cir, 1903).
Sale v Haitian Centers Council Inc., 509 US 155 (1993).
Sandhu v Burke (United States District Court, S.D. New York, No 97 Civ 4608, 2000 WL 191707, 10 February 2000).
Septic Tank Co. v Knoxville, 227 US 39 (1913).
Singh v Ashcroft, F.3d 396 (6th Cir, 2005).
Sosa v Alvarez-Machain, 542 US 692, 735 (2004).
Tel-Oren v Libyan Arab Republic, 726 F.2d 774 (DC Cir, 1984).
US ex rel. Knauff v Shaughnessy, 338 US 543 (1950).
United States v $228,536, 895, F.2d 908 (2nd Cir, 1990).
United States v Aguilar, 883 F.2d 662 (9th Cir, 1989).
United States v Davis, 905 F.2d 245 (9th Cir, 1990).
United States v Degado-Garcia, 374 F.3d 1137 (DC Cir, 2004).
United States v Duarte-Acero, 208 F.3d 1282 (11th Cir, 2000).
United States v Layton, 509 F Supp. 212 (ND Cal, 1981).
United States v Lee, 906 F.2d 117 (4th Cir, 1990).
United States v Merkt, 794, F.2d 950 (5th Cir, 1986).
United States v Munsingwear, 340 US 36 (1950).
United States v Percheman, 32 US 51 (1833).
United States v Postal, 589 F.2d 862 (5th Cir, 1979).
United States v Rendon, 354 F.3d 1320 (11th Cir, 2003).
United States v Rogers, 388 F Supp. 298 (ED Va, 1975).
United States v Verdugo-Urquidez, 494 US 259 (1990).
White v Paulsen, 997 F Supp. 1380 (ED Wash, 1998).
Zadvydas v Davis, 533 US 678 (2001).
Zhen Li Iao v Gonzales, 400 F.3d 530 (7th Cir, 2005).

U.S. Statutes, Notices, Regulations, Executive Orders, Proclamations and Other Related Material

An Act Declaring that War Exists Between the United States of America and the Kingdom of Spain, 30 Stat. 364.

Cuban Adjustment Act of 1966 Pub L No 89–414, 732, 80 Stat. 1161 (1966).

Detainees Treatment Act of 2005 Pub L No 109–148, 119 Stat. 2680, 2742–4.

Executive Order 12324, 46 *Federal Register* 48 (1981).

Executive Order 12807, 57 *Federal Register* 23 (1992).

Executive Order 12807, 57 *Federal Register* 23, 133 (1992).

Executive Order 13276, 67 *Federal Register* 69 (2002).

Executive Order 13286, 68 *Federal Register* 10619 (2003).

Executive Order 13492, 74 *Federal Register* 4897 (2009).

Foreign Affairs Reform and Restructuring Act of 1998, Pub L No 105–277 (1998).

Homeland Security Act, Pub L No 107–296, 116 Stat. 745 (2002).

Immigration and Nationality Act, Pub L No 82–414, 66 Stat. 163 (1952).

INS Memorandum, *Shipboard Processing of Cubans* (9 August 1995).

Liberty and Democratic Solidarity Act, Pub L No 104–114, 110. Stat. 785 (1996).

Migration and Refugee Assistance Act, Pub L No 510, 87th Cong, 1st sess, (1962).

Presidential Proclamation 2523, 3 CFR 270 (1941).

Presidential Proclamation 3447, 27 *Federal Register* 1085 (1962).

Presidential Proclamation 4865, 46 *Federal Register* 48 (1981).

Refugee Act, Pub L No 96–212, 94 Stat. 102 (1980).

Treaties and Other International Agreements

Agreement between the Government of the United States of America and the Government of the Dominican Republic Concerning Maritime Migration Law Enforcement, signed at Washington 20 May 2003 (entered into force 20 May 2003).

Agreement Between the Government of the United States of America and the Government of the Bahamas Concerning Cooperation in Maritime

Law Enforcement, signed at Nassau 29 June 2004 (entered into force 29 June 2004).

Agreement Between the United States and Cuba for the Lease of Lands for Coaling and Naval Stations; Lease to the United States of Lands in Cuba for Coaling and Naval Stations, 16–23 February 1903, US-Cuba, T.S. No. 418.

Agreement Effected by Exchange of Notes Regarding Migrants and Interdiction, 23 September 1981, US-Haiti, 33 U.S.T. 3559, TIAS. No. 10, 241.

Agreement on Interdiction of Haitian Immigration to the US, 23 September 1981, US-Haiti, 33 U.S.T.-3559.

Agreement Relating to the Implementation of Part XI of the United Nations Convention on the Law of the Sea of 10 December 1982, Registration 16 November 1994, 1836 UNTS 3 (entered into force provisionally on 16 November 1994 and definitively on 28 July 1996).

Charter of the United Nations, opened for signature 26 June 1945, 1 UNTS XVI (entered into force on 24 October 1945).

Convention Against Torture and Other Cruel Inhuman or Degrading Treatment or Punishment, opened for signature 4 February 1985, 1465 UNTS 85 (entered into force 26 June 1987).

Convention for the Protection of Human Rights and Fundamental Freedoms, opened for signature 4 November 1950, 213 UNTS 222 (entered into force 3 September 1953).

Convention on Rights and Duties of States, opened for signature 26 December 1933, 165 LNTS 19 (entered into force 26 December 1934).

Convention on the Elimination of all Forms of Discrimination against Women, opened for signature 18 December 1979, 1249 UNTS 13 (entered into force 3 September 1981).

Convention on the High Seas, opened for signature 29 April 1958, 13 UST 2312 (entered into force 30 September 1962).

Convention on the Rights of Persons with Disabilities, opened for signature 30 March 2007, 189 UNTS 137 (entered into force 3 May 2008).

Convention on the Rights of the Child, opened for signature 20 November 1989, 1577 UNTS, 3 (entered into force 2 September 1990).

Convention Relating to the Status of Refugees, opened for signature 28 July 1951, 189 UNTS 150 (entered into force 22 April 1954).

International Convention on Maritime Search and Rescue, opened for signature 27 April 1979, 1405 UNTS 97 (entered into force 22 June 1985).

International Convention on Safety of Life at Sea, opened for signature 1 November 1974, 164 UNTS 113 (entered into force 25 May 1980).

International Convention on Salvage, opened for signature 1 July 1989, 1953 UNTS 33479 (entered into force 14 July 1996).

International Convention on the Elimination of All Forms of Racial Discrimination, opened for signature 21 December 1965, 660 UNTS 195 (entered into force 4 January 1969).

International Covenant on Civil and Political Rights, opened for signature 19 December 1966, 999 UNTS 171 (entered into force 23 March 1976).

International Covenant on Economic, Social and Cultural Rights, opened for signature 16 December 1966, 993 UNTS 3 (entered into force 3 January 1976).

International Maritime Organization, *Resolution MSC.167(78), Guidelines on the Treatment of Persons Rescued at Sea*, 20 May 2004.

Joint Statement on Migration, US Department of State Dispatch, 8 May 1995, Vol. 6, Issue 19, 397.

Lease to the United States by the Government of Cuba of Certain Areas of Land and Water for naval or Coaling Stations in Guantánamo and Bahia Honda, 2 July 1903, US-Cuba, art. III, T.S. No. 426.

Maritime Boundary Agreement between the United States of America and the Republic of Cuba (1977) Senate Treaty Document EX. H, 96–1.

Memorandum of understanding between the Government of the United Kingdom, the Government of the Turks and Caicos Islands, and the Government of the United States to establish in the Turks and Caicos Islands a processing facility to determine the refugee status of boat people from Haiti KAV 3906, Temp. State Dept. No. 94–158 (entered into force 18 June 1994).

Memorandum of Understanding Between the Government of the United States and the Government of Jamaica for the Establishment Within the Jamaican Territorial Sea and Internal Waters of a Facility to Process Nationals of Haiti Seeking Refuge Within or Entry to the United States of America, KAV 3901, Temp. State Dept. No. 94–153 (entered into force 2 June 1994).

North Atlantic Treaty, opened for signature 4 April 1949, 34 UNTS 243 (entered into force 24 August 1949).

Optional Protocol to the International Covenant on Civil and Political Rights, opened for signature 19 December 1966, 999 UNTS 171 (entered into force 23 March 1976).

Organization of American States, *Resolution MRE/RES*,. 1/91 OEA/ SER. F/V.1 (3 October, 1991).

Protocol Against the Smuggling of Migrants by Land, Sea and Air Protocol Against Smuggling of Migrants by Land, Sea and Air, opened for signature 15 November 2000, 2241 UNTS 507 (entered into force 28 January 2004).

Protocol No 4 to the Convention for the Protection of Human Rights and Fundamental Freedoms, Securing Certain Rights and Freedoms other than those Already Included in the Convention and in the first Protocol Thereto, opened for signature 16 September 1963, ETS No 46 (entered into force 2 May1968).

Protocol No 7 to the Convention for the Protection of Human Rights and Fundamental Freedoms as amended by Protocol No 11, opened for signature 22 November 1984, ETS No 117 (entered into force 11 November 1988).

Protocol Relating to the Status of Refugees, opened for signature 31 January 1967, 606 UNTS 267 (entered into force 4 October 1967).

The Situation of Democracy and Human Rights in Haiti, GA Res 46/7, 51st Plen mtg, UN Doc A/RES/46/7 (11 October 1991).

Statute of the Office of the United Nations High Commissioner for Refugees, G.A. Res. 428 (V), annex, UN GAOR Supp. (No 20), 46 UN Doc A/1775 (1950).

Treaty Between the United States and Cuba. Defining Their Relations, May 29, 1934, US-. Cuba, T.S. No. 866.

Treaty of Paris, 30 *Stat*. 1754.

US-Cuba Joint Communiqué On Migration, US Department of State Dispatch, 9 December 1994, Vol. 5, Issue 37, 603.

United Nations Convention on the Law of the Sea, opened for signature 10 December 1982, 1833 UNTS 3 (entered into force 14 November 1994).

Universal Declaration of Human Rights, GA Res 217A(III), UN GAOR, 3rd sess, 183rd plen mtg, UN Doc A/810 (10 December 1948).

Material Relating to the United Nations High Commissioner for Refugees or the Executive Committee of the High Commissioner's Program

UNHCR ExCom, *Conclusion No 2: Function of the Subcommittee and General Conclusion on International Protection*, 27th sess, UN Doc 12A A/10012/Add.1 (14 October 1975).

UNHCR ExCom, *Conclusion No 8: Note on the Extraterritorial Effect of the Determination of Refugee Status under the 1951 Convention and the 1967 Protocol Relating to the Status of Refugees*, 29th sess, UN Doc EC/SCP/9 (24 August 1978).

UNHCR ExCom, *Conclusion No 11: General Conclusion on International Protection*, 29th sess, UN Doc 12A A/33/12/Add.1 (17 October 1978).

UNHCR ExCom, *Conclusion No 14: General Conclusion on International Protection*, 30th sess, UN Doc 12A A/34/12/Add.1 (16 October 1979).

UNHCR ExCom, *Conclusion No 16: General Conclusion on International Protection*, 31st sess, UN Doc 12A A/35/12/Add.1 (16 October 1980).

UNHCR ExCom, *Conclusion No 20: Protection of Asylum-Seekers at Sea*, 31st sess, UN Doc No 12A A/35/12/Add.1 (16 October 1980).

UNHCR ExCom, *Conclusion No 21: General Conclusion on International Protection*, 32nd sess, UN Doc 12A A/35/12/Add.1 (21 October 1981).

UNHCR ExCom, *Conclusion No 25: General Conclusion on International Protection*, 33rd sess, UN Doc 12A A/37/12/Add.1 (20 October 1982).

UNHCR ExCom, *Conclusion No 28: Follow-up on Earlier Conclusions of the Sub-Committee of the Whole on International Protection on the Determination of Refugee Status, Inter Alia, with Reference to the Role of UNHCR in National Refugee Status Determination Procedures*, 33rd sess, UN Doc 12A A/36/12/Add. 12 (20 October 1982).

UNHCR ExCom, *Conclusion No 29: General Conclusion on International Protection*, 34th sess, UN Doc 12A A/38/12/Add.1 (20 October 1983).

UNHCR ExCom, *Conclusion No 44: Detention of Refugees and Asylum-Seekers*, 37th sess, UN Doc 12A A/41/12/Add.1 (13 October 1986).

UNHCR ExCom, *Conclusion No 46: General Conclusion on International Protection*, 38th sess, UN Doc12A A/42/12/Add.1 (12 October 1987).

UNHCR ExCom, *Conclusion No 55: General Conclusion on International Protection*, 40th sess, UN Doc 12A A/44/12/Add.1 (13 October 1989).

UNHCR ExCom, *Conclusion No 71: General Conclusion on International Protection*, 44th sess, UN Doc 12A A/48/12/Add.1 (8 October 1993).

UNHCR ExCom, *Conclusion No 74: General Conclusion on International Protection*, 45th sess, UN Doc 12A A/49/12/Add.1 (7 October 1994).

UNHCR ExCom, *Conclusion No 81: General Conclusion on International Protection*, 48th sess, UN Doc A/52/12/Add.1 (17 October 1997).

UNHCR ExCom, *Conclusion No 82: Conclusion on Safeguarding Asylum*, 48th sess, UN Doc A/52/12/Add.1 (17 October 1997).

UNHCR ExCom, *Conclusion No 85: Conclusion on International Protection*, 49th sess, UN Doc 12A A/53/12/Add.1 (9 October 1998).

UNHCR ExCom, *Conclusion No 87: General Conclusion on International Protection*, 50th sess, UN Doc 12A A/54/12/Add.1 (8 October 1999).

UNHCR ExCom, *Conclusion No 93: Conclusion on Reception of Asylum Seekers in the Context of Individual Asylum Systems*, 53rd sess, UN Doc 12A A/57/12/Add.1 (8 October 2002).

UNHCR ExCom, *Conclusion No 97: Conclusion on Protection Safeguards in Interception Measures*, 58th sess, UN Doc A/58/12/Add.1 (10 October 2003).

UNHCR ExCom, *Conclusion No 99: Conclusions Adopted by the Executive Committee on the International Protection of Refugees*, 55th sess, UN Doc A/59/12/Add.1, (8 October 1997).

UNHCR ExCom, *Note on International Protection*, 52nd sess, UN Doc A/AC.96/951 (13 September 2001).

UNHCR ExCom, *Note on the Extraterritorial Effect of the Determination of Refugee Status under the 1951 Convention and the 1967 Protocol*

Relating to the Status of Refugees, Conclusion No 8., 29th sess, UN Doc EC/SCP/9 (24 August 1978).

UNHCR, *Advisory Opinion on the Extraterritorial Application of Non-Refoulement Obligations under the 1951 Convention Relating to the Status of Refugees and Its 1967 Protocol* (26 January 2007) <http://www.unhcr.org/refworld/docid/45f17a1a4.html>.

UNHCR, *Background Note: The Treatment of Persons Rescued at Sea: Conclusions and Recommendations From Recent Meetings and Expert Roundtables Convened by* (28 November 2007) <http://www.unhcr.org/refworld/docid/4782500d2.html>.

UNHCR, *Briefing Note: Human Rights and Refugee Protection* (1 July 1997) <http://www.unhcr.org/refworld/docid/3ae6b32310.html>.

UNHCR, *Fair and Efficient Asylum Procedures: A Non-Exhaustive Overview of Applicable International Standards* (2 September 2005) 3 <http://www.unhcr.org/refworld/pdfid/432ae9204.pdf>.

UNHCR, *Global Consultations on International Protection/Third Track: Asylum Processes (Fair and Efficient Asylum Procedures)*, UN Doc EC/GC/01/12 (31 May 2001).

UNHCR, *Guidelines on the Applicable Criteria and Standards Relating to the Detention of Asylum-Seekers and Alternatives to Detention* (2012) <http://www.unhcr.org/refworld/docid/503489533b8.html>.

UNHCR, *Handbook and Guidelines on Procedures and Criteria for Determining Refugee Status Under the 1951 Convention and the 1967 Protocol Relating to the Status of Refugees* (1992, reissued 2011).

UNHCR, *Protection Policy Paper: Maritime Interception Operations and the Processing of International Protection Claims* (November 2010) <http://www.unhcr.org/refworld/docid/4cd12d3a2.html>.

UNHCR, *Provisional Comments on the Proposal for a European Council Directive on Minimum Standards on Procedures in Member States for Granting and Withdrawing Refugee Status* (10 February 2005) <http://www.unhcr.org/refworld/docid/42492b302.html>.

UNHCR, 'The Haitian Interdiction Case 1993 Brief amicus curiae', (1994) 6 *International Journal of Refugee Law* 85.

United Nations Ad Hoc Committee on Statelessness and Related Problems, *Summary Record of the Twentieth Meeting* 11–12, <www.unhcr.org/refworld/docid/3ae68c1c0.html>.

United States Mission to International Organizations, Statement of the United States Delegation to the Standing Committee of the Executive Committee of the Program of the UN High Commissioner for Refugees (Geneva, 25 June 1996).

United States Mission to the United Nations and Other International Organisations in Geneva, Observations of the United States on the Advisory Opinion of the UN High Commissioner for Refugees on Extraterritorial Application of *Non-Refoulement* Obligations under the 1951 Convention Relating to the Status of Refugees and its 1967 Protocol (Geneva, 28 December 2007).

Material Relating to United Nations Treaty Bodies

A v Australia, UN Doc CCPR/C/59/D/560/1993 (30 April 1997).

Ackla v Togo, UN Doc CCPR/C/51/D/505/1992 (25 March 1996).

Agiza v Sweden, UN Doc CAT/C/34/D/233/2003 (20 May 2005).

Ahani v Canada, UN Doc CCPR/C/80/D/1051/2002 (15 June 2004).

Alzery v Sweden, UN Doc CCPR/C/88/D/1416/2005 (10 November 2006).

Baban v Australia, UN Doc CCPR/C/78/D/1014/2001 (6 August 2003).

Bahamonde v Equatorial Guinea, UN Doc CCPR/C/49/D/468/1991 (10 November 1993).

Bakhtiyari v Australia, UN Doc CCPR/C/79/D/1069/2002 (29 October 2003).

Burgos v Uruguay, UN Doc CCPR/C/13/D/52/1979 (29 July 1981).

Byahuranga v Denmark, UN Doc CCPR/C/82/D/1222/2003 (9 December 2004).

C v Australia, UN Doc CCPR/C/76/D/ 900/1999 (28 October 2002).

Casafranca de Gomez v Peru, UN Doc CCPR/C/78/D/981/2001 (22 July 2003).

Casariego v Uruguay, UN Doc. CCPR/C/13/D/56/1979 (29 July 1981).

Celepli v Sweden, UN Doc CCPR/C/51/D/456/1991 (18 July 1994).

Chadzjian v The Netherlands, UN Doc CCPR/C/93/D/1494/2006 (5 August 2008).

Committee Against Torture, *Concluding Observations on the Third to Fifth Periodic Report of the United States of America*, 53rd sess, UN DOC CAT/C/USA/CO/3–5 (20 November 2014).

Committee Against Torture, *Concluding Observations: United States of America*: UN Doc CAT/C/USA/CO/2 (25 July 2006).

Committee Against Torture, *Consideration of Reports Submitted by State Parties under Article 19 of the Convention: Initial Reports of State Parties Due in 1995*, UN Doc CAT/C/28/Add.5 (9 February 2000).

Committee Against Torture, *Consideration of Reports Submitted by State Parties under Article 19 of the Convention Conclusions and Recommendations of the CAT Committee: United States of America*, 36th sess, UN DOC CAT/C/USA/CO/2 (25 July 2006).

Committee Against Torture, *General Comment No 2: Implementation of Article 2 by State Parties*, 39th sess, UN Doc CAT/C/GC/2 (24 January 2008).

Committee on the Elimination of Racial Discrimination, *General Recommendation No 26: Article 6 of the Convention*, 56th sess, UN Doc A/55/18, annex V (24 March 2000).

Committee on the Elimination of Racial Discrimination, *Reports Submitted by State Parties Under Article 9 of the Convention, Third Periodic Reports of State Parties due in 1999, Addendum, United States of America*, UN Doc CERD/C/351/Add.1 (10 October 2000).

D & E v Australia, UN Doc CCPR/C/87/D/1050/2002 (11 July 2006).

El Ghar v Libyan Arab Jamahiriya, UN Doc CCPR/C/82/D/1107/2002 (15 November 2004).

Faure v Australia, UN doc CCPR/C/85/D/1036/01(31 October 2005).

Fernando v Sri Lanka, UN Doc CCPR/C/83/D/1189/2003 (10 May 2005).

Gonzalez v Guyana, UN Doc CCPR/C/98/D/1246/2004 (21 May 2010).

Hammel v Madagascar, UN Doc CCPR/C/OP/2 (3 April 1987).

Hudoyberganova v Uzbekistan, UN Doc CCPR/C/82/D/931/2000 (15 June 2004).

Human Rights Committee, *Concluding Observations of the Human Rights Committee: Denmark*, 70th sess, UN Doc CCPR/CO/70/DNK (31 October 2000).

Human Rights Committee, *Concluding Observations of the Human Rights Committee: Israel*, 99th sess, UN Doc CCPR/C/ISR/CO/3 (3 September 2010).

Human Rights Committee, *Concluding Observations of the Human Rights Committee: United Kingdom of Great Britain and Northern Ireland*, UN Doc CCPR/C/GBR/CO/6 (30 July 2008).

Human Rights Committee, *Concluding Observations of the Human Rights Committee: United States of America*, 53rd sess, UN Doc CCPR/C/79/Add.50 (6 April 1995).

Human Rights Committee, *Concluding Observations on the Fourth Periodic Report of the United States of America*, UN Doc CCPR/C/USA/CO/4, (23 April 2014).

Human Rights Committee, *Consideration of Reports Submitted by States Parties Under Article 40 of the Covenant: Concluding Observations of the Human Rights Committee: United States of America*, 87th sess, UN Doc CCPR/C/USA/CO/3 (15 September 2006).

Human Rights Committee, *General Comment No 15: The Position of Aliens Under the Covenant*, 27th sess, UN Doc HRI/GEN/1/Rev.1 (4 November 1986).

Human Rights Committee, *General Comment No 18: Non-Discrimination*, 37th sess (10 November 1989).

Human Rights Committee, *General Comment No 20: Replaces General Comment No 7 Concerning Prohibition Of Torture And Cruel Treatment Or Punishment*, 44th sess, UN Doc HRI/GEN/1/Rev6 (10 March 1992).

Human Rights Committee, *General Comment No 24: Issues Relating to Reservations Made Upon Ratification or Accession to the Covenant or the Optional Protocols Thereto, or In Relation to Declarations Under Article 41 of the Covenant*, 52nd sess, UN Doc CCPR/C/21/Rev.1/Add.6 (4 November 1994).

Human Rights Committee, *General Comment No 27: Freedom of Movement (Art.12)*, 67th sess, UN Doc CCPR/C/21/Rev.1/Add.9 (2 November 1999).

Human Rights Committee, *General Comment No 31: Nature of the General Obligation Imposed on States Parties to the Covenant*, 80th sess, 12 UN Doc CCPR/C/21/Rev1/Add.13 (26 May 2004).

Human Rights Committee, *General Comment No 32: Right to Equality Before Courts and Tribunals and to a Fair Trial*, 90th sess, UN Doc CCPR/C/GC/32 (27 July 2007).

Human Rights Committee, *General Comment No 33: The Obligations of State Parties under the Optional Protocol to the International Covenant on Civil and Political Rights*, 94th sess, UN Doc CCPR/C/GC/33 (5 November 2008).

Human Rights Committee, General Comment No 35 – Article 9: Liberty and Security of Person, 112th sess, UN Doc CCPR/C/GC/35 (28 October 2014).

Human Rights Committee, *Reports Submitted by State Parties under Article 40 of the Covenant: Initial Reports of State Parties Due in 1993: United States of America*, CCPR/C/81/Add.4 (24 August 1994).

Human Rights Committee, *Reservations, Declarations, Notifications and Objections Relating to the International Covenant on Civil and Political Rights and the Optional Protocols Thereto*, UN Doc CCPR/C/2/Rev.4 (24 August 1994).

J.H.A v Spain, UN Doc CAT/C/41/D/323/2007 (21 November 2008).

K. A. L. *and* A. A. M. L *v Canada*, UN Doc CCPR/C/104/D/1816/2008 (26 March 2012).

Karker v France, UN Doc CCPR/C/70/D/833/1998 (26 October 2000).

Kaur v Canada, UN Doc CCPR/C/94/D/1455/2006 (18 November 2008).

Kazantsis v Cyprus, UN doc CCPR/C/78/D/972/2001(19 September 2003).

Kennedy v Trindad and Tobago, UN Doc CCPR/C/74/D/845/1998 (26 March 2002).

Kurbanov v Tajikistan, UN Doc CCPR/C/79/D/1096/2002 (12 November 2003).

Kwok v Australia, UN Doc CCPR/C/97/D/1442/2005 (23 October 2009).

Lee v Republic of Korea, UN Doc CCPR/C/84/D/1119/2002 (23 August 2005).

Madafferi v Australia, UN Doc CCPR/C/81/D/1011/2001 (26 August 2004).

Maroufidou v Sweden, UN Doc CCPR/C/OP/1 (8 April 1981).

Marques de Morais v Angola, UN Doc CCPR/C/83/D/1128/2002 (18 April 2005).

Montero v Uruguay, UN Doc CCPR/C/18/D/106/1981 (31 March 1983).

P.K. v Canada, UN Doc CCPR/C/89/D/1234/2003 (3 April 2007).

Paul Perterer v Austria, UN Doc CCPR/C/81/D/1015/2001 (20 August 2004).

Rameka v New Zealand, UN Doc CCPR/C/79/D/1090/200 (23 November 2003).

Sarma v Sri Lanka, UN Doc CCPR/C/78/D/950/2000 (31 July 2003).

Semey v Spain, UN Doc CCPR/C/78/D/986/2001 (19 September 2003).
Shafiq v Australia, UN Doc CCPR/C/88/D/1324/2004 (13 November 2006).
Shams v Australia, UN Doc CCPR/C/90/D/1255, 1256, 1259, 1260, 1266, 1268, 1270, 1288/2004 (11 September 2007).
Shin v Republic of Korea, UN Doc CCPR/C/80/D/926/2000 (19 March 2004).
Tillman v Australia, UN Doc CCPR/C/98/D/1635/2007 (10 May 2010).
Torres v Finland, UN Doc CCPR/C/38/D/291/1988 (5 April 1990).
Van Alphen v The Netherlands, UN Doc CCPR/C/39/D/305/1988 (15 August 1990).
Voulanne v Finland, UN Doc CCPR/C/35/D/265/1987 (31 October 1987).
Weiss v Austria, UN Doc CCPR/C/77/D/1086/2002 (24 May 2002).
Zundel v Canada, UN Doc CCPR/C/89/D/1341/2005 (4 April 2007).

Decisions of the International Court of Justice

Aegean Sea Continental Shelf, Judgment (Greece v Turkey) (Judgment) [1978] ICJ Rep 39.
Armed Activities on the Territory of the Congo (Democratic Republic of the Congo v Uganda) (Judgment, Merits) [2005] ICJ Rep 168.
Avena case (Mexico v United States) [2004] ICJ Rep 12.
Case Concerning the Application of the International Convention on the Elimination of All Forms of Racial Discrimination (*Georgia v Russian Federation*) (*Provisional Measure*)[2008] ICJ Rep 353.
Case Concerning the Military and Paramilitary Activities in and Against Nicaragua (Nicaragua v United States Of America) (Judgement) [1986] ICJ Rep 14.
Legal Consequences of the Construction of a Wall in the Occupied Palestinian Territory (Advisory Opinion) [2004] ICJ Rep 136.
Maritime Delimitation and Territorial Questions between Qatar and Bahrain (Qatar v Bahrain) (Jurisdiction and Admissibility) [1994] ICJ Rep 112.
S.S 'Lotus' (France v Turkey) (Judgement) [1927] PCIJ (Ser A) No 10.
Temple of Preah Vihear (Cambodia v Thailand) (Preliminary Objection) [1961] IJC Rep 26.

Foreign Domestic and Regional Material

Alkateb v Godwin (2004) 219 CLR 562.

Al-Skeini v United Kingdom (2011) 53 EHRR 18.

American Convention on Human Rights, *Advisory Opinion OC10/89*, July 14, 1989, Inter Am. C.H.R. (Ser. A), Rep. No 10 (1989).

Amuur v France (1996) 22 Eur Court HR 533.

Banković v Belgium (2001) XII Eur Court HR 333.

Decree Law No.2 of 24 February 1977. Entered into force 26 September 1977.

Decree No. 38, entered into Force 8 April 1977 *Le Moniteur* No. 38.

Dominican Republic: Law No. 573, entered into force 1 April 1977.

Guzzardi v Italy (7367/76) [1981] 3 EHRR 333.

Haitian Centre for Human rights et al. v United States, Case No 10.675, Report No 51/96, Inter AmCHR Doc. OEA/Ser.L/V/II.95 Doc. 7.

Hirsi Jamaa and Others v Italy (European Court of Human Rights, Grand Chamber, Application No 27765/09, 23 February 2012).

In Re Guzman & Latamble, Annual Digest, 1933–34, Case No. 43 p 112.

Instrument of Designation of the Independent State of Papua New Guinea as a Regional Processing Country under Subsection 198ab(1) of the Migration Act 1958.

Instrument of Designation of the Republic of Nauru as a Regional Processing Country under Subsection 198ab(1) of the Migration Act 1958.

Migration Act 1958 (Australia).

Migration Legislation Amendment (Regional Processing and Other Measures) Act 2012.

Minister for Immigration & Multicultural Affairs v Ibrahim (2000) 204 CLR 1.

Minister for Immigration & Multicultural Affairs v Savvin (2000) FCA 478.

Minister for Immigration and Ethnic Affairs v Mayer (1985) 157 CLR 290.

Minister for Immigration v Khawar (2002) 210 CLR 1.

Molvan v A.G For Palestine (1948) Ac 351, 369–370 (UK).

Pamuk e Altri Tribunale de Crotone, 27 September 2001 (Italy).

Plaintiff M70/2011 and Plaintiff M106/2011 v Minister for Immigration and Citizenship (2011) 280 ALR 18.

Prevention of Terrorism Act 2005 (UK).

R *(European Roma Rights Centre and Others) v Immigration Officer at Prague Airport* (2004) QB 811.

R (*on the application of Abbasi et al*) *v Secretary of State for Foreign and Commonwealth Affairs* (2002) EWCA Civ 1598 (UK).

Refugee Convention Act, Act No 12 of 2012 (Nauru).

Regina v Immigration Officer at Prague Airport and Anor (*Respondents*) *ex parte European Roma Rights Centre & Ors* (*Appellants*) (2004) UKHL 55 (UK).

Ruddock v Vardarlis (2001) 110 FCR 491 (Australia).

Treaty of Waitangi (Fisheries Claims) Settlement Act 1992 (NZ).

Books and Journal Articles

Acer, Eleanor and Goodman, Jake, 'Reaffirming Rights: Human Rights Protections of Migrants, Asylum Seekers, and Refugees in Immigration Detention' (2010) 24 *Georgetown Immigration Law Journal* 507.

Agnolucci, Simona, 'Expedited Removal: Suggestions for Reform in Light of the United States Commission on International Religious Freedom Report and the Real ID Act' (2006) 57 *Hastings Law Journal* 619.

Akram, Susan, Dumper, Michael, Lynk, Michael and Scobbie, Iain (eds), *International Law and the Israeli-Palestinian Conflict: A Rights-Based Approach to Middle East Peace* (Routledge, 2011).

Allen, Neil, 'Restricting Movement or Depriving Liberty' (2009) 19 *Journal of Mental Health Law* 19.

Anderson III, Edward, 'The Nationality of Ships and Flags of Convenience: Economics, Politics, and Alternatives' (1996) 21 *Tulane Maritime Law Journal* 139.

Bantekas, Ilias and Oette, Lutz, *International Human Rights Law and Practice* (Cambridge University Press, 2013).

Barnes, Richard, 'Refugee Law at Sea' (2004) 53 *International and Comparative Law Quarterly* 47.

Barsky, Robert, *Constructing a Productive Other Discourse Theory and the Convention Refugee Gearing* (John Benjamins Publishing, 1994).

Barsky, Robert, 'The Interpreter and the Canadian Convention Refugee Hearing: Crossing the Potentially Life-Threatening Boundaries between "coccode-e-eh," "cluck-cluck," and "cot-cot-cot"' (1993) 6 *Traduction, Terminologie, Racdaction* 13.

Barsky, Robert, 'The Interpreter as Intercultural Agent in Convention Refugee Hearings' (1996) 2 *The Translator* 45.

Barta, Peter, 'Lambskin Borders: An Argument for the Abolition of the United States' Exclusion of HIV Positive Immigrants' (1998) 12 *Georgetown Immigration Law Journal* 323.

Bellinger III, John and Padmanabhan, Vijay, 'Detention Operations in Contemporary Conflicts: Four Challenges for the Geneva Conventions and Other Existing Law' (2011) 105 *American Journal of International Law* 105.

Bhabha, Jacqueline, 'Boundaries in the Field of Human Rights: Internationalist Gatekeepers?' (2002) 15 *Harvard Human Rights Journal* 155.

Bhabha, Jacqueline, *Seeking Asylum Alone: Unaccompanied and Separated Children and Refugee Protection in Australia, the UK and the US* (Federation Press, 2007).

Bochner, Stephen (ed), *Cultures in Contact* (Oxford University Press, 1982).

Bockley, Karen, 'A Historical Overview of Refugee Legislation: The Deception of Foreign Policy in the Land of Promise' (1995) 21 *North Carolina Journal of International Law and Commercial Regulation* 253.

Bon-Tempo, Carl, *Americans at the Gate: The United States and Refugees During the Cold War* (Princeton University Press, 2008).

Bossuyt, Marc, *Guide to the "Travaux Préparatoires" of the International Covenant on Civil and Political Rights* (Martinus Nijhoff Publishers, 1987).

Briggs, Vernon, 'US asylum policy and the new world order' (1993) 1 *People and Place* 1.

Brinker-Gable, Gisela (ed), *Encountering the Other/s* (SUNY Press, 1995).

Brouwer, Andrew and Kumin, Judith, 'Interception and Asylum: When Migration Control and Human Rights Collide' (2003) 21 *Refuge: Canada's Journal on Refugees* 6.

Brown, Colton, 'Enforcement of ICJ Decisions in United States Courts' (1987) 11 *Maryland Journal of International Law and Trade* 73.

Brown, Donald, 'Crooked Straits: Maritime Smuggling of Humans from Cuba to the United States' (2002) 33 *University of Miami Inter-American Law Review* 273.

Butler, Clark, *Guantanamo Bay and the Judicial-Moral Treatment of the Other* (Purdue University Press, 2007).

Card, David, 'The Impact of the Mariel Boatlift on the Miami Labor Market' (1990) 43 *Industrial and Labor Relations Review* 245.

Carlson, Scott and Gisvold, Gregory, *Practical Guide to the International Covenant on Civil and Political Rights* (Translation Publishers, 2003).

Chesney, Robert, 'Leaving *Guantánamo*: The Law of International Detainee Transfers' (2006) 40 *University of Richmond Law Review* 657.

Chinkin, Christine, 'A Mirage in the Sand? Distinguishing Binding and Non-Binding Relations between States' (1997) 10 *Leiden International Journal of International Law* 223.

Churchill, Robin and Lowe, Vaughan, *Law of the Sea* (Manchester University Press, 3rd ed, 1999).

Clark, Tom and Crépeau, François, 'Human Rights in Asylum Sharing and Other Human Transfer Agreements' (2004) 22 *Netherlands Quarterly of Human Rights* 217.

Clark, Tom and Crépeau, François, 'Mainstreaming Refugee Rights: The 1951 Refugee Convention and International Human Rights Law' (1999) 17 *Netherlands Quarterly of Human Rights* 389.

Clawson, Victoria, Detweiler, Elizabeth and Ho, Laura, 'Litigating as Law Students: An Inside Look at Haitian Center Council' (1994) 103 *The Yale Law Journal* 2337.

Collyer, Michael and de Haas, Hein, 'Developing Dynamic Categorisation of Transit Migration' (2012) 18 *Population, Space and Place* 468.

Colson, David, Smith, Robert and the American Society of International Law, *International Maritime Boundaries* (The American Society of International Law, 1995).

Coltman, Leycester, *The Real Fidel Castro* (Yale University Press, 2003).

Conte, Alex, Davidson, Scott and Burchill, Richard, *Defining Civil and Political Rights* (Ashgate, 2004).

Coomans, Fons and Kamminga, Menno (eds), *Extraterritorial Application of Human Rights Treaties* (Hart Publishing, 2004).

Cooper, Phillip, *By Order of the President: The Use and Abuse of Executive Direct Action* (University Press of Kansas, 2002).

Coppens, Jasmine and Somers, Eduard, 'Towards New Rules on Disembarkation of Persons at Sea' (2010) 25 *The International Journal of Marine and Coastal Law* 377.

Cox, Adam, 'Immigration Law's Organizing Principles' (2008) 157 *University of Pennsylvania Law Review* 341.

Cox, Adam, 'The President and Immigration Law' (2009) 119 *Yale Law Journal* 458.

Crépeau, François and Nakache, Delphine, 'Controlling Irregular Migration in Canada: Reconciling Security Concerns with Human Rights Protection' (2006) 12 *Immigration and Refugee Policy* 1.

Crépeau, François and Nakache, Delphine, 'Critical Space in the Canadian Refugee Determination System: 1989–2002' (2008) 20 *International Journal of Refugee Law* 50.

Crock, Mary, Saul, Ben and Dastyari, Azadeh, *FutureSeekersII* (Federation Press, 2006).

Currie, Robert and Coughlan, Stephen, 'Extraterritorial Criminal Jurisdiction: Bigger Picture or Smaller Frame?' (2007) 11 *Canadian Criminal Law Review* 141.

Damrosch, Lori 'The Role of the United States Senate Concerning "Self-Executing" and "Non-Self-Executing" Treaties' (1991) 67 *Chicago-Kent Law Review* 515.

Dastyari, Azadeh, 'Refugees on Guantánamo Bay. A Blue Print for Australia's "Pacific Solution"?' (2007) 78 *Australian Quarterly* 1.

Dastyari, Azadeh, 'Swapping Refugees: The Implications of the "Atlantic Solution"' (2008) 9 *UTS Law Review* 93.

Dastyari, Azadeh and Effeny, Libbey, 'Immigration Detention in Guantánamo Bay: (Not Going Anywhere Anytime Soon)' (2002) 6 *Shima* 49.

De Genova, Nicholas and Peutz, Nathalie (eds), *The Deportation Regime: Sovereignty, Space, and the Freedom of Movement* (Duke University Press, 2010).

De Schutter, Olivier, *International Human Rights Law: Cases, Materials, Commentary* (Cambridge University Press, 2010).

Deere, Carmen, 'Here Come the Yankees! The Rise and Decline of United States Colonies in Cuba 1898–1930' (1998) 78 *The Hispanic American Historical Review* 729.

Denbeaux, Mark and Hafetz, Jonathan (eds), *The Guantánamo Lawyers: Inside a Prison Outside the Law* (NYU Press, 2009).

Dench, Janet and Crépeau, François, 'Introduction: Interdiction at the Expense of Human Rights: A Long-Term Containment Strategy' (2003) 21 *Refuge: Canada's Journal on Refugees* 1.

Dennis, Michael, 'Application of Human Rights Treaties Extraterritorially In Times of Armed Conflict and Military Occupation (2005) 99 *American Journal of International Law* 119.

Dollar, Jordan and Kent, Allison, 'In Times of Famine, Sweet Potatoes Have No Skin: A Historical Overview and Discussion of Post-Earthquake US Immigration Policy towards the Haitian People' (2011) 6 *Intercultural Human Rights Law Review* 87.

Dupuy, Alex, *The Prophet and Power: Jean-Bertrand Aristide, the International Community, Haiti* (Rowman & Littlefield Publishers, 2006).

Dutton, Yvonne, 'Pirates and Impunity: Is the Threat of Asylum Claims a Reason to Allow Pirates to Escape Justice?'(2011) 34 *Fordham International Law Journal* 236.

Edwards, Alice, 'Articles-Human Rights, Refugees, and the Right "to Enjoy" Asylum' (2005) 17 *International Journal of Refugee Law* 293.

Engstrom, David, *Presidential Decision Making Adrift: The Carter Administration and the Mariel Boatlift* (Rowman & Littlefield Publishers, 1997).

Estevez, Roland, 'Modern Application of the Cuban Adjustment Act of 1966 and Helms-Burton: Adding Insult to Injury' (2002) 30 *Hofstra Law Review* 1273.

Fagen, Richard, Brody, Richard and O'Leary, Thomas, *Cubans in Exile: Disaffection and the Revolution* (Stanford University Press, 1968).

Falkoff, Marc and Knowles, Robert, 'Bagram, Boumediene, and Limited Government' (2010) 59 *DePaul Law Review* 851.

Farbenblum, Bassina, 'Executive Deference in US Refugee Law: Internationalist Paths Through and Beyond Chevron' (2011) 60 *Duke Law Journal* 1059.

Farber, Sonia, 'Forgotten at Guantánamo: The *Boumediene* Decision and Its Implications for Refugees at the Base under the Obama Administration' (2010) 98 *California Law Review* 989.

Feller, Erika, 'Refugees Are Not Migrants' (2005) 24 *Refugee Survey Quarterly* 27.

Feller, Erika, Türk, Volker, Nicholson, Frances and United Nations High Commissioner for Refugees (eds), *Refugee Protection in International Law: UNHCR's Global Consultations on International Protection* (Cambridge University Press, 2003).

Field, Jeannie Rose, 'Bridging the Gap between Refugee Rights and Reality: A Proposal for Developing International Duties in the Refugee Context' (2010) 22 *International Journal of Refugee Law* 512.

Fischer-Lescano, Andreas and Löhr, Tillmann, *Border Control at Sea: Requirements under International Human Rights an Refugee Law* (European Centre for Constitutional and Human Rights, 2007).

Fischer-Lescano, Andreas, Löhr, Tillmann and Tohidipur, Timo, 'Border Controls at Sea: Requirements under International Human Rights and Refugee Law' (2009) 21 *International Journal of Refugee Law* 256.

Fisher, Louis, *American Constitutional Law* (Carolina Academic Press, 2005).

Fitzpatrick, Joan, 'Revitalizing the 1951 Refugee Convention' (1996) 9 *Harvard Human Rights Journal* 229.

Fitzpatrick, Joan, 'The International Dimension of US Refugee Law' (1997) 15 *Berkeley Journal of International Law* 1.

Fletcher, George, 'Black Hole in Guantánamo Bay' (2004) 2 *Journal of International Criminal Justice* 121.

Foster, Michelle, *International Refugee Law and Socio-Economic Rights: Refuge from Deprivation* (Cambridge University Press, 2007).

Foster, Michelle and Pobjoy, Jason, 'A Failed Case of Legal Exceptionalism? Refugee Status Determination in Australia's "Excised" Territory' (2011) 23 *International Journal of Refugee Law* 583.

Francis, Angus, 'Bringing Protection Home: Healing the Schism between International Obligations and National Safeguards Created by Extraterritorial Processing' (2008) 20 *International Journal of Refugee Law* 273.

Franks, Mary Anne, 'Guantanamo Forever: United States Sovereignty and the Unending State of Exception' (2007) 1 *Harvard Law and Policy Review* 259.

Frelick, Bill, '"Abundantly Clear": Refoulement' (2004) 19 *Georgetown Immigration Law Journal* 245.

Frelick, Bill, 'Haitian Boat Interdiction and Return: First Asylum and First Principles of Refugee Protection' (1993) 26 *Cornell International Law Journal* 675.

Frelick, Bill, 'US Refugee Policy in the Caribbean: No Bridge over Troubled Waters' (1996) 20 *Fletcher Forum of World Affairs* 67.

Frohock, Christina '"Brisas Del Mar": Judicial and Political Outcomes of the Cuban Rafter Crisis in Guantánamo Bay' (2012) 15 *Harvard Latin Law Review* 302.

Fullerton, Maryellen, 'Cuban Exceptionalism: Migration and Asylum in Spain and the United States' (2004) 35 *University of Miami Inter-American Law Review* 527.

Gammeltoft-Hansen, Thomas, *Access to Asylum: International Refugee Law and the Globalisation of Migration Control* (Cambridge University Press, 2011).

Garlick, Madeline, 'The EU Discussions on Extraterritorial Processing: Solution or Conundrum?' (2006) 18 *International Journal of Refugee Law* 601.

Gavilan, David, 'Y Que Paso – And Then What Happened: The Plight of Cuban Detainees at Guantanamo Bay' (1996) 4 *Cardozo Journal of International and Comparative Law* 451.

Geltzer, Joshua, 'Of Suspension, Due Process, and Guantánamo: The Reach of the Fifth Amendment after *Boumediene* and the Relationship between Habeas Corpus and Due Process' (2012) 14 *University of Pennsylvania Journal of Constitutional Law* 719.

Gerangelos, Peter, *The Separation of Powers and Legislative Interference in Judicial Process: Constitutional Principles and Limitations* (Hart Publishing, 2009).

Gibbs, Jessica, *US Policy towards Cuba: Since the Cold War* (Routledge, 2011).

Gilbert, Geoff, 'Editorial' (2006) 18 *International Journal of Refugee Law* 487.

Ginsburg, Tom, 'Symposium: Eastphalia as the Perfection of Westphalia' (2010) 17 *Journal of Global Legal Studies* 27.

Gluck, Suzanne, 'Intercepting Refugees at Sea: An Analysis of the United States' Legal and Moral Obligations' (1993) 61 *Fordham Law Review* 865.

Golden, Jason, 'Haitian Refugees Housed at Guantanamo Bay Naval Base Held to Have No Valid Constitutional or International Law Claims to Challenge Forced Repatriation by the US Government' (1992) 22 *Georgia Journal of International and Comparative Law* 515.

Goldstein, Brandt, *Storming the Court: How a Band of Yale Law Students Sued the President – And Won* (Simon and Schuster, 2005).

Gonzalez-Pando, Miguel, *The Cuban Americans* (Greenwood Press, 1998).

Goodwin-Gill, Guy, 'Refugees and Responsibility in the Twenty-First Century: More Lessons Learned From the South Pacific' (2003) 12 *Pacific Law and Policy Journal* 23.

Goodwin-Gill, Guy, 'The Right to Seek Asylum: Interception at Sea and the Principle of *Non-Refoulement*' (2011) 23 *International Journal of Refugee Law* 443.

Goodwin-Gill, Guy and McAdam, Jane, *The Refugee in International Law* (Oxford University Press, 3rd ed, 2007).

Grahl-Madsen, Atle, *The Status of Refugees in International law* (Sijthoff, 1966).

Greenhill, Kelly, 'Engineered Migration and the Use of Refugees as Political Weapons: A Case Study of the 1994 Cuban "Balseros" Crisis' (2002) 40 *International Migration* 39.

Greenhill, Kelly, *Weapons of Mass Migration: Forced Displacement, Coercion, and Foreign Policy* (Cornell University Press, 2010).

Gryll, Sarah, 'Immigration Detention Reform: No Band-Aid Desired' (2011) 60 *Emory Law Journal* 1211.

Guilfoyle, Douglas, 'Maritime Interdiction of Weapons of Mass Destruction' (2007) 12 *Journal of Conflict & Security Law* 1.

Guilfoyle, Douglas, *Shipping Interdiction and the Law of the Sea* (Cambridge University Press, 2009).

Hailbronner, Kay, 'Non-Refoulement and Humanitarian Refugees: Customary International Law or Wishful Legal Thinking' (1986) 3 *Virginia Journal of International Law* 857.

Hailbronner, Kay, 'Principles of International Law Regarding the Concept of Subsidiary Protection' in Daphné Bouteillet-Paquet (ed), *Subsidary Protection of Refugees in the European Union Complementing the Geneva Convention?* (Bruylant, 2000).

Hamilton, Kimberly, 'Immigrant Detention Centers in the United States and International Human Rights Law' (2011) 21 *Berkeley La Raza Law Journal* 93.

Harris, David, *Cases and Materials on International law* (Sweet and Maxwell, 5th ed, 2010).

Harris, Hadar, 'Race Across Borders: The U.S. and ICERD' (2008) 24 *Harvard Blackletter Law Journal* 61.

Hathaway, James, 'Forced Migration Studies: Could We Agree Just to "Date"?' (2007) 20 *Journal of Refugee Studies* 349.

Hathaway, James, 'Leveraging Asylum' (2010) 45 *Texas International Law Journal* 503.

Hathaway, James, *The Rights of Refugees Under International Law* (Cambridge University Press, 2005).

Hathaway, James and Cusick, Anne, 'Refugee Rights Are Not Negotiable (2000) 14 *Georgetown Immigration Law Journal* 481.

Hathaway, James and Foster, Michelle, *The Law of Refugee Status* (Cambridge University Press, 2nd ed, 2014).

Hathaway, James and Gammeltoft-Hansen, Thomas, 'Non-Refoulement in a World of Cooperative Deterrence'. Law and Economic Working Papers, Paper 106, University of Michigan Law School, 1 August 2014.

Hech, Gabrielle, *Entangled Geographies: Empire and Technopolitics in the Global Cold War* (MIT Press, 2011).

Heckman, Gerald, 'Canada's Refugee Status Determination System and the International Norm of Independence' (2008) 25 *Refuge: Canada's Journal on Refugees* 79.

Heckman, Gerald, 'Securing Procedural Safeguards for Asylum Seekers in Canadian Law: An Expanding Role For International Human Rights Law?' (2003) 15 *International Journal of Refugee Law* 212.

Heckman, Gerald, 'Unfinished Business: *Baker* and the Constitutionality of the Leave and Certification Requirement under the *Immigration Act*' (2002) 27 *Queen's Law Journal* 715.

Heeren, Geoffrey, 'Pulling Teeth: The State of Mandatory Immigration Detention' (2010) 45 *Harvard Civil Rights-Civil Liberties Law Review* 601.

Helton, Arthur, 'United States Government Program of Intercepting and Forcibly Returning Haitian Boat People to Haiti: Policy Implications and Prospects' (1992) 10 *New York Law School Journal of Human Rights* 325.

Hemel, Daniel, 'First Amendment's First Word' (2013) 40 *Pepperdine Law Review* 601.

Henkin, Louis (ed), *The International Bill of Human Rights: The Covenant on Civil and Political Rights* (Columbia University Press, 1981).

Henkin, Louis, 'US Ratification of Human Rights Conventions: The Ghost of Senator Bricker' (1995) 89 *American Journal of International Law* 341.

Hiemstra, Nancy, 'The US and Ecuador: Is Intervention on the Table?' (2012) 12 *NACLA Report on the Americas* 20.

Hiemstra, Nancy, *The View from Ecuador: Security, Insecurity, and Chaotic Geographies of U.S. Migrant Detention and Deportation* (PhD Dissertation, Syracuse University, 2011)

Hillgenburg, Hartmut, 'A Fresh Look at Soft Law' (1999) 10 *European Journal of International Law* 499.

Hughes, Joyce and Crane, Linda, 'Haitians: Seeking Refuge in the United States' (1993) 7 *Georgetown Immigration Law Journal* 747.

Jacobson, Jon, 'At-Sea Interception of Alien Migrants: International Law Issues' (1992) 28 *Willamette Law Review* 811.

Johnson, Creola, 'Quarantining HIV-Infected Haitians: United States' Violations of International Law at Guantanamo Bay' (1994) 37 *Howard Law Journal* 305.

Joint Working Group of Non-Governmental Civil, Political, and Human Rights Organizations in the U.S and Sklar, Morton (eds), *The Status of Human Rights in the United States: An Analysis of the Initial US Government Report to the Human Rights Committee of the United Nations Under the International Covenant on Civil and Political Rights* (S.N., 1995).

Jones, Howard, *The Bay of Pigs* (Oxford University Press, 2008).

Jones, Thomas, 'A Human Rights Tragedy: The Cuban and Haitian Refugee Crises Revisited' (1995) 9 *Georgetown Immigration Law Journal* 479.

Joseph, Sarah and Castan, Melissa, *The International Covenant on Civil and Political Right: Cases, Materials, and Commentary* (Oxford University Press, 3rd ed, 2013).

Joseph, Sarah and McBeth, Adam (eds), *Research Handbook on International Human Rights Law* (Edward Elgar Publishers, 2010).

Jowanna, Matthew, '42 USC § 1983: A Legal Vehicle with No International Human Rights Treaty Passengers' (2010) 9 *University of New Hampshire Law Review* 31.

Kagan, Michael, 'Frontier Justice: Legal Aid and UNHCR Refugee Status Determination in Egypt' (2006) 19 *Journal of Refugee Studies* 45.

Kälin, Walter, 'Troubled Communication: Cross-Cultural Misunderstandings in the Asylum Hearing' (1986) 20 *International Migration Review* 230.

Kenney, Fredrick and Tasikas, Vasilos, 'Tampa Incident: IMO Perspectives and Responses on the Treatment of Persons Rescued at Sea' (2003) 12 *Pacific Rim Law & Policy Journal* 143.

Kneebone, Susan (ed), *Refugees, Asylum Seekers and the Rule of Law* (Cambridge University Press, 2009).

Kneebone, Susan, 'The Pacific Plan: The Provision of "Effective Protection"?' (2006) 18 *International Journal of Refugee Law* 696.

Koh, Harold Hongju, 'America's Offshore Refugee Camps Symposium: Human Rights International Law'(1994) 29 *University of Richmond Law Review* 139.

Koh, Harold Hongju, 'On American Exceptionalism' (2003) 55 *Stanford Law Review* 1479.

Koh, Harold Hongju, 'Reflections on *Refoulement* and Haitian Centers Council' (1994) 35 *Harvard International Law Journal* 1.

Lazar, Joseph, 'International Legal Status of Guantanamo Bay' (1968) 62 *The American Journal of International Law* 730.

Leckie, Scott, 'The Inter-State Complaint Procedures in International Human Rights Law: Hopeful Prospects or Wishful Thinking?' (1988) 10 *Human Rights Quarterly* 253.

Legomsky, Stephen, 'An Asylum Seeker's Bill of Rights In a Non-Utopian World' (2000) 14 *Georgetown Immigration Law Journal* 619.

Legomsky, Stephen, 'Deportation and the War on Independence' (2006) 91 *Cornell Law Review* 369.

Legomsky, Stephen, *Immigration and Refugee Law and Policy* (Foundation Press, 5th ed, 2009).

Legomsky, Stephen, 'Refugees, Administrative Tribunals, and Real Independence: Dangers Ahead for Australia' (1998) 76 *Washington University Law Quarterly* 243.

Legomsky, Stephen, 'The USA and the Caribbean Interdiction Program' (2006) 18 *International Journal of Refugee Law* 677.

Levesque, Christian, 'The International Covenant on Civil and Political Rights: A Primer For Raising a Defense against the Juvenile Death Penalty in Federal Courts' (2001) 50 *American University Law Review* 755.

Little, Cheryl, 'InterGroup Coalitions and Immigration Politics: The Haitian Experience in Florida' (1998) 53 *University of Miami Law Review* 717.

Loescher, Gil and Scanlan, John, *Calculated Kindness: Refugees and America's Half-open Door, 1945 to the Present* (Free Press, 1986).

Loescher, Gilburt, 'US Foreign Policy, 1959–80: Impact on Refugee Flow from Cuba' (1983) 467 *The Annals of the American Academy of Political and Social Science* 116.

Loper, Kelley, 'Human Rights, Non-refoulement and the Protection of Refugees in Hong Kong' (2010) 22 *International Journal of Refugee Law* 404.

MacCoun, Robert, 'Voice, Control, and Belonging: The Double-Edged Sword of Procedural Fairness' (2005) 1 *Annual Review of Law and Social Science* 171.

Machura, Stefan, 'Introduction: Procedural Justice, Law and Policy' (1998) 20 *Law & Policy* 1.

Madden, Mike, 'Trading the Shield of Sovereignty for the Scales of Justice: A Proposal for Reform of International Sea Piracy Laws' (2009) 21 *University of San Francisco Maritime Law Journal* 139.

Magill, Frank and Loos, John, *Great Events from History: 1956–1996* (Salem Press, 1997).

Mariam, Alemayehu, 'International Law and the Pre-emptive Use of State Interdiction Authority on the High Seas: The Case of Suspected Illegal Haitian Immigrants Seeking Entry into the US' (1987) 12 *Maryland Journal of International Law and Trade* 211.

Marouf, Fatma and Anker, Deborah, 'Socioeconomic Rights and Refugee Status: Deepening the Dialogue between Human Rights and Refugee Law' (2010) 103 *The American Journal of International Law* 784.

Marsden, Simon, 'Invoking Direct Application and Effect of International Treaties by the European Court of Justice: Implications for International Environmental Law in the European Union' (2011) 60 *International & Comparative Law Quarterly* 737.

Masud-Piloto, Felix, *From Welcomed Exiles to Illegal Immigrants: Cuban Migration to the US, 1959–1995* (Rowman & Littlefield Publishers, 1996).

Mathew, Penelope, 'Australian Refugee Protection in the Wake of the Tampa' (2002) 96 *American Journal of International Law* 661.

Mathew, Penelope, 'Legal Issues Concerning Interception' (2003) 17 *Georgetown Immigration Law Journal* 221.
McAdam, Jane, *Complementary Protection in International Refugee Law* (Oxford University Press, 2007).
McAdam, Jane (ed), *Forced Migration, Human Rights and Security* (Hart Publishing, 2008).
McAdam, Jane, 'Status Anxiety: The New Zealand Immigration Bill and the Rights of Non-Convention Refugees' (2009) *New Zealand Law Review* 239.
McBride, Michael, 'Migrants and Asylum Seekers: Policy Responses in the United States to Immigrants and Refugees from Central America and the Caribbean' (1999) 37 *International Migration* 289.
McCorquodale, Robert, 'An Inclusive International Legal System' (2004) 17 *Leiden Journal of International Law* 477.
McDougal, Myles, The Maintenance of Public Order at Sea and the Nationality of Ships (1960) 59 *American Journal of International Law* 25.
Meron, Theodor, 'Extraterritoriality of Human Rights Treaties' (1995) 89 *The American Journal of International Law* 78.
Meyers, Herman, *The Nationality of Ships* (Nijhoff, 1967).
Miltner, Barbara, 'Irregular Maritime Migration: Refugee Protection Issues in Rescue and Interception' (2006) 30 *Fordham international Law Journal* 75.
Mintz, Sidney, 'Can Haiti Change' (1995) 74 *Foreign Affairs* 73.
Moore, Jennifer, 'Restoring the Humanitarian Character of US Refugee Law: Lessons from the International Community' (1997) 15 *Berkeley Journal of International Law* 51.
Moreno-Lax, Violeta, '*Hirsi Jamaa and Others v Italy* or the Strasbourg Court versus Extraterritorial Migration Control' (2012) 1 *Human Rights Law Review* 1.
Moreno-Lax, Violeta, 'Seeking Asylum in the Mediterranean: Against a Fragmentary Reading of EU Member States' Obligations Accruing at Sea' (2011) 33 *International Journal of Refugee Law* 174.
Moreno-Lax, Violeta, 'The EU Regime on Interdiction, Search and Rescue, and Disembarkation: The Frontex Guidelines for Intervention at Sea' (2010) 25 *The International Journal of Marine and Coastal Law* 621.
Morley, Morris and McGillion, Chris, 'Disobedient Generals and the Politics of Redemocratization: The Clinton Administration and Haiti' (1997) 112 *Political Science Quarterly* 363.
Munton, Don and Welch, David, *The Cuban Missile Crisis: A Concise History* (Oxford University Press, 2011).

Münz, Rainer and Weiner, Myron (eds), *Migrants, Refugees, and Foreign Policy: U.S. and German Policies Toward Countries of Origin* (Berghahn Books, 1997).

Murphy, Marion, *History of Guantánamo Bay 1494–1964* (District Publications, 1962).

Musalo, Karen, Gibson, Lauren, Knight, Stephen and Taylor, J. Edward, *The Expedited Removal Study: Report on the First Three Years of Implementation of Expedited Removal*, Centre for Human Rights and International Justice University of California (Hastings College of Law, 2001).

Musalo, Karen, Moore, Jennifer and Boswell, Richard, *Refugee Law and Policy: Cases and Materials* (Carolina Academic Press, 1997).

Nessel, Lori, 'Externalized Borders and the Invisible Refugee' (2009) 40 *Columbia Human Rights Law Review* 625.

Neuberger, Angelika, 'The Concept of "Jurisdiction" in the Jurisprudence of the European Court of Human Rights' (2012) 1 *Current Legal Problems* 1.

Neuman, Gerald, 'Admissions and Denials: A Dialogic Introduction to the Immigration Law Symposium' (1997) 29 *Connecticut Law Review* 1395.

Neuman, Gerald, 'Closing the Guantánamo Loophole' (2004) 50 *Loyola Law Review* 1.

Neuman, Gerald, 'The Extraterritorial Constitution after *Boumediene v Bush*' (2009) 82 *Southern California Law Review* 259.

Neuman, Gerald, 'The Habeas Corpus Suspension Clause after *Boumediene v Bush*' (2010) 110 *Columbia Law Review* 537.

Nowak, Manfred, *UN Covenant on Civil and Political Rights: CCPR Commentary* (N.P Engel Publisher, 2nd ed, 2005).

Nowak, Manfred, Birk, Moritz and Crittin, Tiphanie 'The Obama Administration and Obligations under the Convention against Torture' (2011) 20 *Transnational Law & Contemporary Problems* 33.

O'Brien, Killian, 'Refugees on the High Seas: International Refugee Law Solutions to a Law of the Sea Problem' (2011) 2 *Goettingen Journal of International Law* 715.

O'Connell, Daniel, *International Law of the Sea* (Clarendon Press, 1982).

Olson, James and Olson, Judith, *Cuban Americans: From Trauma to Triumph* (Twayne Publishers, 1995).

Oppenheim, Lassa, *International Law* (McKay, 8th ed, 1955).

Orford, Anne, 'Jurisdiction without Territory: From the Holy Roman Empire to the Responsibility to Protect' (2009) 3 *Michigan Journal of International Law* 981.

Ortiz Miranda, Carlos, 'Haiti and the United States during the 1980s and 1990s: Refugees, Immigration and Foreign Policy' (1995) 32 *San Diego Law Review* 673.

Pallis, Mark, 'Obligations of States Towards Asylum Seekers at Sea: Interactions and Conflicts Between Legal Regimes' (2002) 31 *International Journal of Refugee Law* 329.

Palmer, Gary, 'Guarding the Coast: Alien Migrant Interdiction Operations at Sea' (1996) 29 *Connecticut Law Review* 1565.

Papastavridis, Efthymios, "Fortress Europe' and FRONTEX: Within or without International Law?' (2010) 79 *Nordic Journal of International Law* 75.

Papastavridis, Efthymios, 'Interception of Human Beings on the High Seas: A Contemporary Analysis under International Law' (2009) 36 *Syracuse Journal of International Law and Commerce* 145.

Papastavridis, Efthymios, *The Interception of Vessels on the High Seas: Contemporary Challenges to the Legal Order of the Oceans* (Hart Publishing, 2013).

Park, James, 'Effectuating Principles of Justice in Ending Indefinite Detention: Historical Repetition and the Case of the Uyghurs' (2010) 31 *Whittier Law Review* 785.

Pastor, Robert, 'The Clinton Administration and the Americas: The Postwar Rhythm and Blues' (1996) 38 *Journal of International Studies and World Affairs* 99.

Penovic, Tania and Dastyari, Azadeh, 'Boatloads of Incongruity: The Evolution of Australia's Offshore Processing Regime' (2007) 12 *Australian Journal of Human Rights* 33.

Perez, Alberto, 'Wet Foot, Dry Foot, No Foot: The Recurring Controversy between Cubans, Haitians and the United States Immigration Policy' (2004) 28 *Nova Law Review* 437.

Pingeton, Matthew 'United States Immigration Policy: Detaining Cuban Refugees Taken from the Sea' (1999) 8 *Journal of Transnational Law & Policy* 329.

Plant, Glen, 'Ship Registration' (1992) 41 *International & Comparative Law Quarterly* 504.

Pobjoy, Jason, 'Treating Like Alike: The Principle of Non-Discrimination as a Tool to Mandate the Equal Treatment of Refugees and Beneficiaries of Complementary Protection' (2010) 34 *Melbourne University Law Review* 181.

Pugh, Michael, 'Drowning Not Waving: Boat People and Humanitarianism at Sea' (2004) 17 *International Journal of Refugee Studies* 50.

Ramjii-Nogales, Jaya, Shoenholtz, Andrew and Shrag, Philip, 'Refugee Roulette: Disparities in Asylum Adjudication' (2007) 60 *Stanford Law Review* 295.

Ratner, Michael, 'How We Closed the Guantanamo HIV Camp: The Intersection of Politics and Litigation' (1998) 11 *Harvard Human Rights Journal* 187.

Rayfuse, Rosemary, *Non-Flag State Enforcement in High Seas Fisheries* (Martinus Nijhoff Publishers, 2004).

Renda, Mary, *Taking Haiti: Military Occupation and the Culture of US Imperialism, 1915–1940* (The University of North Carolina Press, 2001).

Reynolds, Heather, 'Irreconcilable Regulations: Why the Sun Has Set on the Cuban Adjustment Act in Florida' (2011) 66 *Florida Law Review* 1013.

Riesenfeld, Stefan and Abbott, Frederick, 'The Scope of US Senate Control over the Conclusion and Operation of Treaties' (1991) 67 *Chicago-Kent Law Review* 571.

Risse, Thomas, Ropp, Stephen and Sikkink, Kathryn (eds), *The Power of Human Rights: International Norms and Domestic Change* (Cambridge University Press, 1999).

Rivera, Mario, *Decision and Structure: US Refugee Policy in the Mariel Crisis* (University Press of America, 1991).

Roberts, Priscilla, *Cuban Missile Crisis: The Essential Reference Guide* (ABC-CLIO, 2012).

Robinson, Nehemiah, *Convention Relating To The Status Of Refugees: Its History, Contents And Interpretation: A Commentary* (1953, reprinted UNHCR-Division of International Protection, 1997).

Rodley, Nigel, 'The Extraterritorial Reach and Applicability in Armed Conflict of the International Covenant on Civil and Political Rights: A Rejoinder to Dennis and Surena' (2009) 5 *European Human Rights Law Review* 628.

Romero, Victor, 'On Elián and Aliens: A Political Solution to the Plenary Power Problem' (2000–2001) 4 *NYU Journal of Legislation and Public Policy* 343.

Rosenberg, Lory, 'International Association of Refugee Law Judges Conference: The Courts and Interception: The United States' 'Interdiction Experience and Its Impact on Refugees and Asylum Seekers' (2003) 17 *Georgetown Immigration Law Journal* 199.

Rosenberg, Lory, 'The Courts and Interception: The United States' Interdiction Experience and Its Impact on Refugees and Asylum Seekers' (2003) 17 *Georgetown Immigration Law Journal* 1999.

Rothwell, Donald, Kaye, Stuart, Akhtarkhavari, Afshin and Davis, Ruth, *International Law Cases and Materials with Australian Perspectives* (Cambridge University Press, 2011).

Ryan, Bernard and Mitsilegas, Valsamis (eds.), *Extraterritorial Immigration Control: Legal Challenges* (Martinus Nijhoff, 2010).

Saladin Meckled-García and Basak Çali (eds), *The Legalization of Human Rights: Multidisciplinary Perspectives on Human Rights and Human Rights Law* (Routledge, 2006).

Sartori, Maria, 'Cuban Migration Dilemma: An Examination of the United States' Policy of Temporary Protection in Offshore Safe Havens' (2001) 15 *Georgetown Immigration Law Journal* 319.

Satterthwaite, Margaret, 'Rendered Meaningless: Extraordinary Rendition and the Rule of Law' (2007) 75 *George Washington Law Review* 1333.

Scanlan, John and Loescher, Gilburt, 'US Foreign Policy, 1959–80: Impact on Refugee Flow from Cuba' (1983) 467 *The Annals of the American Academy of Political and Social Science* 116.

Schlochauer, Hans-Jürgen and von Münch, Ingo (eds), *Staatsrecht – Völkerrecht – Europarecht* (Walter de Gruyter, 1981).

Schmidt, Hans, *The United States Occupation of Haiti, 1915–1934* (Rutgers University Press, 1995).

Schoenholtz, Andrew and Jacobs, Jonathan, 'The State of Asylum Representation: Ideas for Change' (2002) 16 *Georgetown Immigration Law Journal* 739.

Schrag, Philip, A *Well-Founded Fear: The Congressional Battle to Save Political Asylum in America* (Routledge, 2000).

Shearer, Ivan, 'Problems of Jurisdiction and Law Enforcement against Delinquent Vessels' (1986) 35 *International & Comparative Law Quarterly* 320.

Sinclair, Ian, *The Vienna Convention on the Law of Treaties* (Manchester University Press, 2nd ed, 1984).

Skolnick, Andrew, 'Doctors Help HIV-Positive Haitian Refugees Gain Freedom from US Government Detention Camp' (1993) 270 *Journal of American Medical Association* 563.

Smith, Marius (ed), *Human Rights 2006: The Year in Review* (Castan Centre, 2007).

Smith, Paul, 'Military Responses to the Global Migration Crisis: A Glimpse of Things to Come' (1999) 23 *Fletcher Forum of World Affairs* 77.

Smith, Robert, *Exclusive Economic Zone Claims: An Analysis and Primary Documents* (Martinus Nijhoff Publishers, 1986).

Sperotto, Federico, 'Ten Years after *Bankovic*' (2012) 12 *Global Jurist* 1.

Spiro, Peter, 'Explaining the End of Plenary Power' (2002) 16 *Georgetown Immigration Law Journal* 339.

Steiner, Niklaus, Gibney, Mark and Loescher, Gil (eds), *Problems of Protection: The UNHCR, Refugees and Human Rights* (Routledge, 2003).

Steyn, Johan, 'Guantanamo Bay: The Legal Black Hole' (2004) 53 *International and Comparative Law Quarterly* 1.

Stotzky, Irwin, 'Haiti: The Human Rights Struggle in a Land without Oil' (2004) 61 *Guild Practitioner* 151.

Stotzzky, Irwin, *Silencing the Guns in Haiti* (University of Chicago Press, 1986).

Stratē, Anastasia, Gavouneli, Maria, Gavouneli and Gavouneli, Nikolaos, *Unresolved Issues and New Challenges to the Law of the Sea: Time Before and Time After* (Martinus Nijhoff Publishers, 2006).

Sweeney, Joseph, '*Guantánamo* and U.S. Law' (2007) 30 *Fordham International Law Journal* 673.

Taifa, Nkechi, 'Civil Forfeiture vs. Civil Liberties' (1994) 95 *New York Law School Law Review* 95.

Tanzi, Attila, 'Problems of Enforcement of Decisions of the International Court of Justice and the Law of the United Nations' (1995) 6 *European Journal of International Law* 539.

Thwaites, Rayner, *The Liberty of Non-Citizens: Indefinite Detention in Commonwealth Countries* (Hart Publishing, 2014).

Triggs, Gillian, *International Law: Contemporary Principles and Practices* (LexisNexis Butterworths, 2nd ed, 2011).

Tucker, Eric, 'The Political Economy of Administrative Fairness: A Preliminary Enquiry' (1987) 25 *Osgoode Hall law Journal* 555.

Tyler, Tom, 'Procedural Fairness and Compliance with the Law' (1997) 133 *Swiss Journal of Economics and Statistics* 219.

UNHCR, 'Expert Meeting on Refugees and Asylum-Seekers in Distress at Sea – How Best to Respond? Djibouti, 8–10 November 2011' (2012) 2 *International Journal of Refugee Law* 485.

UNHCR, 'Outline of Submissions on Behalf of the Office of the United Nations High Commissioner for Refugees (as Amicus Curiae)' (2007) 19 *International Journal of Refugee Law* 360.

UNHCR, 'The Haitian Interdiction Case 1993 Brief Amicus Curiae' (1994) 6 *International Journal of Refugee Law* 85

Van Houten, Mary, 'The Post-*Boumediene* Paradox: Habeas Corpus or Due Process' (2014) 67 *Stanford Law Review* 9.

Vazquez, Carlos, 'The Four Doctrines of Self-Executing Treaties' (1995) 89 *American Journal of International Law* 695.

Vladeck, Stephen, '*Boumediene*'s Quiet Theory: Access to Courts and the Separation of Powers' (2009) 84 *Notre Dame Law Review* 2107.

Wachs, Jonathan, 'Recent Development: The Need to Define the International Legal Status of Cubans Detained at Guantánamo' (1996) 11 *The American University Journal of International Law & Policy* 79.

Watts, Arthur, *The International Law Commission 1949–1998: Volume Two: The Treaties* (Oxford University Press, 1999).

Weis, Paul, *The Refugee Convention, 1951: The Travaux Preparatoires Analysed, with a Commentary* (Cambridge University Press, 1995).

Weissbrodt, David, and Bergquist, Amy, 'Extraordinary Rendition and the Torture Convention' (2006) 46 *Virginia Journal of International Law* 586.

Weissbrodt, David and Hortreiter, Isabel, 'The Principle of *Non-Refoulement*: Article 3 of the Convention Against Torture and Other Cruel, Inhuman or Degrading Treatment or Punishment in Comparison with the *Non-Refoulement* Provisions of Other International Human Rights Treaties' (1999) 5 *Buffalo Human Rights Review* 1.

Wilde, Ralph, 'Complementing Occupation Law? Selective Judicial Treatment of the Suitability of Human Rights Norms' (2009) 42 *Israel Law Review* 80.

Wilde, Ralph, 'Legal Black Hole – Extraterritorial State Action and International Treaty Law on Civil and Political Rights' (2006) 26 *Michigan Journal of International Law* 739.

Willheim, Ernst, 'MV Tampa: The Australian Response' (2003) 15 *International Journal of Refugee* 159.

Wilsher, Daniel, *Immigration Detention: Law, History, Politics* (Cambridge University Press, 2011).

Wilson, Thomas and Donnan, Hastings (eds), *A Companion to Border Studies* (Wiley-Blackwell, 2012).

Wise, Charles, 'Organizing for Homeland Security' (2002) 62 *Public Administration Review* 131.

Wong, Diana, 'Semantics of Migration' (1989) 4 *Journal of Social Issues in Southeast Asia* 275.

Yoo, John, 'Transferring Terrorists' (2004) 79 *Notre Dame Law Review* 1183.

Zagor, Matthew, 'Uncertainty and Exclusion: Detention of Aliens and the High Court' (2006) 34 *Federal Law Review* 127.

Zhang, Sheldon and Chin, Ko-Lin, 'Enter The Dragon: Inside Chinese Human Smuggling Organizations' (2002) 40 *Criminology* 737.

Zimmermann, Andreas (ed), *The 1951 Convention Relating to the Status of Refugees and Its 1967 Protocol: A Commentary* (Oxford University Press, 2011).

Newspaper Articles, Reports, Websites and Other Secondary Sources

'A refugee mother opens her heart', *Miami Herald* 19 February 2001 <www.latinamericanstudies.org/immigration/arelys.htm>.

American Law Institute, *Restatement (Third) of the Foreign Relations Law of the United States* (1987).

Americas Watch & National Coalition for Haitian Refugees, *Half the Story: The Skewed US Monitoring of Repatriated Haitian Refugees* (1992) National Coalition of Haitian Rights <www.nchr.org/mnd/reptlist.htm>.

Amnesty International, 'Haiti: The Human Rights Tragedy: Human Rights Violations Since the Coup' (1992).

Associated Press, 'Aristide Says US Policy on Haiti Is Criminal, Racist, *Desert News* (Sale Lake City) 19 March 1994 <www.deseretnews.com/article/342492/ARISTIDE-SAYS-US-POLICY-ON-HAITI-IS-CRIMINAL-RACIST.html?pg=all>.

Atkins, Vincent, Testimony of Rear Admiral Vincent Atkins, US Coast Guard, before the House Subcommittee on Homeland Security, on Department of Homeland Security Air and Marine Operations and Investments, 19 April 2010. Reproduced (2010) <www.dhs.gov/ynews/testimony/testimony_1271690315007.shtm>.

Canty, Lt Rachel, 'Limits of the Coast Guard Authority to Board Foreign Flag Vessels on the High Seas', Unclassified Report, Naval War College (29 April 1997).

CNIS, *GTMO Entry Clearance Information* <www.cnic.navy.mil/guantanamo/InstallationGuide/GTMOEntryClearanceInformation/index.htm>.

Defence System Journal, *Inside GTMO* <www.dsjournal.com/insidegtmo.html>.

Department of Defense, 'Media Ground Rules for Guantanamo Bay, Cuba' (10 September 2010) <http://media.mcclatchydc.com/static/pdf/guantanamo-rules.pdf>.

Department of the Navy Office of the Chief of Naval Operations and Headquarters, US Marine Corps, Department Of Homeland Security And US Coast Guard, *United States Commander's Handbook on the Law of Naval Operations* (2007).

Devroy, Ann and Gellman, Barton, 'Exodus from Haiti Strains US Policy', *Washington Post*, 2 July 1994, A1.

Devroy, Ann and Williams, Daniel, 'Serious Alarm Bells Led to Talks with Cuba: Congressmen Warned of Exodus, Riots at Camp', *Washington Post*, 5 May 1995, A4.

Federal Business Opportunities, *Guard Services for the Migrant Operations Center* (8 February 2012) <www.fbo.gov/index?s=opportunity&mode=form&tab=core&id=264814fc2dd263475076cde797036ee>.

Franklin, Jane, *How Did Guantánamo Become a Prison* (2005) History News Network <http://hnn.us/articles/11000.html>.

French, Howard, 'US Is Holding 200 Haitians on 2 Ships', *New York Times*, 8 November 1991 <www.nytimes.com/1991/11/08/world/us-is-holding-200-haitians-on-2-ships.html>.

Friedman, Jonathan, et al., *Maritime Interception: History, Practice and Emerging Issue*, Yale Law School, Allard K. Lowenstein International Human Rights Clinic (Unpublished, 2002).

Garcia, Michael, 'Renditions: Constraints Imposed by Laws on Torture', *Congressional Research Service*, 12 October 2007 <http://assets.opencrs.com/rpts/RL32890_20071012.pdf>.

Garcia, Michael, 'The U.N. Convention Against Torture: Overview of US Implementation Policy Concerning the Removal of Aliens', *Congressional Research Service*, 21 January 2009 <www.au.af.mil/au/awc/awcgate/crs/rl32276.pdf>.

GEO Group, *Guantánamo Bay (GTMO) Migrant Operations Center* (2008) <www.thegeogroupinc.com/locations_na.asp>.

Goshko, John, 'Aristide Renounces Treaty Allowing Return of Haitians', *Washington Post*, 7 April 1994 <www.highbeam.com/doc/1P2-884384.html>.

Greenhouse, Steven, 'Aristide to End Accord that Allows US to Seize Refugee Boats', *New York Times*, 8 April 1994, A6. See also Migration News, *Aristide to Cancel US Return Policy* <http://migration.ucdavis.edu/mn/more.php?id=302_0_2_0>.

Helton, Arthur, 'Haitian Refugees in Political Limbo', *Miami Herald*, 24 November 1991, L1.

Human Rights Watch, *Cuba: Repression, the Exodus of August 1994, and the US Response* (1994) <www.hrw.org/reports/pdfs/c/cuba/cuba940.pdf>.

International Law Association, 'Resolution 6/2002 on Refugee Procedures (Declaration on International Minimum Standards for Refugee Procedures)' (70th Conference of the International Law Association, New Delhi, India, 2–6 April 2002).

International Law Commission, 'Report of the International Law Commission Covering the Work of Its Eighth Session (April 23–July 4, 1956)' (1956) II *Yearbook of the International Law Commission* 253.

Koh, Harold Hongju, 'Memorandum Opinion on the Geographic Scope of the Convention Against Torture and Its Application in Situations of Armed Conflict' (21 January 2013) <www.documentcloud.org/documents/1053901-state-department-cat-memo.html>.

Koh, Harold Hongju, 'Memorandum Opinion on the Geographic Scope of the International Covenant on Civil and Political Rights' (19 October 2010) < <www.documentcloud.org/documents/1053853-state-department-iccpr-memo.html>.

Lawyers Committee for Human Rights, *Refugee Refoulement: The Forced Return of Haitians Under the US-Haitian Interdiction Agreement* (1990) 24.

Marcario, John, 'Immigration Assist: The Coast Guard Is Making Fewer Migrant Interdictions at Sea as Tougher Laws, Partnerships Take Hold' (2012) *Seapower* 44.

Migration News, 'Haitian Zig-Zags' (1994) <http://migration.ucdavis.edu/mn/comments.php?id=383_0_2_0>.

Miller, Greg, 'Obama Preserves Rendition as Counter-Terrorism Tool', *L.A. Times*, 1 February 2009, A1.

Mohn, Sid, 'Haitians in Cuba Need Compassion', *Chicago Tribune*, 18 March 1993 <http://articles.chicagotribune.com/1993-03-18/news/9303180009_1_haitian-refugees-hiv-positive-detainees>.

Musalo, Karen, *Chronology of US Policy on Haitian Refugees – 1980 to the Present*, UC Hastings (1993) <www.uchastings.edu/site_files/musalo/chronology.pdf>.

Musalo, Karen, Gibson, Lauren, Knight, Stephen and Taylor, J. Edward, *The Expedited Removal Study: Report on the First Three Years of Implementation of Expedited Removal*, Centre for Human Rights and International Justice University of California, Hastings College of Law (2001).

Oakley, Phyllis, Assistant Secretary for Population, Refugees, and Migration United States, 'The Pursuit and Implementation of Durable Solutions' (Geneva, 7 October 1996).

Ocker, Lisa, 'Haitians at Guantánamo Bay Exempt from HIV Legislation', *South Florida Sun Sentinel*, 20 February 1993 <http://articles.sun-sentinel.com/1993-02-20/news/9301100780_1_guantanamo-haitians-haitian-refugees-guantanamo-bay>.

Preston, Julia, 'US shifts on Haiti, Gets Tougher on Army', *Washington Post*, 29 April 1994 <http://www.highbeam.com/doc/1P2-888227.html>.

Reagan, Ronald, Statement on United States Ocean Policy, 19 Weekly Comp. Pres. Doc. 383 (10 March 1983).

Rosenberg, Carol, 'Cuban Migrants at Guantánamo Base 'Broke Rules' Face Restrictions', *Miami Herald*, 7 February 2012 <www.miamiherald.com/2012/02/07/2629897/cuban-migrants-at-Guantánamo-base.html>.

Savage, Charlie, 'U.S. Seems Unlikely to Accept That Rights Treaty Applies to Its Actions Abroad', *New York Times*, 6 March 2014 <www.nytimes.com/2014/03/07/world/us-seems-unlikely-to-accept-that-rights-treaty-applies-to-its-actions-abroad.html>.

Senate Committee on Foreign Relations, 'Report on the International Covenant on Civil and Political Rights', S. Rep. No 23, 102d Cong., 2d sess. 25 (1992), reprinted in (1992) *International Legal Materials* 645.

The White House, *Expect More: Coast Guard Migrant Interdiction Program* <www.whitehouse.gov/sites/default/files/omb/assets/OMB/expectmore/summary/10002406.2004.html>.

The White House, *President Bush Welcomes Georgian President Saakashvili to White House* (25 February 2004) <http://georgewbush whitehouse.archives.gov/news/releases/2004/02/20040225-1.html>.

Thomas-Hope, Elizabeth and World Institute for Development Economics, *Irregular Migration and Asylum Seekers in the Caribbean*, No. 2003/48 (2003).

United Nations, *Haiti Background* (1994) <www.un.org/en/peace keeping/missions/past/unmihbackgr2.html>.

US Department of Justice Press Release No 09-835, *Special Task Force on Interrogations and Transfer Policies Issues Its Recommendations to the President* (24 August 2009) <www.justice.gov/opa/pr/2009/August/09-ag-835.html>.

US Department of State, *List of Issues to Be Taken Up in Connection with the Consideration of the Second and Third Periodic Reports of the United States of America* (17 July 2006) <www.state.gov/g/drl/rls/70385.htm>.

US Department of State, *Opening Statement by Matthew Waxman on the Report Concerning the International Covenant on Civil and Political Rights (ICCPR)* (17 July 2006) <http://2001–2009.state.gov/g/drl/rls/70392.htm>.

US Department of State, *United States Written Response to Questions Asked by the Committee Against Torture* (2006) <www.state.gov/documents/organization/68662.pdf>.

US Immigration and Customs Enforcement, *Fact Sheet*: *Guantánamo Bay Migrant Operations* (23 July 2004) <http://web.archive.org/web/20070711063736/http://www.ice.gov/pi/news/factsheets/072304gitmo.htm>.

US Coast Guard, *Alien Migrant Interdiction* (2014) <www.uscg.mil/hq/cg5/cg531/AMIO/amio.asp>.

US Coast Guard, *Maritime Law Enforcement Manual* <www.uscg.mil/hq/cg5/cg531/AMIO/FOIA_Docs.pdf>. Accessed 1 November 2014.

US Coast Guard, *Maritime Safety*. Accessed 1 February 2012. <www.uscg.mil/top/missions/M_Safety.asp>.

US Coast Guard, *Statistics*, '*Alien Migrant Interdiction*' (2014) <www.uscg.mil/hq/cg5/cg531/AMIO/FlowStats/currentstats.asp>.

Wasem, Ruth, Congressional Research Service, 'Cuban Migration to the United States: Policy and Trends' (2 June 2009) <www.fas.org/sgp/crs/row/R40566.pdf>.

Wasem, Ruth, Congressional Research Service, 'US Immigration Policy on Haitian Migrants' (2 February 2009) <www.fas.org/sgp/crs/row/RS21349.pdf>.

Index

Legal Sources

For EU product safety concerns, contact us at Calle de José Abascal, 56–1°, 28003 Madrid, Spain or eugpsr@cambridge.org.

www.ingramcontent.com/pod-product-compliance
Lightning Source LLC
LaVergne TN
LVHW011524200926
848484LV00001B/140

* 9 7 8 1 1 0 7 1 0 1 0 0 5 *